SCANDINAVIA – BETWEEN EAST AND WEST

Scandinavia

Between East and West

EDITED BY

HENNING FRIIS

Adviser in Social Science to the
Danish Ministry of Social Affairs

———

A Publication of the New School for Social Research

CORNELL UNIVERSITY PRESS

ITHACA AND NEW YORK, 1950

Foreword

SCANDINAVIA'S position geographically between East and West is obvious to anyone who looks at a map. Scandinavia's middle position between East and West in the conflict of political ideas is equally obvious.

In that conflict it is inevitable that particular interest should be aroused by a group of countries that seem to have pursued "the middle way" successfully; by countries in which much, if not most, of the driving force of economic life is still geared to individual initiative and enterprise, while at the same time the state has become a potent factor in controlling economic individualism to the end that the benefits of individualism shall be more widely shared and the evils mitigated.

The middle way is often thought of in this country as an end in itself—as a condition to be achieved or avoided, depending upon one's point of view. And perhaps the middle way is an end in itself in the sense that any democratic form of government, based on respect for the individual, must inevitably involve a whole framework of compromises and balances between the political and economic forces within the country where it exists.

But certainly the people of the countries of the middle way do not consider that they have reached any final solution of their governmental and social problems. Rightly so. They, like the rest of the world, are on the move; and they cannot stop where they are if they wish to live. To become static is to die—or to be on the point of death. The Scandinavian countries have no thought of committing suicide through inanition. They may continue on *a* middle road, but it is certainly a road that is not a dead end. It leads somewhere. The question whither it leads is a matter of moment, not only to the inhabitants of those countries but to the rest of the world.

For those now in command of the destinies of Scandinavia, there is nothing final in the present political and economic procedures and institutions. In all the Scandinavian countries the dominant political parties are composed of Social Democrats, whose political philosophy is based on the doctrines of Karl Marx at least as much as is that of the Kremlin Communists. And so far as one can foresee, these Social Democrats will retain political control in Scandinavia for at least several years to come. They are an important group of people, for they seem to have made substantial progress toward finding an effective, if still partial, answer to some serious modern problems—at least in their own countries.

Their record is an interesting one. Long before they were charged with the responsibilities of government their agitation was responsible for most of the measures of social security and for mitigating the effects of uncontrolled economic individualism brought about by more conservative elements. And as time has passed, they have been largely successful in converting these same conservative forces to a definite acceptance of what has already been done. It may be doubted whether any government controlled by parties of the Right in any Scandinavian country, even though it had a large parliamentary majority, would undo any of the so-called socialistic measures now on the statute books.

The issue today between the Right and Left in Scandinavia has become: Where and how and how fast do we go from here?

There seems little danger that the Scandinavians will go fast. There will be no plunge into extremism in the course of which the rights of individuals are thrown overboard. That is not the Scandinavian way. Still more decisive is the fact that Scandinavian socialists are also democrats, and, I believe, very convinced democrats who have not the slightest intention of betraying their guarantees of the rights of the individual. Within the limitations of these guarantees, however, they are intent on going as far as possible toward social and economic equalitarianism.

Probably the most crucial political question of our time, so far as concerns domestic government, is: What degree of planned and managed economy can a people have and still retain political liberty for the individual?

That question has not, of course, bothered the totalitarians. In Nazi Germany, in Fascist Italy, and in Soviet Russia, the answer has simply been: To hell with the individual; he exists solely for the state, and as an individual he has no rights whatsoever.

I am not enough of a student of political science to know whether or not that is sound Marxian doctrine, as it seems to be accepted Nazi-Soviet doctrine. But I have a hunch that Karl Marx is writhing uneasily in his grave at some of the absurdities and the brutalities now being committed in his name by those who profess to revere him most and who plaster their country with his pictures.

In any case, the Scandinavian followers of Marx give no such answer. The socialism in which they believe is a socialism of conviction or consent on the part of the majority, which, under democratic forms of government, can reverse itself and undo its socialization at any time it changes its mind and so records itself by the freely spoken and freely written word and by the votes freely cast at the polls.

The answers, partial or complete, which the Scandinavian democracies have found, are finding, and may find to the problem of a managed economy that does not infringe on the established rights of the individual, and the ways and means these democracies use to implement those answers, are, I take it, the true subject matter of this book. The extent of the possible applicability of those answers to our own problems here in the United States, I leave to the American readers of this book to determine. Certainly there must be something important to be learned from these Scandinavian countries whose political and social philosophy and whose methods of implementing it have brought them—or at least have been accompanied by—such a high degree of political stability, economic prosperity, and cultural development.

There does not exist in English, to my knowledge, any volume that examines contemporary developments throughout Scandinavia as integral parts of one important cultural development. It was therefore with great interest that the American-Scandinavian Foundation agreed to participate in the sponsorship of a series of lectures on recent Scandinavian developments given at the New School for Social Research in New York during the latter half of 1948 under the direction of a distinguished young Danish social scientist, assisted by a group of American and Scandinavian scholars who know whereof they speak. The result of their collaborative efforts is this book.

The American-Scandinavian Foundation is very proud to participate in the sponsorship of a project of such consequential design and is hopeful that the book will reward all who reflect upon its meaning.

LITHGOW OSBORNE
*President, The American-
Scandinavian Foundation*

Preface

WHEN I visited American universities in 1948 to lecture on Scandinavian problems, it appeared to me that there was a great need for a general survey text on the main contributions of the Scandinavian countries to contemporary culture. Popular books on each of the countries and scholarly works on special aspects of Scandinavian culture are numerous. But there is no single-volume presentation of the most important features of the social, political, and economic systems of Scandinavia.

The occasion for remedying this situation presented itself when the New School for Social Research permitted me to call upon a number of American specialists and Scandinavian scholars temporarily in the United States to take part in a series of lectures on major aspects of Scandinavian political, economic, and social life. I took this opportunity to persuade the lecturers to examine their manuscripts with a view to publication.

I have found it necessary to limit the coverage of the book to Denmark, Norway, and Sweden, as Finland and Iceland, though historically and culturally close to the Scandinavian countries, are too different in many respects to be profitably included in this survey.

It is fundamental to the thinking of those who worked together on this book that there is a cultural harmony in the separate efforts of each of the Scandinavian countries to preserve democratic principles in the midst of experimentation with new forms of economic and social organization. Although the writers have frequently emphasized the experiences of the countries with which they are best acquainted, such discussions are to be understood as illustrations of common traits unless differences in the development between the three countries have been specifically stressed.

The title of the book, *Scandinavia—Between East and West,* is based on the conception that Scandinavian culture is a distinctive culture somewhere between that of free-enterprise democracy in the United States and that of the Communist dictatorship in Soviet Russia. This title also indicates the position of the Scandinavian countries in world affairs on the border between the Eastern and Western blocs. The fact that the Scandinavian countries recently failed to agree on a common policy for defense and foreign affairs and that Norway and Denmark, but not Sweden, have entered into the Atlantic pact has not changed the basic problem, which is founded upon the geographic position of Scandinavia.

The editor wants to express his gratitude to the president of the New School, Dr. Bryn J. Hovde, who initiated the series of lectures on contemporary Scandinavia at the New School, and to the president of the American-Scandinavian Foundation, Mr. Lithgow Osborne, who actively sponsored the project. For encouragement and advice, the editor is also indebted to Dr. Arne Björnberg, formerly of the United Nations secretariat; Mr. Allan Kastrup of the American-Swedish News Exchange; Dr. Henry Goddard Leach, president emeritus of the American-Scandinavian Foundation; Mr. Finn T. B. Friis and Mr. Henning Ravnholt of the Danish Ministry of Foreign Affairs; Mr. Erik Schmidt of the Danish Ministry of Finance; Mr. Halvor Gille of the Danish Ministry of Social Affairs; Mr. Einer Engberg of the Danish Ministry of Housing; and Mr. Clemens Pedersen of the Danish Central Cooperative Committee.

HENNING FRIIS

Summer, 1949

Contents

I

Scandinavian Democracy

By HENNING FRIIS

I

COMMUNIST doctrine asserts that there is no fundamental difference between the Scandinavian countries
and other countries based on a capitalistic system.
Laissez-faire liberals declare that there is no important distinction
between the government-controlled economy of the Scandinavian
countries and the Russian economic system, and that the political
democracy of the Scandinavian countries is gradually being undermined by government planning of economic life. Between these
two extremes stands the conception of Scandinavian culture
known as "the middle way." Under this system the Scandinavian
countries, during this century, have developed a type of welfare
economy with more government planning than many other European countries have, while extending their political democracy,
defined as a form of government in which the political functions
are exercised by the people through representatives elected in free
elections and in which there is freedom for all groups of citizens to
speak and organize.

In the following pages, I shall outline the special features of
political democracy in Scandinavia [1] and try to explain why these
democracies have been able to survive in a Europe where most of
the other nations have become totalitarian in our generation.

---

[1] For a comparative study of the Scandinavian governments, see Herbert
Tingsten, "Folkestyret i Norden," in *Nordisk gemenskap* (Stockholm, 1940).
The most comprehensive survey and discussion of Scandinavian democracy is
presented by Hal Koch and Alf Ross (eds.), *Nordisk demokrati* (Copenhagen,
1949).

THE DEVELOPMENT OF SCANDINAVIAN DEMOCRACY

The decay of democratic institutions took place particularly in those European countries that introduced political democracy after 1918. In the older democracies, such as the Scandinavian, democracy became more firmly entrenched during the period between the wars. This development can be ascribed, at least in part, to the older traditions of the Scandinavian type of government. Although full democracy with universal suffrage for both men and women was not introduced in any of the Scandinavian countries before the present century, basic democratic institutions are much older, and the peaceful struggle for democracy through the years has in itself been a strong political education for these nations.

The Swedish parliament celebrated its quincentennial in 1935. Even though the influence of the parliament during long periods of this five hundred years was quite small, the right to representation for the four estates (nobility, clergy, burghers, and farmers) was always acknowledged. In 1866 the old legislature based on the four estates was replaced by a two-chamber one, but voting for the members of the upper house was restricted to large landowners and civil servants, and for the members of the lower house it was largely restricted to very well-to-do farmers. At the turn of the century universal suffrage was demanded by the Liberal and Social Democratic parties, and the democratization took place through the constitutional reforms of 1907–1909 and 1918–1921. Universal male suffrage was instituted in 1909 for elections to the lower house and to the upper house in 1918. Women obtained voting rights in 1921. Since 1921 various lesser reforms have brought complete political democracy closer. The voting age was reduced to twenty-one years. The lower house is now elected by direct popular vote every fourth year, the upper house by municipal and county electoral bodies, which, in turn, are elected by direct popular vote every fourth year.

The parliamentary system of government, with appointment of the cabinet from the majority party in parliament, was not definitely established in Sweden until 1917. Before that time Sweden had a few governments of a parliamentary character, but the persistent and active opposition of the king and of the Conservative party did not end until 1917. Because it often happens that no single party commands a majority, the practice has developed of forming minority or coalition governments, which are able to obtain the necessary parliamentary support.

The tradition of self-government in Denmark is not as old as in Sweden, but when Denmark finally got its democratic constitution in 1849, it was a very radical one for its time. The members of both the lower and the upper house were elected on the basis of free and equal suffrage for all adult males. The background of this radical constitution was the revolutionary wave in Europe after the February Revolution in France, but in Denmark the absolute monarchy, which had held power since 1660, was abolished without bloodshed.

After such a bold advance some reaction was to be expected, and through a revision of the constitution in 1866, the manor owners succeeded in gaining control of the upper house by instituting restrictive election rules. The lower house, however, was kept in its original democratic form and was dominated by the farmers. Against this background a struggle developed between the two houses, which was aggravated by the fact that the king chose the cabinet according to the majority in the upper house alone. Danish political history in the last decades of the nineteenth century was marked by the fight of the farmers for the principle of parliamentarism under which the king would be obliged to choose his cabinet from the majority party in the lower house. At last the king gave way, and since 1901 all Danish governments have been appointed in this manner.

The struggle to democratize the upper house continued, with the small farmers and the growing labor movement the leading forces. In 1915 Denmark acquired her present constitution through a compromise among all political parties. Women were granted suffrage, and restrictions on voting in elections for the upper house were modified.

The lower house is elected by direct popular vote every fourth year, but the government can call for elections whenever political conditions demand them. The members of the upper house are elected for eight years. One fourth of the members are elected by their fellow members before retiring, the remainder being chosen by electors for eight years, half of them retiring every fourth year.

The age requirement for voting in elections for, and for eligibility to, the upper house is thirty-five years as against twenty-five for the lower house. Particularly during recent years the age limit for both the upper and the lower houses has been challenged, and the political parties have now reached a preliminary agreement on revision of the constitution in this respect.

Norway got her first constitution in the historic year of 1814, when the Danish crown was forced to cede Norway to Sweden after Norway had been a part of the Danish-Norwegian monarchy for four hundred years. The constitution of 1814 gave the Norwegian people greater freedom than was enjoyed by any other European people at that time. The parliament then, as now, had one chamber; members were chosen by direct vote. For a long time, however, suffrage was rather limited, the electorate totaling only 7 per cent of the adult population. In the 1880's a parliamentary majority was won by the Liberal party, which, comprised largely of farmers and middle-class townspeople, demanded parliamentarism and extended suffrage. In 1884 the king yielded and parliamentary government was introduced in Norway, the first of the Scandinavian countries to have it. In the following years an intense struggle for extension of suffrage went on until in 1898 universal suffrage for men was introduced. After the dissolution of the union with Sweden in 1905, women obtained the vote under the census system, and in 1913 they were granted full voting rights equal with men. Through amendments to the constitution the voting age has been lowered; since 1946 it has been twenty-one years.

In all the Scandinavian countries the process of democratization has included two important features:

1. The termination of the personal power of the monarch, including the absolute right to choose the government. The Scandinavian kings of today are important solely as symbols of national unity. The executive authority rests with a cabinet chosen according to the parliamentary principle.

2. The abolition of the rules that gave the more well-to-do a dominant position in the parliament or in one of the chambers and the introduction of suffrage for women. Today all adult citizens in Scandinavia are entitled to vote in free and general elections.

These reforms have been sought by slow and peaceful processes. The social basis of the struggle has been a coalition between most of the farmers, the labor movement, and the liberal intelligentsia of the cities. Opposition to democratization has come from the upper middle class and the large landowners, but today no political group of importance regrets the development of political democracy.

THE PARTY SYSTEM

The basis of the parliamentary system in Scandinavia is the existence of solid party groups in the parliaments. The first parties in the modern sense were the Liberal parties in Norway and Denmark, which were established in the latter half of the nineteenth century. The first modern party in Sweden was the Social Democratic party, which was founded in 1889. The party system has a rather similar structure in all the Scandinavian countries.[2] The parties to the right of the Social Democrats have made up the majority, except in Sweden since 1936 and in Norway since 1945, but these groups have been separated into three parties, which very

---

[2] For statistics on the distribution of the seats in the parliaments since 1930, see Appendix, pp. 365–366.

often have had different attitudes toward co-operation with the Social Democrats.

The Conservative parties originally opposed the development of democracy and later were active in supporting national traditions, military establishments, and the existing economic order. Before the war—under the impact of Fascism and Nazism—some groups inside the Conservative parties tended to sympathize with totalitarian ideas, but since the wartime experience with the Germans in Scandinavia nearly all of these people have expressed strong sentiments in favor of democracy. The most important supporters of the Conservative parties are the industrialists, but these parties get most of their votes from the lower middle class and white-collar workers. In the last elections Conservative support was reduced in all three countries.

The Farmers' parties have a very clear electoral basis among farmers with middle-sized farms, but they also get support from a number of small farmers. The Farmers' parties in Sweden and Norway co-operated during the last part of the thirties with the Social Democrats, but the Danish Farmers' party (Venstre), which has a relatively conservative laissez-faire philosophy, has been the leading opposition party in Denmark, except during the period from 1945 to 1947 when the party controlled the government.

Finally, among the parties to the right of the Social Democrats we have the Liberal parties, which were very important during the struggle for democracy and parliamentarism but which gradually lost support in the elections during the period between the wars. In Denmark the Liberal party, which gets its main support from small farmers and the intelligentsia, was represented in the Social Democratic government in the thirties. For a time after the war it supported the Farmers' party government, but it now gives its parliamentary support to the Social Democratic government, which has been in office since 1947. It did not, however, wish to take part in the Social Democratic government and, with its background of pacifism, has tried to limit increases in expenditures for the military establishments and has voted against Denmark's participation in the Atlantic pact.

The Liberal parties in Sweden and Norway have attracted some of the farmers as well as a portion of the middle class in the cities. In the last two elections the Swedish Liberal party gained considerably; it is now the strongest opposition party in Sweden.

The Social Democratic parties represent the political branch of the labor movement. Since their beginning in the 1880's they have grown from small opposition parties to the largest of the political groups. For many years they have been stronger than any single party to the right of them. With few exceptions, the Social Democrats have controlled the governments in all three countries throughout the last fifteen to twenty years. During the war they were leading members of coalition governments. All three parties have advocated nearly identical policies aiming at economic planning and social welfare, but socialization, which is in their programs, has played a rather modest role in their actual policy.

Originally consisting mainly of industrial workers, the Social Democratic parties have gradually attracted an increasing number of the lower middle class and the small farmers, a fact that has had an impact on their policies. The Marxist ideology, which had a certain, if not very deep, influence in the earlier years, has given way to a spirit of gradual reform. The only deviation from the reformist line is to be found in the history of the Norwegian Labor party, which, in the years after World War I, had a strong revolutionary tendency and for a short period was a member of the Communist International. The Norwegian Labor party now adheres to the same principles as the Social Democratic parties in Denmark and Sweden, although socialist ideals still play a more vital part in the Norwegian party than in the other two.

Apart from the short period when the Norwegian Labor party was a member of the Communist International, the Communist parties have been fairly unimportant in Scandinavian political life. They have followed the same political line as in other European countries, changing their tactics according to the trends in Russian foreign policy.

The Scandinavian type of party system provides a marked contrast to American political parties. The electoral basis is, of course, the voters, but the strength of the parties in the long run is founded upon party organizations, which are made up of members paying dues regularly. The number of actual party members is much smaller than the number of voters, but the Social Democrats in particular have succeeded in organizing a rather high proportion of their supporters in Sweden and Norway, partly through affiliation with trade unions. Members represented about 40 per cent of the total votes of the Social Democratic parties in the last elections. Local party organizations arrange regular lectures, political meetings, and social events. None of the parties, however, have been able to inspire more than a small fraction of their membership to political activity and a few leaders determine policy.[3]

The principal leader is generally chairman of the parliamentary group as well as chairman of the national party organization, and he keeps the latter position even if he acts as prime minister. Political leadership has been very stable, particularly in the Social Democratic parties. Hjalmar Branting headed the Swedish Social Democratic party for thirty-five years; Per Albin Hansson succeeded him, maintaining his leadership for twenty years. In Denmark Thorvald Stauning was the undisputed leader of the Social Democratic party for thirty-two years; in 1942 he was succeeded by Hans Hedtoft. This stable political leadership can also be found in other parties. For example, Admiral Lindmann was the leader of the Swedish Conservative party for twenty years and Gunnar Knudsen headed the Norwegian Liberal party for seventeen years.

The aim of a party is common action on the basis of a common program. Membership in the party, and especially in the parliamentary group, therefore, imposes upon the members a certain

---

[3] A thought-provoking discussion of this problem may be found in Johan Vogt's *Tanker om politik* (Oslo, 1947).

amount of discipline. This view of party discipline has been much discussed in Scandinavia. There is no doubt that it sometimes limits the individual activity of members of parliament and makes parliamentary debates less interesting; but it does not mean that differences of opinion are not discussed inside the parliamentary groups. When a certain position on a major issue wins a majority inside a party, all members of that parliamentary group are supposed to vote according to the majority decision. On points of minor political interest, however, each member may vote according to his own best judgment.

The problem of domination by the party leadership and lack of activity among the rank-and-file party members has often been criticized. The fact is, however, that political education today reaches broader masses in the Scandinavian countries, through the activity of the parties, than at any prior time, and that the political interest of the people both on the local and the national level is greater than it is in most other countries. Seventy to eighty per cent of the electorate take part in the parliamentary elections. In the last Danish election 86 per cent of the electorate actually voted.

In addition to political parties, there are many popular movements of all kinds that have acted as citizen-training schools. The pioneers were the farmer organizations and the temperance groups; then came the trade unions and the rural and urban co-operatives, health insurance clubs, organizations for adult education, and political and cultural youth groups. All these and many other popular movements are extending the basis of political democracy, partly by educating their members through lectures and study circles, partly by creating many opportunities for active participation in the work of these organizations. At the same time the popular movements, especially the economic organizations, have a strong influence on the policies of the political parties, an influence that in recent years has been criticized as a threat to the supremacy of parliamentary democracy.[4] The trade unions and

[4] See Gunnar Heckscher, "Pluralist Democracy—The Swedish Experience," *Social Research,* XV (Dec., 1948), 417–461.

the urban co-operatives have very close contacts with the Social Democratic parties; the agricultural organizations, including the rural co-operative movement, with the Farmers' parties; and the employers' associations and the organizations of industry and trade with the Conservative parties.

An important element in Scandinavian democracy is the system of proportional representation, by which seats in the parliament are distributed among the parties in proportion to the total number of votes obtained by each party in the election. There is common agreement that proportional representation has worked out well in Scandinavia. Although only in the last decade has any party been able to get a majority of the votes, no parliamentary regime in Europe, with the exception of that of England, has had as much governmental stability as has that of Denmark, where the average government tenure during the period between the wars was five years. In Norway and Sweden it was about two years.

Most governments have been minority governments that have either had the permanent support of one of the other parties in parliament or have secured support for each measure in their program as it came up. The Social Democratic government now in office in Denmark is an example of the latter type.

GOVERNMENT PLANNING AND CONTROL

The basis for this kind of parliamentarism is a certain degree of common interest between different political parties and a willingness to discuss and compromise. The government in office has to judge carefully whether or not its proposals will be able to get the necessary support in parliament. The government often knows the position of the other political parties on certain issues from work done in government committees, whose work, in Scandinavia, normally precedes the introduction of bills. This committee system dates far back in Scandinavian political administration, especially in Sweden where the system has a history of more than two hundred years. The purely fact-finding objective of the committees in earlier days has gradually been combined with a more political one.

The committees are normally appointed by the government, either at the request of parliament or on the government's own initiative. In addition to experts on the problem under investigation, representatives of political parties and of organizations especially concerned may be appointed members. The representation on committees of interested groups and public authorities is normally broader in Denmark than in Sweden. Denmark has therefore not introduced the very interesting and unique Swedish system of sending out the finished reports to various private organizations and public authorities for criticism before the cabinet makes its final decision on proposals.

When a government bill is presented to parliament, it will normally be studied in a parliamentary committee where necessary compromises are worked out. Committee work is looked upon as the most important parliamentary activity; debates in the chamber are, as a rule, relatively short and not very exciting. For the work of the parliament, and especially of the committees, it is fortunate that experts in many different fields are active in Scandinavian politics. It is looked upon as an honor to be charged with a political task, and politics has attracted a number of competent people from various professions and from the ranks of the farmers' organizations, the co-operatives, the labor unions, and other popular organizations. The social stratification of Scandinavian parliaments, therefore, corresponds very closely to the stratification in the population as a whole.

In the Scandinavian countries civil servants may hold elective offices, including seats in parliament, and they may speak and vote against the government. In its government work, however, the civil service is politically neutral. Civil servants, even in the highest ranks, are not removable except through the retirement system, and very few appointments are made on partisan grounds. This adds to popular confidence in government intervention and administration, an attitude that is an important element in Scandinavian life. For centuries the Scandinavians have lived in an orderly society, and the people as a whole believe in the possibility of achieving social progress along rational lines and through the medium of parliamentary government. They have confidence in the laws and in the impartiality of the administration. Politics has never been altogether dominated by doctrinaire laissez-faire ideology, and it is important to note that government control dates back to a period long before the Social Democratic parties rose to their present political power.

Legal development has followed the gradual trend toward more government control of economic life. At no point has there been any definite break with the past. From the latter part of the nineteenth century there has been a slow but constant change in the attitude of the legislature toward freedom of contract and of unrestricted competition. The concept of government interference with private enterprise has little by little gained a foothold in legal practice. This idea first grew out of practices unfair to individual competitors or customers. Later, however, this trend was merged with the idea of government interference in the interest of society as a whole.

Social welfare legislation, free education, and subsidized housing were originally introduced by Conservative or Farmers' governments, and even public ownership has a very long tradition behind it. Since the Middle Ages the state, in both Sweden and Norway, has owned vast forest areas and waterfalls.

Public control of Norwegian and Swedish mineral resources and of the production of electric power (water power) dates back to the beginning of this century. In Sweden the state is responsible for 40 per cent of the total energy production, municipal authorities for 6 per cent, and private companies for the remaining 54 per cent. In a number of the privately owned companies, however, municipal authorities are part owners.

The railways, as a general rule, have been owned and operated by the state in all three Scandinavian countries since the first railways were built in the middle of the last century. The chief reasons for this were: (1) that it was recognized that only in this way could the new means of transport be developed according to some sort of national plan and (2) that the state was more capable of raising the necessary capital than was private business. The postal service and the telephone and telegraph systems have been public enterprises almost from their establishment. From the beginning radio facilities in all three countries have been publicly owned.

Local authorities are very active in the development of public utilities. As we have already seen, the production of electric power is taken care of, to a large extent, by cities and communities. The retail distribution of electric energy is nearly always handled by local authorities. Gas- and water-works are also, as a rule, owned and operated by communities. This applies also to streetcar and bus systems in cities. Other similar activities that have traditionally been regarded as belonging to the sector of public enterprise are sanitation and the operation of ports, slaughterhouses, and meat markets.

In both Sweden and Norway the state has a monopoly of the production and distribution of liquor and wine. In Sweden the government has gone a step further and established a state monopoly of the processing of tobacco. Distribution, however, is left to private enterprise.

It should be added that during the last decade the Swedish and Norwegian governments have also entered some industries, not as monopolists, but in competition with private enterprise, as in the steel mills. In Norway German-owned or controlled property, including a large portion of stock in the aluminum industry and in Norsk Hydro, the great electrochemical works, was taken over by the government after the war. In Denmark the government has taken part in the financing of a new steel mill. Privately owned enterprise is, however, still dominant, and in general manufacturing as well as commercial banks and insurance companies are under private ownership.

The fact that the state and municipalities have started and have continued to operate most public utilities and public services has not caused much political disagreement. The enlargement of the sector of public enterprise that has been effected in the last decade, for instance, by the inclusion of private railways in the state railway system and by the establishment of such an enterprise as the state steel mills has been endorsed by all political parties.

The extension of government control during the 1930's took the shape mainly of a compensatory fiscal policy aimed at restoring economic activity to a predepression level. As early as 1932 British restrictions on the import of Danish farm products forced the introduction of direct control of Danish foreign trade, necessitating a system of allocation on the home market. After World War II the international trade and exchange situation also forced Norway, and later Sweden, into controls of a similar kind. In all three countries government control over private enterprise was greatly extended in the postwar period.[5]

The battle against the depression in the thirties was fought by the Social Democratic parties—in Sweden and Norway in cooperation with the Farmers' party and in Denmark with the Liberal party. Together they protected the farmers against the results of the agrarian crises by means of different types of subsidies and combated unemployment of industrial workers through public works and government loans to semipublic housing societies.

THE POSTWAR POLITICAL SCENE

In the postwar period the Social Democrats in Sweden and Norway have been able to carry out their economic policies as majority parties.[6] Since their majorities, however, have been very slight, they have tried to get support from the other parties. In Norway the four major parties—Labor, Agrarian, Conservative, and Liberal—shortly after the liberation formulated a Joint Program to

---

[5] For the background of this development see Chapter II, and for the postwar system of government economic planning and control see Chapter III.

[6] On the political development in Scandinavia since the war, see Eric C. Bellquist, "Political and Economic Conditions in the Scandinavian Countries," *Foreign Policy Reports*, vol. XXIV (May 15, 1948), no. 5.

serve them as a guide in the period of postwar reconstruction, and the Labor government that succeeded the postwar coalition government in November, 1945, accepted the program as the basis for its policy. The Joint Program dealt with economic, military, and foreign policy and also with policies relating to social welfare, education, and the church. The program was couched in very general terms and has been subject to different interpretations. Nevertheless it represented a certain measure of agreement, and it was helpful during the first years after the war by creating an atmosphere of moderation and accommodation when controversial questions came up for discussion in parliament.

In Sweden the wartime coalition government, which included representation from all parties except the Communists, came to an end in July, 1945, when a Social Democratic government took over. The Social Democrats had at that time an absolute majority in the parliament, but this position was not maintained. In the election for the second chamber in 1948 the Social Democrats won 112 seats out of 230. Although the nine Communist members are not to be regarded as supporters of the government, they cannot be expected to vote with the parties to the right of the Social Democrats. The position of the Social Democrats is therefore practically the same as it was before.

Political discussion in Sweden has been somewhat more tense during the postwar period because the program of Swedish labor, which was published in 1944,[7] included plans for the socialization of certain industries. These plans, however, have been buried in government committees. In coping with the economic difficulties of the postwar period the Social Democratic government has been occupied chiefly with day-to-day policy and with broad social welfare reforms that have been passed by a nearly unanimous vote in parliament. The Swedish neutrality policy and the expansion of the defense program have also been carried out with the strong backing of all political parties.

---

[7] Landsorganisationen, *The Post-War Program of Swedish Labor* (Stockholm, 1946), English translation.

Political developments in Denmark since the war have differed somewhat from those in Norway and Sweden. When the first election after the liberation was held in November, 1945, the Social Democrats suffered a heavy loss to the Communists. At the same time the Agrarian party increased its representation at the cost of the Conservative and the Liberal parties. Under the circumstances, the Social Democrats did not want to take office, and an Agrarian government was formed that received the parliamentary support of the Conservatives and Liberals. The free-trade policy of the Agrarians under which import controls were relaxed was unable to cope with the problems of an increasing deficit in the balance of trade, and when the prime minister lost the confidence of the Liberal party because of his activist line in the South Schleswig question,[8] new elections were held in November, 1947. The Social Democrats regained a considerable number of lost seats from the Communists and took office as a minority government, which through compromises has succeeded in getting sufficient support from the parties to the right to stay in power.

The general picture in all three countries is the same: The Social Democratic parties have had to postpone the prosecution of their more far-reaching nationalization programs, resigning themselves to immediate necessities and to the expansion of their traditional social welfare policy. The other parties have accepted various kinds of government intervention that they formerly would have denounced. They are also supporting social welfare measures that they would never have considered twenty years ago. The ideological dispute between free enterprise and socialism is still alive, but the antagonism has a tendency to disappear or change its character when the dispute is carried over from the ideological to the concrete level.

Thus the multiparty system has not resulted in national disunity. On the contrary, the parties have grown closer to one another during the last twenty years, and their differences have, as a rule, been worked out in a peaceful manner. The fact is that most laws

---

[8] See Chapter IX.

in Scandinavia are passed with the backing of all or nearly all parties. It is also interesting to note that a change of government results only to a minor degree in the revocation of decisions made by the previous government.

The negative side of the system is that it makes long-range planning difficult and that the necessity for continuous compromising has a tendency to weaken straightforward political thinking.

THE BACKGROUND OF POLITICAL SOLIDARITY

What is the explanation of the rather high degree of national solidarity upon which the Scandinavian democracies are based? The question has never been thoroughly studied, but the homogeneity of the countries with respect to race, nationality, language, religion, and education is undoubtedly an important factor.

The Scandinavian countries have no racial problems. Except for the nomadic Lapps in the North and the German-speaking or German-born population group on the Danish border next to Germany, there are no minorities of race or nationality. Immigration from other countries has always been unimportant.

The problem of language has had some importance in Norway, which now has two official languages, one rather close to Danish and the other similar to the old Norwegian dialects. Since supporters of each of the two languages are represented in nearly every party, the problem has never caused a serious political split. Sweden and Denmark have had no such problem.

With respect to religion, the Lutheran State Church has been dominant in all the countries since the Reformation in the sixteenth century. The number of Roman Catholics is about 23,000 in Denmark and 3,500 in Sweden, and the number of Jews is about 6,000 in each country. At times there have been conflicts between the state church and larger or smaller groups of Lutheran dissenters, especially in Sweden and Norway, but on the whole the problem of religion has never caused much strife in cultural or political life.

In the nineteenth century some of the religious movements actually played an important role in democratic development.

Compulsory elementary education was introduced in the Scandinavian countries at the beginning of the nineteenth century and, together with expanding adult education [9] as exemplified by the people's colleges in the rural districts and the educational activities of the labor movement, it has given the people a fairly homogeneous educational background.

But even if the population is homogeneous in the respects mentioned, there might still be strong conflicts in interest between the different social classes. The fact is that class distinctions have never been as sharp as they are in other European countries. The contrast between an impoverished proletariat and a small wealthy class of great landowners or mighty industrialists has not been prominent for the simple reason that in the Scandinavian countries such groups are of slight importance. Norway is in the peculiar situation of never having had a dominant aristocracy, and the power of the large landowners in Denmark and Sweden was broken long ago.

It is true that in the Scandinavian countries as elsewhere the distance between the two ends of the income scale is very great and that there are sections of the population living under difficult circumstances, sections that the community recognizes it must assist through constructive social planning and social security legislation. It is a fact, however, that for large sectors of the Scandinavian population the standard of living is rather high compared with that of other countries in Europe.

Over a period of fifty years preceding World War II the standard of living of the less well-to-do sections of the Scandinavian people steadily improved along with the greatly increased industrial and agricultural production and favorable trade relations with foreign markets. The relative distribution of the national income between the classes has not changed essentially, but national production has been growing continuously, and the different social

---

[9] See Chapter VIII.

groups have been able to secure their share of this growth through the activities of the industrial organizations and the political parties. From 1914 to 1939 real wages in industry increased by 35 per cent in Denmark and by 50 per cent in Sweden. In order to secure a correct picture we must add the extended social benefits enjoyed by the workers and other less well-to-do people through social insurance [10] and paid vacations, though it should be remembered that the groups receiving most of the benefits of these schemes carry no small share of their cost through the contributions and taxes that they pay.

The wage policy of the trade unions has been to obtain the largest wage increases for the lower income groups. This policy at the same time has been based on and has contributed to the unity inside the labor movement that is characteristic of the Scandinavian countries [11] and that has been so important for political stability.

In large parts of Western Europe the working class is almost a separate nation. Even where Communist leadership is not strong, the sense of being apart and cut off from the other classes persists. During this century and especially during the last twenty years labor in Scandinavia has developed an active co-operative relationship with other classes, and all other social groups look upon the workers as equals.

Also important for the stability of democracy has been the fact that small holdings in agriculture and small units in industry, handicraft, and trade have been and still are important in Scandinavian politics. These rather large groups in the population have acted as a balance in two ways: on the one hand, the Social Democratic parties have modified their policies in order to get votes from these groups, and, on the other hand, these groups are important factors in modifying policy in all other parties. Because of the political weight of the lower middle class no party today dares to introduce economic legislation that would threaten the position

---

[10] See Chapter V.
[11] See Chapter IV.

of small business, and government policy has traditionally safe-guarded the small holders. From the point of view of economic efficiency these policies may be rather questionable, but they have been a very important factor in political stability.

THE FUTURE OF SCANDINAVIAN DEMOCRACY

What are the future prospects of the Scandinavian democracies? In his book on collective bargaining in Scandinavia, *This Is Democracy* (1938), Marquis W. Childs suggested the possibility that the labor governments of Scandinavia might be only

a transitory manifestation of the particular phase of industrial de-velopment that these countries have now reached; the result of singularly fortunate circumstances. With new technological develop-ment, industrialization of those countries that are still "backward," sharper competition in the world market, this orderly structure may give way; and labor having held power over the political but not the major economic forces of the state may be swept aside.[12]

We have now experienced the critical years of the war and the economic difficulties of the postwar period, and the dominating force in modern Scandinavian democracy, the Labor parties, still occupies the same strong position it held before the war. No threat against a peaceful democratic development is now to be found in Scandinavia. The immediate danger lies in a military clash be-tween the Eastern and the Western blocs, in which event the Scandinavian countries may be occupied by Soviet armies.

But even if it is possible to avoid the disaster of war, other threats are in the air. The Scandinavian economy is part of Euro-pean economy and of world economy. The rather high degree of prosperity and stability in the Scandinavian countries through-out the last fifty years has been based on the free interchange of goods with other sections of the world. Before the war the total import value per head in Scandinavia was 180 gold kroner, or

[12] Page xii.

about six times the corresponding United States figure, and the Scandinavians were able to pay for these imports through their export and shipping incomes. The main markets were the European countries, especially Germany and England. Denmark felt the impact of the economic decline of Great Britain as early as the 1930's. The collapse of Germany and the economic difficulties of Great Britain since the war have caused serious troubles for all the Scandinavian countries.[13] If plans for reorganizing the economy of Europe are successful and a period of extended and reciprocal trade relations between the United States and Europe follows, then the Scandinavian countries will benefit. If not, the gradual rise in the standard of living of all population groups in the Scandinavian countries, which has been so important to the stability of political democracy during the last fifty years, will come to an end, and a painful process of adjustment to the new situation will have to take place. The margin for further equalization of the distribution of income through taxation and social welfare policies is narrow, and a decline in the national income might endanger the welfare gains already achieved.

If this pessimistic forecast is realized, even in part, the Scandinavian democracies will be put on trial. In the past they have shown a sufficient degree of flexibility to adjust themselves to the economic and social problems of the modern world. In view of their long and successful experience with self-government, it is to be hoped that the Scandinavian people will find solutions through democratic means to their new problems. Their sober approach to the problems now confronting them provides the basis for optimism on this score.

[13] See Chapter II.

The Scandinavian Countries in a

Changing World Economy

By SVEND LAURSEN

Assistant Professor of Economics,
Williams College

II

I T IS the main thesis of this chapter that the economic problems facing Scandinavia today are not limited to that region and hence can be analyzed only in the broader context of Europe's present economic and political ills. In other words, without an understanding of the general nature of the European crisis it is difficult, if not impossible, to understand the problems of Scandinavian economies.

One way to approach our subject matter would be to describe the basic changes in the world economy in order to show how they have affected the Scandinavian economies. Instead of doing that I propose to follow another procedure that will lead to the same result. First an attempt will be made to outline, however briefly, the economic development in Sweden, Denmark, and Norway since the end of the war. Next will be taken up the question of the measures that the various governments propose in order to meet the present difficulties. Because of the existence of the European Recovery Program it seems natural to center that part of the discussion on the present American aid program and the long-term planning as formulated by the governments in the so-called "four-year programs" submitted to the Organization for European Economic Co-operation and the Economic Co-operation Administration. An evaluation of Scandinavian plans will show how much their success depends on events in other parts of Europe and on world economy in general. This fact follows, as I hope to show, from the traditionally great dependence of Scandinavian countries on trade with other nations. A dislocation of world trade is bound to have serious repercussions for them, whereas an expanding world economy is likely to restore their external as well as domestic equilibrium.

THE STATUS OF POSTWAR RECOVERY

The first broad complex of questions is concerned with post-war economic development in the three countries. The most important single fact that must be emphasized at the outset is the substantial recovery that has been achieved so far. For the sake of comparison it should be added, however, that the rate of industrial recovery in Europe in general has been much faster than it was after the First World War. In the Scandinavian countries the level of industrial output is now from 20 to 40 per cent higher than it was before World War II (Table 1).

Table 1. Industrial production. 1938 = 100.

	Sweden	Denmark	Norway
1946	136	101	94
1947	138	116	108
1948 *	143	130	118

* Provisional.
Source: Economic Commission for Europe of the United Nations, *Economic Survey of Europe in 1948* (Geneva, 1949), p. 4.

In agriculture the picture is not quite so favorable even though here again the level of output is above the average for Europe as a whole (Table 2). A great many factors have been responsible for this: lack of fodder and fertilizers, loss of livestock, deterioration of agricultural machinery, scarcity of manpower, and, finally, unfavorable weather conditions. The production trend is, however, definitely upward.

Table 2. The level of agricultural production. 1934–1938 =100.

	Sweden	Denmark	Norway
1946–47	103	94	95
1947–48	103	76	86
1948–49 *	105	100	95

* Provisional.
Source: Economic Survey of Europe in 1948, p. 17.

Gross national income statistics, expressed in terms of stable prewar prices, confirm our conclusions about the rate of recovery. In brief, they indicate that the prewar level of real income has been reached in all three countries. However, considering the population increase during the last decade, there has been a slight decrease in the real income on a per capita basis.

It must be pointed out that such aggregates as gross national product have to be used with caution. To say that national products have reached the prewar level is not identical with saying that living standards are equal to those achieved in the thirties. A breakdown of the income statistics shows that there were significant changes in the composition of the national income during and after the war.

In Table 3 an attempt has been made to show these changes in the allocation of national expenditure. Detailed analysis of this table is left to the reader, but a few conclusions may be pointed out. In the first place, the percentage of national income devoted to government expenditures has increased in all three countries, while personal consumption has either remained constant or declined somewhat. The proportion of net investment to net national income shows a definite upward trend in Denmark and Norway, but the picture is less clear in the case of Sweden. An increasing

Table 3. The allocation of national income (in percentage of net national income).

	Sweden			Denmark			Norway		
	1938–9	1947	1948	1938	1947	1948	1939	1947	1948
Current expenditure									
Personal consumption	77	76	75	80	81	76	74	75	73
Government consumption	12	15	15	10	13	12	11	17	16
Capital formation									
Net capital formation	11	17	12	9	9	14	15	25	21
Balance of payments on current account		−8	−2	1	−3	−2		−17	−10
Net national expenditure	100	100	100	100	100	100	100	100	100

Source: *Economic Survey of Europe in 1948*, p. 45.

proportion of investment is dependent on savings by public authorities, but even so total savings have been insufficient to bring about a volume of savings that balances the rate of investment. This fact is reflected in the postwar deficit that all three countries show in their balance of payments on current account. In other words, the available resources of the countries have been augmented through an import surplus.

It might seem to follow from this brief survey that the three Scandinavian economies are in excellent shape today and that the difficulties of the transition period have been overcome. This conclusion would not, however, be correct, as a more detailed analysis will show. It is true, as we have seen, that large strides have been made toward restoration of the prewar level of production, but it does not follow that these countries have restored their economic equilibria. Let me substantiate this statement by listing some of the principal factors that have retarded recovery.

1. In the field of money and prices some problems still remain to be solved. First a few facts. In April, 1949, wholesale prices were 89 per cent higher than before the war (1937) in Sweden, 119 per cent higher in Denmark, and 80 per cent higher in Norway. Similar rises have taken place in money wages, but the cost-of-living index has risen somewhat less in the three countries.[1]

A comparison with the United States will show about the same degree of inflation. There are, however, important differences. To use current terminology, American postwar inflation has been "open" since the lifting of controls in the summer of 1946, whereas the Scandinavian inflation has been "suppressed," i.e., postwar prices have been kept relatively stable by direct controls. Since all three countries at the present time have approximately full employment, the principal way to close the inflationary gap without price rises is to reduce the rate of money spending. The alternative is, of course, open inflation. Both courses of action have ad-

---

[1] United Nations Secretariat, Statistical Office, *Monthly Bulletin of Statistics*, III (July, 1949), 27 and 29.

vantages, as well as disadvantages, that I cannot go into here. One special point will be taken up later in connection with the Foreign Aid Program.[2]

2. I now turn to what is undoubtedly the most critical feature of Scandinavia's current economic situation, the dislocation of her foreign trade. It is a general rule that small countries are more dependent on foreign trade than are large ones. The Scandinavian countries are no exception to this rule; on the contrary, it can be stated categorically that the high standard of living of the area before the war was closely correlated with an intensive participation in world trade.

On a per capita basis the value of their exports and imports was three to six times higher than that of those of the United States. If the value of exports (or imports) is expressed as a percentage of national income, the contrast is even greater. It has been as high as 30 to 40 per cent, while the corresponding figure for the United States was about 5 per cent before the last war.

In view of this great dependence on foreign trade, it is obvious that postwar disturbances in the international economic field have had serious repercussions on the Scandinavian economies. The loss of Germany both as a market for their export products and as one of their chief suppliers of raw materials and industrial goods has been serious enough. In more general terms it can be stated that intra-European trade so far has not kept up with European recovery in other fields. The diminished importance of the international division of labor is the joint result of many factors: insufficient production in certain fields, unwillingness to export vital raw materials, and monetary and financial difficulties. The existence of a whole network of bilateral trade and payment agreements made possible a certain expansion of trade in the immediate postwar period; gradually their inflexibility and the exhaustion of

---

[2] Since this was written the inflationary gap has been reduced in both Sweden and Denmark. Norway, on the other hand, has continued a policy of easy money that necessitates a stricter system of direct controls than that in the other two countries.

limited financial resources have made it clear that a further expansion will require a new approach, but more about this later.

A comparison with the prewar volume of trade is presented in
Table 4. From this table is clearly seen the uneven development of
exports and imports. All three countries have substantial import

Table 4. Total exports and imports, expressed in real terms. 1938 =
100.

		1947	1948
Sweden:	Imports	125	109
	Exports	74	80
Denmark:	Imports	80	81
	Exports	67	72
Norway:	Imports	119	100
	Exports	82	85

Source: Economic Survey of Europe in 1948, p. 58.

surpluses. Even if invisible items are included (freight, tourism,
and so forth), there is still a very substantial deficit on current
account in their balance of payments.

What cannot be seen from this table are the important changes
in the geographic pattern of trade, especially on the import side.
Although the Scandinavian countries have fairly balanced trade
with other European countries, they have developed since the
end of the war a huge deficit with the Western hemisphere and
in particular with the United States. Since this deficit constitutes
the hard core of the long-run adjustment problem for Scandinavia,
it might perhaps be appropriate to say a few words about it at this
juncture; I shall come back to it again in connection with long-
term planning under the European Recovery Program.

For Sweden the normal prewar pattern of trade was one of an
export surplus in relation to the United Kingdom, the sterling
area in general, and the other Scandinavian countries, and an import surplus with Germany and the Western hemisphere. The

central point in this multilateral system was the convertibility of pound sterling that made it possible for Sweden to finance her trade deficits with Germany and the Western hemisphere out of her sterling area surplus. This pattern has been distorted in some important respects. Sterling convertibility is something of the past, and at the same time Swedish imports have been transferred from Europe to overseas markets, especially to the United States. As previously mentioned, this transfer is related to the heavy decline in German production of such commodities as solid fuels, iron, chemicals, machines, and textiles. The working of these and other factors is clearly indicated in the Swedish balance of payments for 1947: the global deficit on current account was $400,-000,000, of which $358,000,000 was with the dollar area.

The Danish problem is not very different from the Swedish. The dependence on a multilateral system and on convertibility of pound sterling into dollars is an exact duplication of the Swedish example. Imports from Germany and other continental countries must now come from the dollar area. In 1947 the balance of trade showed a $132,000,000 deficit with the Western hemisphere and a $72,000,000 surplus with the rest of the world.

A high percentage of Norway's receipts from abroad are derived from shipping; in the interwar period this surplus financed the deficit on the trade balance with the Western hemisphere as well as with the sterling area and continental Europe (Germany). In the postwar period the dollar incomes from her shipping have not been sufficient to cover the abnormal increase in imports from this continent. Thus, in 1947 the over-all deficit on current account was $250,000,000, of which $160,000,000 was with the United States and Canada.

THE EUROPEAN RECOVERY PROGRAM
AND SCANDINAVIA

After this brief outline of the current economic problems, let us consider those aspects of the European Recovery Program that relate to the Scandinavian countries. In general it can be said that the economic objectives of ERP are (1) to achieve a distribution of European production and American aid among the participating countries that will contribute most effectively to European recovery; and (2) to make it possible for participating countries to balance their accounts with hard currency areas by the end of the ERP period.

First let us study the annual program prepared by the Organization for European Economic Co-operation (OEEC) in Paris, covering the period from July 1, 1948, through June 30, 1949. The OEEC agreement contains production, consumption, and trade programs and a proposed division among the participating nations of American financial aid amounting to a total of $4,875,000,000. Paul Hoffman, the Economic Co-operation administrator, has stated that these programs would be used as an operating guide by ECA in making its allocations of funds and in authorizing procurement of specific commodities by each participating country.

The first annual program for the three Scandinavian countries is summarized in Table 5. The first column of figures, the direct dollar aid, does not require much explanation. It is supposed to

Table 5. Division of American financial aid, July 1, 1948, to June 30, 1949, expressed in millions of dollars.

	Direct aid	Net indirect aid	Total aid
Sweden	47	—25	22
Denmark	110	6.8	116.8
Norway	84	32.8	116.8
Total	241	14.6	255.6

Source: ECA press release no. 232, 1948, and OEEC, *Agreement for Intra-European Payments and Compensations* (Paris, October, 1948).

cover the programed deficit; that means, among other things, that the receiving country has to spend the money in accordance with plans accepted by OEEC and reviewed by ECA, in both Europe and Washington. The aid is partly on a loan basis and partly in the form of grants. Sweden has not received any grants so far, whereas the major part of the aid to Denmark and Norway has been on a grant basis. The loans that have been extended so far call for an interest rate of 2½ per cent per annum starting in 1952. Repayment of the principal will begin in 1956, and the entire sum is to be repaid in thirty-five years.

How are the recipients spending their first annual appropriation? No information is as yet available about Sweden. In the case of Denmark the most important categories of purchases are coarse grains and feeds for the cattle, petroleum products, tobacco, machinery, and various metals. The Norwegian list is not very different from that of Denmark except that bread grains play a more important role in imports.

The second column in the table, indirect aid, requires more explanation. One of the primary objectives of the European Recovery Program is, of course, to cover the Western hemisphere deficit of each participating country. In the course of these efforts it soon became evident that re-establishment of more normal trade relations among the participants themselves would materially enhance the achievement of the primary aim. For this reason the OEEC has devised a new scheme for the expansion of European trade that is commonly referred to as the "intra-European payments plan." Briefly the scheme works as follows: The participating nations determine through negotiations how much each country can export to and import from the other OEEC members during the next year. This programing of intra-European trade determines a country's position as a creditor or debtor nation vis-à-vis each of the other members of the organization. If a country's balance of payments on current account shows a surplus with another member country, it is obligated to make available sufficient funds in local currency to its trading partner to cover the discrepancy between receipts and expenditures. In this manner all bilateral deficits are to be financed. For example, during the first year of the program Sweden must make available to Norway the equivalent in Swedish kronor of Norway's deficit with Sweden ($21,-800,000). All the members of the payment scheme are receivers of the so-called drawing rights from some countries, and at the same time they must establish drawing rights for other countries. The net figures for the Scandinavian countries are indicated in the second column in Table 5. The last column shows the total aid received, i.e., direct plus indirect aid.

THE FOUR-YEAR PROGRAMS

So far I have dealt with the first phase of the economic reconstruction and the aid the three Scandinavian countries are now receiving under the European Recovery Program. I now turn to what I consider the most important question in this field: the long-term planning of the economic development within these countries. This centers largely on the problem of finding a satisfactory solution to their payment difficulties. In this section I shall discuss the salient features of the planning as it is expressed in the four-year programs submitted by the three governments to OEEC and ECA. In the following section I shall discuss certain questions raised by this planning, first of all, the long-run prospects, i.e., the possibility of achieving viability by 1951 or 1952.

Sweden.[3] In Sweden as in the other Scandinavian countries, the problem is essentially one of making adjustments to structural changes in the world economy that are outside the control of Sweden. More concretely, it involves decisions as to the best use of domestic resources, that is, the relative importance to be given to consumption, investment, and foreign trade.

Since the labor force cannot be expected to change materially over the next four years (and there is no unemployment at the present time), the possibilities of developing Swedish production are thus primarily dependent on improved productivity. In view of the current high rate of investment and modernization an estimated increase of 10 per cent in productivity from 1947 to 1952

---

[3] *The Long-Term Program of Sweden* (Stockholm, 1948).

does not seem unreasonable. A few words about the production and export targets might be in order here. In agriculture a planned increase in output will permit cuts in import requirements of foodstuffs. On the other hand, the success of the program will necessitate additional imports of fertilizer and agricultural machinery. Complete self-sufficiency in foodstuffs will not be achieved at the end of the period. Meat and sugar are imported from abroad and will presumably continue to be in short supply for some time, thus leading to a continuation of the present rationing system.

In the all-important forest industries a maximum output seems to have been reached. Exhaustion of old reserves of virgin forest limits future output to the annual growth of the forests. An expansion of exports is nevertheless programed; it will be in manufactured products rather than in timber and low-quality pulp. The increase is made possible in part by various timber-saving devices in domestic construction combined with a greater domestic use of stone as a building material.

The expansion of Sweden's hydroelectric resources has been given a high priority within the framework of the long-term program because of its great importance to industrial development in general. The same holds true for the iron and steel industries as well as for engineering.

In general, the program calls for an estimated increase in gross national product in 1952–1953 of 10 per cent over 1947. A net decrease of imports by 7 per cent will, however, reduce the total available supply of goods to 9 per cent above the 1947 level. One third of this increase will be needed to fulfill the export program. That will still permit an improvement in per capita consumption of about 5 per cent, together with approximate maintenance of the 1947 rate of investment. (Investment was rather high in the base year because of an abnormal increase in stocks.)

Those aspects of the program that deal with Sweden's international payments are summarized in Table 6. The aim is an over-all balance in Sweden's international payments. This is to be achieved through a 7 per cent decrease in the volume of imports, a 25 per cent increase in the volume of exports, and an improvement of the "invisibles" item.

Table 6. Sweden's balance of payments, 1947 and 1952–53, expressed in millions of dollars.

	1947	1952–53 (at 1947 prices)
Imports	−$1,279	−$1,183
Exports	900	1,127
Balance of trade	−379	−56
"Invisibles"	−21	56
Balance of payments on current account	−400	0

What is of equal importance but cannot be seen from this table is the attempt to establish more balanced trade with separate regions and currency areas. In particular, it is the intention to close the substantial gap in the trade with the dollar area.

Denmark.[4] The present high level of employment means that most of the production effort must be concentrated on activities that will increase efficiency in agriculture and industry. The most obvious approach is to invest more, and that is one of the keynotes in the Danish recovery program. In general it can be said that new investment activity will be undertaken in several fields and that, as a consequence, a balanced expansion can be expected without great structural changes.

For agriculture, of vital importance for Danish economy, the production targets have been set to accomplish two purposes:

1. To bring export capacity back to the 1938 level. For some of the chief products—butter, bacon, and eggs—1947 exports were considerably below the prewar level. Certain changes are also contemplated in the composition of the output: there is to be more bacon than other meat and there are to be more canned and processed food products.

2. To bring domestic food consumption back to the 1938 level.

---

[4] *The Long-Term Program of Denmark* (rev. ed.; Copenhagen, 1948).

Here again there are to be certain changes in the composition of the output.

This production program cannot be carried out without considerable expansion in livestock. In addition it will require substantial investment in machinery and new farm buildings. As part of a much longer program lasting fifteen to twenty years, it is planned to modernize the dairies. Many of these are obsolete, and the number of units is too great while the size of the individual unit is too small to be efficient. The implementation of the farm program will necessitate increased imports of grains, oil cakes, and other feeding stuffs.

In industry the targets are, in general, to increase production so that Danish industry can cover the same proportion of the domestic demand as it did before the war (approximately two thirds). An expansion of industrial exports is also planned.

Danish shipping was harder hit by the war than was any other section of the economy. About one half of the tonnage was lost through acts of war, and replacements were quite insufficient to offset these losses. Since shipping has been an important dollar earner in the past, a determined effort is being made to enlarge the merchant marine and at the same time increase its ability to compete.

As for the gross national product, the target is a 14 per cent increase in relation to 1947. It is expected that the increase in output will, on the whole, be used to increase investments. For the total period, net investment is planned to be about 10 per cent of the gross national product.

The strategic balance-of-trade figures are presented in Table 7. Other items in the balance of payments, such as shipping and the service of the foreign debt, are not shown here. The main outline is, however, clear enough: an attempt is being made to restore equilibrium by the end of the planning period. It is also worth pointing out that in contrast to Sweden a considerable expansion is programed for over-all imports as well as exports. In trade with the Western hemisphere there will still be a deficit at the end of the period. The program is based on the assumption of at least limited convertibility of other currencies into dollars.

Table 7. Denmark's balance of trade, 1947 and 1952–53, expressed in millions of dollars.

		1947	1952–53
Imports	All countries	520	903
	Western hemisphere	145	157
Exports	All countries	460	898
	Western hemisphere	13	98
Balance of trade	All countries	—60	—5
	Western hemisphere	—132	—59

Norway. The destructive effects of the war were greater in Norway than in Denmark, the other enemy-occupied country. It has been calculated that real capital was reduced by nearly one fifth at the end of hostilities. Norway, moreover, is less developed industrially than the other two Scandinavian countries. These two factors go a long way in explaining the general outline of present economic planning, which is an attempt, first, to make up for war losses and, second, to industrialize the country. To make the ambitious investment program possible, consumption cannot exceed the prewar level.

Let us investigate for a moment the production and investment targets in some of the major sectors of the economy. In agriculture the production effort is directed toward greater mechanization and self-sufficiency, especially as concerns bread grains. Should this effort meet with success, it still does not follow that there will be a corresponding saving in foreign exchange, at least not in the short run. An increased output will not be possible without great imports of farm machinery and fertilizers. In mining and manufacturing industries the over-all target is an increase of about 20 per cent by the end of the period. The expansion will take place on a wide front: in textiles, electrochemicals, iron, steel, and ferroalloys and in the mining of coal and iron ores. To mention only one specific example, the provisional plans for aluminum entail a trebling of the output.

Because of its key importance in Norwegian economy, shipping calls for special mention. Half the tonnage was sunk during the war, and, compared to the losses, replacements were negligible. As a consequence, after the end of hostilities top priority was given to the rebuilding of the merchant fleet, but it is not yet complete. By 1953 this total tonnage should be 5,600,000 gross tons as compared with 4,800,000 before the war. Whether the increased tonnage will reflect a corresponding increase in the fleet's earning capacity is, however, doubtful. The importance of this question follows from the fact that shipping receipts in the thirties paid for about one third of total imports.

Table 8 summarizes programed exports and imports as well as "invisibles," which in Norway are receipts derived mainly from shipping. The general outline is clear enough: an attempt is being

Table 8. Norway's balance of payments, 1947 and 1952–53, expressed in millions of dollars.

	1947	1952–53
Imports	$730	$740
Exports	384	536
Balance of trade	—346	—213
"Invisibles" (mainly shipping)	97	193
Balance of payments on current account	—249	—10

made to eliminate the present deficit through a freezing of the level of imports at the same time as a substantial increase is planned for exports and shipping.

AN EVALUATION OF THE
RECOVERY PROGRAMS

What are the long-term prospects of these three recovery programs? The answer must be considered in relation to other Western European countries. As was stated earlier, the problems facing

Scandinavia are not peculiar to that region and hence can only be analyzed in a broader context. Evaluation of the programs and their results will take the form of raising basic questions rather than providing definite answers. That precise conclusions cannot be drawn should not surprise anybody. The number of political and economic unknowns is unfortunately greater than the number of equations that we can construct.

1. One of the basic problems will be how to keep the standard of living within reasonable bounds. As the national income increases, it will be necessary for a time to maintain a fairly stable level of consumption in order to guarantee the success of the investment and export programs. In the Scandinavian plans the definition of adequate standards seems to imply a per capita consumption of about the prewar level. The possibilities for carrying through that part of the program are good. I base that statement on the political and social stability of the region and the fact that the Labor governments in the three countries have been largely responsible for the formulation of the plans.

There is no denying, however, that there may be a constant pressure on money wages in view of the high level of employment. Inflationary gaps have not yet been eliminated. On the other hand, the aid program will of course reduce the inflationary pressure and hence the demand for higher money wages. The anti-inflationary effect will follow partly from the greater supply of goods made available and partly from some mopping up of purchasing power. The latter results from a provision in the Foreign Aid Act that obligates countries receiving assistance in the form of grants to deposit in a special account an amount of their currencies (called "counterpart funds") equal to the full dollar cost to the United States government of the commodities or services furnished. In Denmark and Norway, which are both receiving grants, this will, other things being equal, lead to a contraction in the supply of money and hence will contribute to monetary stability. After agreement with ECA, these funds may be released to finance reconstruction.

While this provision in the Foreign Aid Act might serve a useful purpose in certain continental countries where inflation is a major problem, its importance should not be overestimated in the case of the Scandinavian countries. Their monetary and financial position has shown great stability since the war, and a contraction in the supply of money could and undoubtedly would have been possible without these special accounts. It can also be argued that the establishment of the special funds might lead to an undesirable tightening in the money markets and hence retard the investment programs that are essential to recovery. This device for mopping up purchasing power cannot and should not be a substitute for a flexible monetary and financial policy.

2. Another basic problem is how to reach the investment targets and direct investment into the right channels. One aspect of this problem is related to the relative weight to be given to short-term and long-range investment schemes. The former, replenishment of inventories in particular, will be highly productive for a time. This phase of the reconstruction has not yet been completed in the Scandinavian countries, even though the situation has improved a great deal within the last two years. As for longer investments, the question must be raised whether the schemes we have reviewed are overambitious. The answer seems to be in the negative. Without going into detail I think it can be stated that the program, viewed as a whole, will not lead to an overextension of the capital structure. In none of the countries will the economic structure at the end of the period be radically different from what it is today. On the contrary, a balanced expansion of natural resources, agriculture, and industry seems to be the aim of the four-year programs.

It must be realized that the investment decisions are exceedingly difficult to make in view of the great dependence of these economies on development in the rest of the world. The planners have had to make a number of assumptions about events that are outside their control. Hence it is likely that subsequent revisions will have to be made if the initial assumptions are not in accordance with facts. We shall come back to that point later.

3. The Atlantic pact may change the picture substantially. Even if membership in that alliance should lead to additional aid in the form of military supplies, serious economic problems would undoubtedly be raised. The labor shortage would be increased, and the plans could probably not be carried out in their current form. A similar condition would, of course, result if increased international tension demanded an intensified rearmament program.

4. Apart from international political events the greatest uncertainties are, as already mentioned, in the field of foreign trade. It is not too much to say that the prospects of the four-year programs in the last analysis will depend on the success of the export and import plans. If, for instance, the targets for exports to the dollar area are not reached, there will be serious repercussions. Barring new loans or additional ECA aid, imports of vital materials would have to be curtailed, thus retarding progress in other fields.

While the implications of divergences of actual trade from programed trade are quite clear, it is unfortunately difficult to say anything very precise about the likelihood of such divergences. For one thing, they will depend on the prospects of the European Recovery Program in general. To be more specific, the German and above all the British development will be of vital importance to the Scandinavian countries. As has been mentioned previously, the decline in German production and exports has been one of the major factors contributing to the present dependence on imports from the dollar area. It follows that an expansion of German exports would lead to considerable dollar savings in the Scandinavian countries. In the case of Britain the key problems are (1) how much she is going to import from the European continent and (2) whether it will again be possible to convert sterling receipts into dollars. The present austerity program in Britain has been criticized by other countries participating in the Recovery Program because, it is said, the British policy through import restrictions will make sterling almost as hard a currency as dollars. What the final outcome will be is not yet clear, but the vital importance of this point for the Scandinavian countries does not need to be emphasized.

As for the second point, the prewar system of multilateral trade was, of course, based on convertibility. For the Scandinavian countries that meant that they could use their surplus with the sterling area to finance their deficit with the dollar area. Britain's ability, before the war, to support a large passive balance in its trade with continental Europe and to convert the sterling earned by its trading partners into dollars depended largely on two factors: its substantial income from overseas investments and the dollar-earning capacity of Southeast Asia. These factors are no longer operative. A resumption of at least limited dollar convertibility is of utmost importance to the Scandinavian economies, but I find it hard to believe that Britain will be able to meet all demands for dollars a few years hence. If the present British export drive succeeds, it is possible, however, that partial convertibility might be attained.

In addition to dollar convertibility, the Scandinavian programs visualize a direct way of earning dollars through increased sales in the Western hemisphere or, in the case of Norway, through an expansion of the merchant marine. Whether this effort will meet with success depends on a number of factors. First, can or will the present high level of economic activity be sustained in the United States? Second, the degree of protection in this country is another determinant of the volume of American imports. In postwar commercial negotiations tariff concessions have been made, in some cases amounting to considerable reductions, but barriers still exist, especially in the field of administrative protection (embargoes, licenses, etc.). For example, at the present time certain Danish dairy products are not allowed to enter the American market. There are also special restrictions on the scale of Norwegian silver foxes. Third, increased exports to the dollar area in most cases will depend on intensive and well-organized sales campaigns. This applies particularly to various high-quality and luxury products that might have potential markets in this country.

As has been mentioned previously, steps are now being taken to promote intra-European trade through the so-called Payments Plan. Insofar as payment difficulties have retarded the recovery of European trade, they have contributed to Europe's present dependence on supplies from the Western hemisphere. A resumption of European multilateral trade on a full scale will reduce that dependence and will thus be of the utmost importance to the Scandinavian countries.

5. An evaluation of the four-year programs also calls for a brief discussion of trade relations with Eastern and Central European nations that are not members of OEEC. Before the war these countries were the source of imports that, while low in value, were still of vital importance to the Scandinavian countries. Coal, oil, and various metals and ores are examples. Commodities that flowed the other way were primarily manufactured goods and industrial equipment.

An attempt to restore the prewar pattern of trade has been made since the end of hostilities. A series of bilateral trade and payment agreements have been concluded leading to a certain revival of trade. In this complex of agreements the most important ones are undoubtedly the Swedish-Russian agreement of 1946 and the coal agreements with Poland. The former agreement covers a five-year period, but actual deliveries are determined on a yearly basis. For certain commodities an annual balancing of exports and imports is contemplated, while for other commodity groups the Swedish government has agreed to extend credits to a total value of one billion Swedish kronor (approximately $240,000,000) over the five-year period. Some of the chief Swedish export products are steel, ball bearings, electrical and mining equipment, and building materials. The Soviet government has agreed to deliver various ores, metals, and petroleum products. Both countries have fallen short of the targets; Swedish deliveries in particular are substantially below the anticipated volume of exports at the present time. The explanation given for the failure is shortages of materials and labor.

6. The question is often raised whether greater economic co-operation between the three countries would not be beneficial. The United States has enjoyed such advantages through the existence of a large domestic market with no internal trade barriers. Could not similar advantages accrue to the countries of Europe? I cannot here give a detailed discussion of a Scandinavian customs or economic union. Let me point out, however, that the idea is not a new one. The great similarities in culture and language and in political and social structure seem to be natural arguments in favor of close economic co-operation. On the other hand—and this is of greater importance—the natural endowment of resources and the economic structures are not too different. Insofar as differences do exist, a substantial volume of trade has always taken place. In peacetime, intra-Scandinavian trade fluctuates between 12 and 15 per cent of the total foreign trade. During the two World Wars the percentages have been somewhat higher because of economic blockades. My conclusion is that even complete absence of trade barriers would not produce a substantial rise in trade within the region and hence would not increase its self-sufficiency by a great deal.

I do not want to be misunderstood as saying that closer co-operation would be of no value. On the contrary, I believe that freer movements of labor and capital, for instance, would be a good thing. Productivity would undoubtedly increase with fewer and larger industrial units.

An interesting development is taking place in this field. During the preparation of the long-term programs that have now been submitted to OEEC the Scandinavian ministers of commerce and technical experts have had meetings where common problems have been discussed. The negotiations are still in their initial phase, but it seems likely that they, among other things, will result in important agreements about new investment activity. To be more specific, an attempt is being made to prevent duplication of investment through prior agreements about the tasks to be undertaken by each participant.

To indicate the scope of this work, let me list some of the commodities and fields that might be covered by joint investment control: iron and steel, aluminum, magnesium, fertilizers, cement, shipbuilding, automobiles, sugar, and hydroelectric power. It remains to be seen how much can be accomplished along these lines, but the prospects may be rather good in view of the fact that these plans are related to new investment that will not interfere too much with the existing industrial structure and vested interests.

SUMMARY

As we have seen, the economic problems facing the Scandinavian countries are basically quite similar. On the domestic front the economic policy is one of production recovery, primarily through measures intended to increase productivity. Much of the emphasis is on the achievement of a high rate of investment. The Norwegian policy, in particular, is based on a substantial volume of new investment. This can be explained, in part, by the fact that Norway is less developed industrially than either Denmark or Sweden and that it possesses important undeveloped resources. In Denmark, on the other hand, natural resources are very limited. As a consequence, much of the effort must be concentrated on types of investment that increase efficiency in industries using imported raw materials. For Sweden the key problem is perhaps one of finding investment outlets that will ease the foreign exchange situation.

The chances of reaching the domestic recovery targets are good. The ultimate challenge to the ERP programs lies in another field. Briefly the problem can be stated as one of finding markets for Scandinavian export products. Unless such markets are found, reconstruction will be seriously endangered. This follows, of course, from the fact that imports would have to be curtailed if the export programs failed.

Because of the extreme importance of the foreign trade programs it might perhaps be appropriate to recapitulate some of the basic assumptions on which they are based:

1. A high and stable level of employment and output in the United States;
2. Expanding trade relations with Germany without which the present dependence on the Western hemisphere cannot be reduced;
3. Expanding trade relations with Eastern Europe for the reason indicated under (2);
4. No deteriorations during the reconstruction period of the terms of trade, i.e., the ratio between Scandinavian export and import prices;
5. Continuation of ERP aid for the full four-year period;
6. A considerable increase in exports to the Western hemisphere.

This last point is the hard core of the problem. Whether the planned export targets can be reached seems questionable at the present time. The situation is more serious for Denmark than for the other countries. Even assuming that the dollar drive is successful, the Danish plan still contemplates a significant dollar deficit in 1952 to be covered by a convertible surplus with the sterling area. The prospects for such a convertibility within a few years do not seem too good. It is also true for all three countries that they probably must find outlets for new commodities in addition to increased sales of traditional export articles.

All of this raises basic questions as to the efficiency of the Scandinavian economies, first of all vis-à-vis the United States. It is true that the four-year programs contemplate a substantial increase in productivity, but it should not be forgotten that productivity is also increasing in the United States. Other important variables are, of course, movements of money wages and exchange rates.

Responsible leaders in the Scandinavian countries are fully aware of these problems, and much effort is devoted to searching for solutions. In the final analysis it is clear that only an expanding world economy will provide an answer to these questions. The political and economic fate of the Scandinavian nations will depend largely on a successful integration of their economies into the European economy—and into the world economy as well.

Government Economic Planning

and Control

By PETTER JAKOB BJERVE

Director, Norwegian Central Bureau of Statistics;
formerly Chief of the Division for the National Budget,
Norwegian Ministry of Trade

THE purpose of the present chapter [1] is to give a broad outline of postwar economic planning and control in Scandinavia: the basic objectives, the system of control, the
form of the plans, the allocation of resources, and the procedure
in the planning. An attempt to make a final appraisal of the postwar economic policy in Scandinavia would still be premature, but
some comments on this subject will be made in the conclusion.
Primarily we shall try to answer the following questions: Why
do the Scandinavian countries today apply an extensive system of
direct control over prices and quantities as a means of implementing their economic policy? Why do they plan beforehand how
to use these and other means of economic control? How does the
control and planning actually work? Concrete economic problems
will be discussed only so far as such discussion may help in answer-
ing these questions.

No attempt will be made to present a complete picture for each
of the three countries. Most of the concrete illustrations as well

[1] This study was written during tenure of a fellowship of the Rockefeller
Foundation. I take this opportunity to express my gratitude for the excellent
opportunities for research which have been provided by this grant, and by the
Cowles Commission for Research in Economics, the University of Chicago,
Harvard University, and the University of California. Also I want to acknowl-
edge the valuable comments and criticism of friends who read the first draft of
this paper. These were Kenneth J. Arrow, Odd Aukrust, Jean Bronfenbrenner,
Carl Christ, Henning Friis, Ragnar Frisch, Joseph Grunwald, Otto Hiorth, Lau-
rence R. Klein, Julius Margolis, N. P. Minsky, O. D. Koht Norbye, Ingvar Ohl-
son, John H. Paxal, Harvey S. Perloff, A. R. Prest, and Erik Ruist. Mr. Christ
has even taken the pains to suggest a large number of improvements in language
and organization. In particular I am indebted to the Cowles Commission staff,
with whom I had many fruitful discussions on subjects related to this paper. Of
course, all responsibility for shortcomings falls on the author.

as the descriptions of planning procedure are related to Norway. The reason for this is the fact that the practical experiences of the author are primarily confined to that country; the justification may be the similarity between Norway and the other two Scandinavian countries in the nature of their economic problems as well as the ways in which they handle them. However, to the extent that there are important differences in their approaches to government control and planning, this will be pointed out explicitly.

It may be well to mention that the main differences of approach have their roots not so much in the attitude toward economic control and planning in general as in the different economic positions in which the three countries found themselves at the end of the war: Norway came out of the war with two northern provinces and several cities further south almost completely flattened out, with half of the merchant marine and two thirds of the whaling fleet sunk, and with stocks depleted and fixed capital depreciated, making altogether a 19 per cent reduction of her domestic real capital; Sweden emerged with her capital equipment intact and in some fields even modernized and expanded; and Denmark was in a position in between. Thus the war had increased considerably the differences in industrial development that existed previously among the three countries.

Although the problem of reconstruction is limited to Denmark and Norway, all three countries have encountered severe difficulties in settling foreign payments balances,[2] and internally they have had to struggle against a rather strong inflationary pressure. On the part of Sweden, both of these problems have been intensified by her generous aid in the form of gifts and credit to other countries.[3] Unfavorable terms of trade as well as the general price increase on the world market (increasing the money costs of the

---

[2] See Chapter II.

[3] The Swedish gifts and credit granted to Denmark, Finland, and Norway during and after the war aggregate almost 1,500,000,000 kronor (approximately 6 per cent of one year's gross national product). A similar sum has been granted to other European nations, in addition to the one-billion-kronor credit to Soviet Russia.

import surplus) have not only added to the balance-of-payments problem of all three countries, but have simultaneously made the struggle against inflation much more difficult.

A typical feature of Scandinavian economic policy is that it is not conducted according to any single and simple general formula. On the contrary, attacks on the economic problems are made on a number of fronts by means of differentiated measures adapted to the circumstances under which the problems occur. The guiding principle behind these efforts is to maximize social welfare (in a wide sense) regardless of whether the measures applied may be classified as belonging to one ideology or another. Typically enough, the nationalization question has received relatively little attention during the last ten to fifteen years. Even among those who believe most in the benefits of government control, nationalization is regarded as only one means alongside many others by which the government may increase welfare under certain conditions and circumstances, and this measure is not to be applied in any field of the economy until careful investigations have proved that it may be expected to lead to desirable results. On the other hand, most businessmen agree that a considerable amount of government control and planning has been necessary during the postwar years, and that in normal times also the government must undertake the responsibility of securing at least a minimum standard of living and of preventing mass unemployment. This rather unbiased attitude toward economic control and planning, together with a relatively strong feeling of social responsibility among the leading men of all classes, explains in the main why the Scandinavian countries developed an extensive social security system earlier than most other countries, why in the 1930's they tackled the unemployment problem and the agriculture crisis rather successfully, and why they now attempt to tackle the postwar economic problems in their special manner regardless of the ideological labels that might be attached to the methods.

Another characteristic important to remember when one is judging Scandinavian economic controls is the high degree of honesty of government officials on all levels, in local as well as central administration. Similarly the centuries-old respect for law among the broad masses is extremely significant.

In the discussion to follow a distinction will be made between control and planning, two terms that are often used synonymously. The term government economic "control" will be used to designate all measures taken by the government in order to influence the course of economic development in a particular direction. The term "planning" will be applied only to the elaboration of blueprints in advance of the actual control, that is, the devising of ways to perform the control activity. This control activity must, to a large extent, be carried on by trial and error. What is attempted by means of economic planning is to carry out as much as possible of this trial-and-error process on paper before the actual control commences and, further, to tie the policy of the government control units to the plan in a manner specified separately for each unit.

The terms "government variable" and "private variable" are used for economic magnitudes that are fixed by the government and the private sector, respectively. "Exogenous" variables are ones that may influence government or private behavior but that are not themselves influenced by government or private action. A private variable is said to be more or less "modifiable" according to how easily it is modified by government policy. Other technical terms will be explained in the context where they are applied.

THE BASIC OBJECTIVES

Although the fundamental ideas regarding ends and means of economic policy are similar in the three Scandinavian countries, the formulation of concrete objectives and the emphasis put on each objective varies from country to country, largely reflecting differences in economic conditions.

In Norway, on one hand, the dominating objective, to which many others are subordinated, has been reconstruction, i.e., the rebuilding of real capital that was destroyed, depleted, or depreciated during the war. A quick reconstruction is one of the central ideas of the Joint Co-operation Program, which was adopted by all political parties in the summer of 1945.[4] In Sweden, on the other hand, greater emphasis is put on the problem of achieving a balance between consumption demand and supply, and for this purpose capital formation has been reduced since 1947 by means of a deliberate government policy of strengthening restrictions on building and construction. In Denmark also during the first few years after the liberation monetary problems were emphasized more than reconstruction, and as in Sweden the government started out with the intention of releasing and abolishing the wartime direct controls within a relatively short period. However, the Danish labor government that resumed power in 1947 adopted a policy of speeding up reconstruction. In the National Budget of Denmark for 1948 it was pointed out that capital formation had been too low during the previous postwar years, and that it should be increased considerably in order to complete reconstruction within a reasonable period of time. Actually net capital formation increased about 30 per cent from 1947 to 1948, and a further increase is expected for 1949.[5]

One of the reasons why reconstruction was stressed so much from the outset in Norway was the widespread feeling among all classes of the population that it was a national duty to aid, as much as possible, those who suffered from war destruction, in their efforts to rebuild their homes and resume their old businesses. Furthermore, in spite of the sacrifices involved in the form of lower present consumption, a quick reconstruction was considered a necessary condition for lasting improvements in the future standard of living. In the first place, it was unlikely that such improvements could be made with 19 per cent less capital equipment and 5 per cent larger population than before the war, i.e., with only a little more than three fourths of the prewar real capital per

---

[4] See Chapter II.

[5] See *Danmarks Nationalbudget,* 1948 and 1949 (Copenhagen, 1948 and 1949).

capita. In the second place, with the high concentration of capital reduction in five out of six major export industries—approximately 50 per cent in shipping, 68 per cent in whaling, 43 per cent in fishing, 40 per cent in mining, and 35 per cent in the paper and pulp industry—it was obvious that exports could not be increased to an optimal level without considerable capital formation, particularly in the export industries. Thus, a quick reconstruction might be expected to bring considerable advantages in the future. On the other side had to be weighed the sacrifices of present consumption involved, the risks and disadvantages in the form of a stronger inflationary pressure, and the future costs of eventual foreign disinvestment and borrowing, to the extent that foreign loans could be expected to be obtainable at all. Balancing these gains and losses, the Norwegian government suggested in the National Budget for 1946[6] that reconstruction and rehabilitation be completed in the course of the five years from 1946 to 1950, and later this was made an integral part of the government's economic program. The reasoning behind the present Danish attitude toward capital formation is in many respects the same; but, whereas in Norway the necessity of certain new investments has been stressed, in Denmark relatively more emphasis has been put on capital formation in connection with modernization and rationalization.

The figures in Table 9 on gross capital formation as a percentage of gross national product illustrate well the differences in attitude pointed out above. In spite of the fact that the higher figures for Norway are partly due to a different technique of calculation, it may be presumed that the relative capital formation has been considerably higher in Norway than in Denmark, but until 1947 probably not much higher than in Sweden.

The differences described above have had their counterparts in the external policies of the three countries. The Norwegian reconstruction plan implied an extensive use of available reserves of

---

[6] *Særskilt vedlegg nr. 11 til statsbudsjettet (1945–46), Nasjonalregnskapet og nasjonalbudsjettet* (Oslo, 1946).

foreign currency plus a relatively large amount of foreign borrowing in order to acquire an import surplus without which, it was
realized, the plan could not be contemplated. Large imports were
necessary, partly for merely technical reasons (the facilities for
producing quickly the ships and equipment required were not

Table 9. Capital formation, import surplus, and savings in the Scandinavian countries.

	1946	1947	1948	1949 National Budget
Gross capital formation as a percentage of gross national product				
Denmark	20	19	21	23
Norway	32	37	34	35
Sweden	27	29	26	24
Import surplus of goods and services as a percentage of gross national product				
Denmark	6	2	1	3
Norway	8	12	7	9
Sweden	0	6	2	1
Savings as a percentage of national income *				
Denmark	2	4	7	8
Norway	6	9	11	10
Sweden		8 †	5 †	

* United States gifts not included.
† Approximate figures.
Sources: For Denmark, *The National Budget of Denmark for 1949;* for Norway,
The National Budget for 1949; and for Sweden, *The Economic Survey for 1949.*
Differences between the three countries are partly due to different definitions;
see the text.

available), partly for economic reasons (foreign countries would
be able to produce much of the equipment more cheaply than
Norway), and partly for the reason that it was not found feasible

to restrict consumption more than assumed in the reconstruction plan, i.e., to a total of 95 per cent of prewar in the average for the five years. Even this implied a very severe restriction on imports of consumer goods and on imports of raw materials for the production of such goods. The policy of restricting consumption and at the same time providing for a high import surplus is well illustrated by comparatively high Norwegian figures for both the import surplus ratio and the savings ratio (see Table 9).

For Denmark and Sweden a weakening of direct controls, particularly of the restrictions on imports, resulted in large import surpluses in 1946 and 1947, respectively, primarily due to a sharp increase in the imports of consumers' goods. This is reflected in comparatively low savings ratios, particularly for Denmark (Table 9). Because of the ensuing balance-of-payment difficulties, which of course also had other roots besides the release of import controls, both countries were later forced to retighten considerably the restrictions on imports.

The future external policy of all three countries is characterized by the four-year programs submitted to the Organization for European Economic Co-operation,[7] which assume among other things the attainment of a balance in the total external economy by 1952, although not a balance toward the dollar area. The major means by which the three countries hope to achieve this goal are somewhat different. While Sweden, with her capital equipment in excellent condition, still puts the main emphasis on an early establishment of internal balance, the crucial point in the Norwegian program is capital formation in the export industries, without which foreign trade, at a balanced future level, cannot be so large as a high standard of living requires. The same point of view appears in the Danish program, although perhaps somewhat less emphasized.

In Norway and Sweden the government consumption of goods and services is now, primarily because of higher expenditures for defense, higher than it used to be before the war. There has been

---

[7] See Chapter II.

a reluctance to restrict government consumption for monetary reasons only. Expenditures of this kind appear to be determined largely on the basis of direct security and welfare considerations. This also holds regarding the choice between private and government capital formation (see p. 96). Even such direct welfare considerations, however, have resulted in a restriction of certain kinds of government consumption alongside of restriction of private consumption, viz., for the sake of releasing resources for other purposes.

The equalization of incomes can be regarded as a major objective of economic policy in all Scandinavian countries, and if it is not stated formally by the government, it is in the Labor party programs to which the governments are committed. This objective has two aspects: equalization between industries and equalization within each industry.

Between industries, equalization has taken place primarily as a result of the general and relatively sharp rise in prices of food and manufactured lumber products, particularly paper. This increase has improved considerably the relative incomes of small farmers, fishermen, and forest workers—groups that before the war had the lowest incomes.[8] The governments have admitted relatively large price increases for these groups, partly with the intention of stimulating production and partly for reasons of equity.

Equalization within industries has been furthered by a large number of measures; we shall enumerate several without specifying the countries where they were introduced. The so-called "stabilization policy" (see p. 70) has a definite equity purpose; it protects wage earners against attempts to reduce the inflationary pressure by a policy that would allow prices to increase more than wages; it also increases equality, because the price subsidies, which

---

[8] The total number of persons earning their living from agriculture, fishing, and forestry amounts to approximately 30 per cent of the population in all three countries. Consequently, the relative improvement for these groups has been felt rather severely by the remaining groups, particularly in Norway where national income during the first postwar years was lower than before the war.

are integrated with it, benefit the lower-income groups and families relatively more than higher-income groups and single persons. The social security system has been extended by child pensions, invalid pensions, an increase in old-age pensions, and so forth. The tax policy has been carried still further in an equalitarian direction. The housing policy has taken important steps toward providing a "social housing standard" for everybody. The so-called "solidarity wage policy" has reduced differences between the various wage levels. The imposition of maximum dividend rates and a cheap money policy by and large exert an equalizing effect. Rationing equalizes real incomes by way of consumption.

Besides their equalitarian effects, these measures have evidently affected the balance between labor input (conceived of in the widest sense) and leisure through an increase in taxes that vary with and consequently have a discouraging effect on labor input; by way of increased inflationary pressure; by a reduction of wage differences that has weakened the incentives to education in skilled trades, and so forth. Some of these effects were acknowledged when the decisions on the measures were taken, others not. On the other hand, the securing of practically complete peace on the labor market and a remarkably stable political development in general can be credited in the main to the equalization policy.

Finally, full employment is an objective to which all Scandinavian governments are committed, doubtless with the support of an overwhelming majority among the voters. The financing of the German occupation in Denmark and Norway and of defense in Sweden demonstrated throughout the war years that full employment can be provided for by means of government intervention, if desired. This lesson has been understood by practically everybody, although not in all its implications. As a result any government that does not prevent severe unemployment will be in danger.

To sum up, major goals of Scandinavian postwar economic policy have been as follows: (1) a quick reconstruction, implying a relatively large capital formation; (2) a balance in the external economy to the extent that this is consistent with the preceding objective; (3) allocation of government funds for goods and services on the basis of direct security and welfare considerations, smaller weight being given to their monetary effects; (4) equalization of the distribution of incomes and of the consumption of important consumer goods; and (5) full employment. In the following pages these points are referred to as the "basic objectives," without explicit mention but nevertheless with full cognizance of the qualifications pointed out above regarding the differences between the countries.

Two long-term objectives may also be added, viz., the achievement of higher efficiency in production by means of industrial reorganization—e.g., by nationalization in cases where this is found practical—and the achievement of an "industrial democracy," which will be explained later (pp. 72–73).

Behind and above the economic policy, as well as the policy in other fields, it is assumed that no restrictions can be placed upon political democracy nor upon the fundamental freedoms of speech, writing, and religion. No policy will be permitted to interfere with these ends.

Freedom of choice on the part of the consumer and of enterprise may be partially superseded if required in order to attain the basic objectives. Full sovereignty of individual households is not regarded as an unmodifiable end. The subsequent sections will, I hope, clarify further the attitude toward these ends.

THE CONTROL SYSTEM

We can now answer the question of why the Scandinavian countries during the postwar years applied an extensive system of direct as well as indirect economic controls. The economic problems that have forced upon the Scandinavian countries their postwar systems of economic controls are partly a consequence of the general European and world economic difficulties and partly a consequence of internal circumstances. In Chapter II the international aspects are discussed. Therefore we shall concentrate our attention on the national part of the problem, particularly the problem of inflationary pressure.

At the end of the war a vast need for consumer goods, particularly durable and semidurable goods, existed. In Norway consumption had dropped between 30 and 40 per cent of the prewar level, and in Denmark approximately 20 per cent. In Denmark and Norway these needs were backed by vast sums of liquid assets created by German occupation finance measures, and in Sweden the high expenditures for defense during the war had increased the liquidity far above the prewar level. In addition to the extraordinary demand for consumer goods originating from these sources, a corresponding backlog demand had accumulated for investments in real capital. On the side of supply, Denmark and Norway were left with a considerably reduced per capita production. Consequently there existed in both countries a large inflationary gap that would have brought disastrous effects if not controlled. Even in Sweden an inflationary pressure was felt, but to a much smaller degree.

The battle against inflation has been waged on two fronts. First, steps have been taken to reduce the inflationary pressure. Second, direct controls have been applied with the purpose of preventing the adverse effects of the inflationary pressure, in particular of preventing an uncontrolled price inflation. This application of controls will be discussed later in connection with a description of their institutional setup.

The policy of reducing the inflationary pressure has been limited by the nature of the basic objectives and certain institutional difficulties connected with the effectuation of such a policy:

1. The determination to complete reconstruction within a relatively short period, which required a high rate of saving when the deflated national income was relatively low per capita (Denmark and Norway), has precluded the possibility of increasing the supply of consumer goods at the expense of capital formation. As

already pointed out, Denmark resorted to this expedient during the first few years after the liberation but later switched over to a policy of rapid reconstruction similar to the Norwegian. Sweden, as already mentioned, reduced the volume of building and construction somewhat below the prewar level with the purpose of reducing the inflationary pressure, but, not having any need for reconstruction, such a policy for her did not contradict the basic objectives.

2. The necessity of keeping the import surplus within definite limits has restricted the possibility of relieving the inflationary pressure by increasing supplies from abroad.

3. The desire to allocate government funds on the basis of security and welfare considerations (or the reluctance to reduce government expenditures for these purposes on anti-inflationary grounds only) has restricted the possibility of adopting a deflationary budget policy. Denmark, however, has obtained some relief by abstaining, for monetary reasons, from some expenditures.

4. The policy of equalizing incomes has precluded application of deflationary measures that have their major effect via a less equal income distribution, and has to some extent even required measures with a distinct inflationary effect.

5. The objective of full employment has further restricted the use of over-all monetary measures as a means of combating inflation and decreasing the deficit on the balance of payments. A vigorous use of such measures would probably have created unemployment.

6. The effects on the composition of capital formation of a general increase in the interest level or of a general restriction of credit would have restricted highly desirable investments as well as those less desirable from a social point of view. Particularly they might have prevented certain key investments yielding high external economies from being undertaken or from being completed as early as desirable.

With the exception already mentioned for Sweden, practically the only deflationary measure permitted within the framework of the basic objectives has been a further reduction of the deflated disposable private income at a constant relative distribution. Such a reduction might conceivably have been achieved by increased taxation and decreased government subsidies and transfers, without weakening the possibility of realizing the basic objectives. This policy would have been confronted with a number of institutional difficulties: (1) The wage level, and to some extent also agricultural prices, are tied closely to the cost-of-living index, as described later. Since indirect taxes as well as price subsidies (even direct taxes in Denmark and until recently also in Sweden) affect this index, an increase in these taxes, or a decrease in subsidies, would initiate an upward price-wage spiral and thereby create the effects that they are supposed to prevent. (2) The possibility of tax evasion imposes a limit on direct taxation. Although the tax systems in Scandinavia are rather efficient compared with those of many other countries, there are still loopholes, particularly for farmers, business enterprises, and the non-wage-earning professions. The higher the taxes, the more these loopholes are taken advantage of, and the greater the injustice felt by those who pay the taxes in full. With the present tax system and level of taxation a further increase in direct taxation might also, via incentives, create larger marginal adverse effects on the allocation of resources than the marginal adverse effects created by the inflationary gap. (3) The Bretton Woods agreement, which limits the possibility of changing the exchange rates, imposes another and obvious restriction even on internal policy.

Even if institutional difficulties had not prevented a reduction of deflated disposable private income sufficiently drastic to restore equilibrium on the consumers' goods market, such a restoration might not have been found desirable, at least not during the first postwar years in Norway. To explain this it must be pointed out that the categories of consumption primarily alternative to capital formation—i.e., the categories the restriction of which might have released resources for investment purposes—are textiles and certain kinds of highly important foods such as sugar (66), meat (68), margarine (77), eggs (24), and coffee (70), the figures in parentheses indicating the Norwegian per capita consumption in 1948 as a percentage of prewar consumption.[9] An increase in the consumption of these commodities would have required either imports of finished goods or relatively large imports of raw materials, e.g., feedstuff for the production of meat and eggs, and most of such imports would have had to be paid for in hard currencies. On the other hand, a restoration of equilibrium on the consumers' goods market by means of a drastic reduction of deflated disposable private income would scarcely have reduced the consumption of these goods beneath the level in 1948. Furthermore, it would have reduced the expenditures on liquor, which is heavily taxed, and on travel, movies, and other services that are of such a nature that a reduction in their consumption would release resources and to a large extent leave them idle, i.e., the national income would have been reduced simultaneously.

Another effect of such a policy of restoring equilibrium on the consumers' goods market (with the obvious purpose of abolishing all rationing) would have been to provide an opportunity for people in the higher-income groups and for those possessing assets to increase their purchases of textiles, sugar, meat, and the other goods that are now rationed, thus forcing the lower-income classes and non-asset-owning people to reduce theirs. To avoid this consequence, which would have been undesirable, not only would a still further equalization of incomes have been required but also a radical cut in private wealth. Such a policy might have been more harmful to incentives than the inflationary gap, particularly during the transition period. Whether or not this is true, it has been argued on purely equalitarian grounds that as long as income distribution is not equitable, rationing should be applied to ensure that everyone gets the same amount of the more important goods that are in scarce supply relative to a certain conventional basis, e.g., the prewar per capita consumption.

---

[9] In the course of 1949 the consumption of meat and eggs has increased substantially.

These are the main arguments explaining why the Scandinavian countries have emphasized the necessity of keeping inflationary pressure under control more than the desirability of reducing the pressure. Not until the last year (1948–1949) has the inflationary pressure been substantially reduced. The major factors contributing to this development have been the increase in production, particularly the excellent harvest in 1948; the maintenance of a considerable import surplus, partly by means of Marshall Plan aid; a vigorous tax policy, which in Denmark and Norway was coupled with monetary reform; a more favorable development in terms of trade; the price decline in the United States, which among other things created expectation of price declines even for home products; an increase in the interest level in Denmark; and a cut in capital formation in Sweden.

In the summer of 1949 the total demand in Denmark had been reduced so far that the problem of unemployment was arising. In Sweden also the consumers' goods market was fairly well balanced. Even in Norway more and more goods have changed from a sellers' to a buyers' market, although demand still exceeds supply, particularly for textiles. This development has permitted the abolition of rationing for a number of consumers' goods. Although an extensive system of direct controls is retained, this is a consequence of international difficulties rather than of internal inflationary pressure.

The interest policy of the Scandinavian countries is established by the government. In Denmark the long-term interest rates have again reached the prewar level. In Norway and Sweden the interest rates have been stabilized at a very low level (2.5 to 3 per cent on long-term loans), and consequently the central banks have practically no means of enforcing a restriction of credit. However, by means of recommendations to the private banks via their associations, the central bank backed up by the Ministry of Finance still exerts some influence on the granting of new credit.

A considerable part of the credit to private business is granted by special government and semigovernment banks for real estate, housing, agriculture, fisheries, manufacturing industries, and municipalities. In Denmark particularly there is a highly developed system of co-operative credit associations. All these credit institutes compete with the private banks and the savings banks. The latter are supervised by a government bank inspection agency, by means of which the government can also influence the credit policy to some extent.

The preparation of the state fiscal budget is co-ordinated by the Ministry of Finance. Municipalities and counties adopt their own budgets, which altogether represent almost as large a sum of expenditures on goods and services as the state budget, while subsidy expenditures and tax incomes are much lower. Central control over the local budget policy is rather weak. Considerably stronger are the controls via government investment and material allocation, which apply to the local governments as well as to the various branches of the central government.

The Scandinavian social security systems are among the most extensive in the world, comprising socialized medicine, old-age pensions, family allowances, unemployment insurance, and other benefits.[10]

Commodity imports and exports are controlled by the Ministry of Trade by means of a licensing system, which is supplemented by a direct control of the demand and supply of foreign currencies, which in Denmark has existed since 1932. Most of the foreign trade is regulated by bilateral trade agreements, i.e., agreements with a second country on the quantities for which each of the two countries is obliged to issue import or export licenses during a given period, usually a year. As a part of the efforts to liberalize inter-European trade, proposals for lists of products free of import and export restrictions were to be submitted to the Organization for European Economic Co-operation before October 1, 1949.

The tasks of the import control agency are (1) to allocate the disposable currency among the various groups of imported goods; (2) to distribute the currency allocated to a given group among

---

[10] See Chapter V.

the individual importers of these goods; (3) to ensure that the currency is used for importing goods that, in quality and price, are "import worthy"; (4) to control the fulfillment of the regulations. Number 1 will be discussed later (see pp. 92–93); no. 4 will not be discussed. The tasks specified in nos. 2 and 3 have more and more been transferred to the various trade associations, which operate in contact with and according to general instructions from the Ministry of Trade. The importers of some commodities have even deliberately transferred to their trade association all of their foreign purchasing activities and retain only the task of distributing the goods to their customers within the country. The delegation of control activity to the trade associations has many obvious advantages, but on the other hand it gives these organizations a power that may be liable to misuse. The decisions on which of the importers shall be given the right to import and how much each of them shall be allowed to import are, to a large extent, made on the basis of conditions during a previous base year, e.g., 1946 or 1938. Although there are provisions for the acceptance of new importers and for a modification of the quotas, this system favors old importers and those who happened to import relatively much in the base years. The delegation of control activity to the trade associations presumably further strengthens the position of the older importers.

For some commodities an element of competition has been introduced by means of a system that fixes the quotas to individual importers in relation to the favorable terms of the contracts they have obtained abroad. From an economic point of view this system has many advantages, but it has met considerable opposition from the trade associations.

To understand the importance of import controls as a means of allocating resources in the Scandinavian countries, one must be aware of the magnitude and structure of their foreign trade. Before the war their commodity imports amounted to approximately a fourth of the net national product, and of these imports only a fifth was consumer goods (for Norway in 1948 only 13 per cent), the remaining part consisting of a large variety of goods: fuel, raw materials, and capital equipment of various kinds. Many of the imported raw materials are essential to current production at home, and even for replacements and other capital formation direct imports are required to a relatively large extent. Because of this peculiarity it is possible, to a large degree, to control consumption as well as capital formation indirectly by means of import control. On the other hand, the possibility of increasing currency incomes by directing goods from the home market to foreign markets is rather small, since currency is earned primarily by shipping and by a few other major export industries that produce goods that have a relatively small market at home.

Various kinds of fuel and materials (particularly imported) are allocated to producers by the Ministry of Supply. The quotas of individual purchasers (producers) are fixed largely according to their purchases in a previous base year. However, attempts are being made to establish a system favoring the most efficient firms. Since these commodity controls, to some extent, also include goods produced at home, they supplement the import controls in their influence on consumption and capital formation.

Rationing of consumer goods has been most extensive in Norway, where between 40 and 50 per cent of private consumption still was rationed in 1948. Since that time, however, the situation has improved considerably in all three countries. In the summer of 1949 only sugar, coffee, and gasoline were rationed in Sweden. In addition to these goods, meat, butter, and tea were rationed in Denmark; in Norway even textiles (but not tea and gasoline) were rationed. The rationing system has been based partly on the use of coupons for particular commodities, partly on a coupon system comprising a number of related commodities, partly on individual licensing, and partly on a system of quotas allocated to merchants, who undertake the responsibility of rationing their customers.

Building and construction are controlled by means of a licensing system. A building or construction project employing more than three men cannot be started without such a license, not even by government agencies. In Denmark and Norway the major building materials are also under government allocation.

There are practically no enforced production and delivery quotas, although Norway has made legal provision for such quotas in connection with price controls. Production prohibitions are negligible. There is no direct control of the labor supply in the form of forced labor or prohibitions against accepting certain jobs. The government has, however, an important influence on the total labor supply by means of its Employment Exchange system, which is particularly extensive and efficient in Norway and Sweden. Here the period of unemployment between jobs has been greatly shortened. By its recommendations to employees the Employment Exchange has some directing influence on the labor supply. Other forms of persuasion are applied, and great emphasis is put on the training and retraining of labor. Apart from this, various forms of pricing are used, e.g., travel subsidies and extra ration coupons. Obviously the government has a considerable influence on the demand for labor via the various rationing controls already described.

Rents and a number of prices are fixed as maximum prices that cannot be increased without the permission of the price control agency. Other prices may be increased without special permission when costs rise, but only according to definite rules imposed by law or by the price control agency. Instead of going further into the principles of price fixing, it may suffice to state that the conditions that must be satisfied before the prices of manufactured goods can be raised have, by and large, been very strict. Agreements on prices of the products of agriculture, forestry, and fisheries are made for definite periods after negotiations with the respective industrial organizations. In Norway and Sweden the negotiations on agricultural prices and eventually the agreements are based on a budget for the aggregate incomes of agriculture during the next price period. The decrease in inflationary pressure has permitted the abolition of a number of maximum prices in the course of 1949.

The immediate objective of Scandinavian price control has been to stabilize the cost of living as expressed by the official cost-of-living index. For this reason increases in profits have not been granted if they were not a necessary condition for sustaining or increasing production in fields where increases have been highly desired. For the same reason price subsidies have been used to counteract inevitable increases in import prices and prices charged by producers. Particularly because of price increases abroad, the total amount of these subsidies increased rapidly from 1947 to 1949. It still constitutes a large part of governmental expenditures (more than a fourth of the total in the 1948–1949 state budget of Norway).

This so-called "stabilization policy" is closely linked to wage policy. In Norway there has been a formal agreement between the trade unions and the Employers' Association on a proportional adjustment of wage rates to changes in the cost-of-living index above or below certain limits. As long as the index stays within these limits, no claims for general wage revisions can be raised within the bargaining periods. Practically the same scheme prevails in Denmark and Sweden. By means of the stabilization policy a climbing price-wage spiral has been prevented in spite of the inflationary pressure, and peace on the labor market has been secured with few exceptions. In the summer of 1949 two rather important modifications were made in the Norwegian index agreement: (1) the limits were widened, and (2) whereas formerly wages had to be adjusted automatically as soon as the cost-of-living index reached the upper or lower limit, the new agreement provides only for the right to open new wage negotiations (half automatic price-wage agreement).

The central quantity and price control agencies mentioned above have been supplemented by local control agencies, which have had a relatively great responsibility for the fulfillment of the regulations. In Sweden the central control agencies have been governed by special boards with representatives of business, trade unions, and so forth, while in Denmark and Norway the corresponding agencies have been headed by civil servants.

The government sector of the economy must also be discussed as a part of the control system, in addition to what already has been said about the budget policy. Practically all public utilities are owned and operated by either the state or the local governments, e.g., most of the railroads, the streetcar systems, postal service, telephone, telegraph, and radio. In one or more of the three countries the government has a monopoly on tobacco (import and production but not distribution), liquor, and grain (not production of course). Furthermore the central or local governments own and operate large forest areas; in Norway they own the most important mines, a large part of the hydroelectric power works, and also a number of manufacturing firms. However, by far the largest part of the manufacturing industry is still privately owned. Relatively few publicly owned enterprises have been expropriated from private ownership. Most of them were originally built and developed with public funds. The question of whether certain branches of production should be nationalized is under investigation, but the development of new government enterprises of high significance for the community as a whole is still regarded as more important than the expropriation of existing private enterprises. This view is, perhaps, most pronounced in Norway, which is the least industrialized of the three countries. Here the new government enterprises that have been established in recent years are organized as independent companies in which the government owns more than 50 per cent of the stock.

Co-operatives play an important role in the Scandinavian economies.[11] In agriculture most of the distribution and refinement of products has been taken over by the farm co-operatives, and even in agricultural production co-operation is expanding in the form of co-operative machine stations and in other ways. In the Nor-

---

[11] See Chapter VII.

wegian fisheries the same development is proceeding rapidly. Particularly in the war-devastated provinces, where fishing is the main industry, is co-operation far advanced. In these as well as in other fields the government has stimulated the co-operative movement.

Within the larger factories so-called "production committees" have been or are being organized. The purpose of these committees is to further the co-operation between management and labor, and to give employees the opportunity to influence the policy of the firm by their advice in such matters as improvements in methods of production, training of new workers, and layoffs.

In Norway trade councils with representatives of the employees, the employers, and the government are being organized for the major industries. Their task is to investigate technological and organizational problems within the trades themselves, as well as supervise relationships with other trades. In order to co-ordinate the activity of the trade councils and to advise the government on general economic policy, an Economic Co-ordination Council has been established with representatives of the organizations of private industry, the trade unions, the consumers, and the government. By means of the production committees, the trade councils, and the Economic Co-ordination Council, it is intended to establish an "industrial democracy," which is regarded not only as a good thing in itself but also as an incentive to great efficiency of production.

It must be stressed that the production committees, and in Norway the trade councils as well as the Economic Co-ordination Council, are only advisory bodies. Political power still rests completely with the cabinet and the parliament. But advice goes not only from these bodies to the government, but also from the government via these bodies to the various trades and enterprises. Thus these bodies act as a kind of machinery for mutual economic co-operation between the government, business (including public enterprises), labor, and the consumers. This machinery has been established since the war and is still in an early phase of development. It is too early to appraise its importance. In Norway, however, the Economic Co-ordination Council has already played an important role as a conciliator of different interest groups, and through its advice it has, in many cases, influenced the attitude of cabinet and parliament.

As already mentioned, many of the control institutions described above are emergency measures that have been forced upon the Scandinavian countries by the war and its aftereffects. They will be superfluous as soon as these effects have been overcome. Among the first to be abolished, obviously, is rationing of consumers' goods. International agreements also call for the early abolition of direct import and export control. It is, however, scarcely possible to predict which kinds of control will be abolished and which retained in the long run. The problem will be solved, not on the basis of general ideological principles, but by practical experience, which is still to be gained.

THE NATIONAL BUDGET

Having stated the basic objectives for the economic policy and having described the instruments applied in order to achieve the objectives, we shall now turn to a discussion of how the application of the various means of control is planned. The Scandinavian form of elaborating and presenting plans is the National Budget.

Technically the National Budget is a statistical arrangement, in the form of a double-entry bookkeeping system, of economic flows during a future period. The flows included are so defined as to be pertinent to the decisions on economic policy that must be taken during the same period. The corresponding arrangement of figures calculated ex post facto, i.e., after the flows have occurred, is called the National Account. In its most detailed form the National Budget consists of a large number of accounts and entries. The accounts are so related, however, that, if desired, it is easy to consolidate them and to add their entries pyramidically into simpler systems. The degree of simplification must, of course, depend upon the purpose for which the budget is used.

Table 10 shows a rather simplified version of the Norwegian National Budget for 1949. This system consists of eight accounts,

Table 10. A simplified version of the Norwegian National

| | Production account (a) | | Government and private business enterprises | | | |
			Use of income account (b)		Capital variation account (c)	
	D	C	D	C	D	C
1. Net national product at market price	9,872			9,872		
2. Import surplus of goods and services	1,033					
3. Wages			5,340			
4. Net interest payments			23			
5. Transfers						
a. From government and private enterprises			89			
b. From government (as consumer)				131		
c. From private consumers						
d. From foreign countries						
6. Indirect taxes, etc.			1,491			
7. Subsidies				693		
8. Direct taxes			520			
9. Dividends and profits (net)			3,033			
10. Consumption		8,874				
11. Refunds to government						
12. Saving = net increase of wealth			200			200
13. Net capital formation						
a. Government		512			319	
b. Private		1,519			1,304	
14. Net financial investment					−1,423	
Total	10,905	10,905	10,696	10,696	200	200

Source: *Nasjonalbudsjettet* (1949), p. 127.

one production account for the country as a whole, one account for foreign countries, and two accounts for each of the three economic sectors: government and private business enterprises, government as a consumer, and private consumers, viz., one use of income account and one capital variation account. It

Budget for 1949, expressed in millions of Norwegian kroner.

Government as a consumer				Private consumers				Account for foreign countries (h)	
Use of income account (d)		Capital variation account (e)		Use of income account (f)		Capital variation account (g)			
D	C	D	C	D	C	D	C	D	C
									1,033
					5,340				
74					70				27
	39				50				
918					771				16
	312			322					10
	4				10			14	
	1,491								
693									
	2,081			1,561					
	—91				3,114				10
1,513				7,361					
	130			130					
768			768	—19			—19		
		193							
						215			
			575			—234		1,082	
3,966	3,966	768	768	9,355	9,355	—19	—19	1,096	1,096

would carry us too far to discuss all subdivisions of these accounts and entries. Neither can we deal with the definitional
problems involved in the construction of such a system. It
should be pointed out, however, that the accounts for business
enterprises form a consolidation of corresponding accounts for all

major industries; the accounts for government form a consolidation of corresponding accounts for the central government, the local government, the social insurance system, and public funds; and the account for foreign countries is a consolidation of similar accounts for the major currency areas. Entries 1, 2, 10, and 13, which elsewhere also are calculated "gross," are broken down into commodities, although this breakdown is not yet as detailed as desired. The same holds for the regional breakdown, which is still rather incomplete.

It will be noticed that the fiscal budgets of the central and local governments appear as a part of the National Budget. A statistical difficulty, which may be mentioned here, is created by the fact that the fiscal budget runs from July 1 to June 30, while the National Budget is related to the calendar year. So far this difficulty has been met by making rough half-year estimates for the fiscal budget. The feasibility of adopting the calendar year as the fiscal budget year is being investigated.

In addition to the money figures of the National Budget, certain commodity entries are expressed in physical units. Furthermore, alongside the money figures for the input of various sectors, corresponding employment figures are calculated. These commodity and employment figures are usually arranged separately also in the form of commodity budgets and a manpower budget, which, broken down in various ways, indicate national supply and demand for commodities and manpower. The entries expressed in monetary units are calculated in prices that either exist at the time of calculation or that have been contracted for at this time. In regard to export and import prices, however, special forecasts are made and introduced into the budget as "price fluctuation entries."

For goods that are controlled quantitatively (by import, export, and internal commodity control) there are separate licensing accounts. The definitional relationship between the entries of a licensing account and the entries of the corresponding account for the commodity transaction is:

$$\text{Delivery of commodities against licenses} = \begin{array}{l}\text{issuance of new licenses}\\ -\text{net increase in the}\\ \text{amount of licenses issued}\\ \text{but not used.}\end{array}$$

Of course all entries in this equation are assumed to be related to the same period and measured in the same unit. If the lag between the issuance of licenses and the delivery of commodities against license increases (or decreases) for one reason or another, this will result in a larger (or smaller) net increase in the amount of circulating licenses to the extent that the issuance of new licenses is not diminished (or increased) correspondingly. Eventual changes in these lags are of great importance for the licensing policy.

A complete double-entry budget of the type illustrated above is termed a "general budget." For separate entries or accounts of this general budget the term "special budget" or "subbudget" is used.[12]

The general purpose of the National Budget may be to serve as (1) a systematic diagnosis of the consistency of existing individual plans, (2) a hypothetical prognosis of future development, or (3) a program for the economic policy of the government. In a budget of type 1 a given flow may be estimated differently by its debitor and its creditor, e.g., there may be a "demand surplus" or a "demand deficit" for a particular commodity or aggregate of commodities. The diagnosis of such inconsistencies is often of great importance for economic policy. In a prognosis budget and a program budget such inconsistencies are eliminated, i.e., the expectation value of the various entries in principle ought to be determined by means of a complete model in which the entries and identities contained in the National Budget form only a part. The main difference between the latter two types of budget is that

---

[12] For a description of some of the Norwegian subbudgets for 1947, see Lawrence R. Klein, "Planned Economy in Norway," *American Economic Review*, XXXVIII (1948), 802–808.

while the entries of a prognosis budget are intended only to give information about an expected development, the entries of a program budget define goals for the policy of particular agencies, e.g., the various control institutions of the government.[13] The nature of these three types of national budget is, I hope, clarified further in the next section.

To the extent that a national budget entry can be modified by government intervention, the possible forms of government action must be considered and a decision on such action taken in order to determine the magnitude of the entry. Administratively, the estimation in such cases might be done in two different ways. The policy might be decided upon separately and the affected entries of the National Budget estimated under the assumption of the government variables having the values so decided upon. Another way is to decide upon the policy in close relation to the elaboration of the estimates, so that the estimates are allowed to influence the decisions. In the beginning the elaboration of the Scandinavian National Budgets was undertaken the first way, but it has more and more shifted to the second. Hardly any important decision on economic policy is now taken without previous consideration of the changes in the National Budget that such a policy would entail.

The Danish and the Norwegian National Budgets are both declared to be programs for the economic policy of those governments. However, while each of the budgets as a whole may be regarded as a program budget, the term "program" has no meaning for single entries, which cannot be modified by governmental action. These must be regarded as assumptions underlying the program. The Swedish National Budget in its published version is not declared to be the government's program; rather it is presented as a committee report analyzing the consistency of the economic policy.

Subbudgets of the diagnosis and prognosis type are constructed

---

[13] For a further discussion of this subject see Petter Jakob Bjerve, "Nasjonalbudsjettering," *Ekonomisk Tidskrift* (Stockholm, 1947), pp. 105–109; and also *Nasjonalbudsjettet*, pp. 10–12.

and found useful as tools for the elaboration of the program budget, e.g., surveys are made of investments, of import and export plans of business enterprises, and of savings plans of consumers. As a matter of fact, all the tentative national budgets that are elaborated until the final program budget is determined (see the next section) may be regarded as budgets of the diagnosis or prognosis type.

In addition to the budget for the calendar year, which is published once a year, each of the Scandinavian countries has recently presented a four-year economic program for the period 1949–1952 as a part of the planning for European recovery.[14]

The National Budget does not present explicitly all the governmental, private, and exogenous variables that must be taken into consideration in the construction of a general economic plan, e.g., commodity prices, wages, interest rates, and tax rates. But these figures, as far as is considered practical, are stated in the textual comments to the budget. Together with these comments the National Budget may be regarded as a national plan. In the following discussion the two terms will be used interchangeably.

PLANNING THE ALLOCATION OF RESOURCES

As we have seen, the Scandinavian governments exert a considerable influence on the allocation of resources by means of the present system of economic controls. It is not the purpose of this chapter to evaluate this influence but to explain how it operates and, in particular, how it is planned in advance. In the next section the administrative setup of the planning machinery will be described. It will be pointed out that the planning work is decentralized in the sense that a large number of more or less independent units take part in it. Furthermore, the relationships between these planning units, and the administrative steps taken from time to time, will be sketched.

In this section we shall devote ourselves to the economic aspect of allocation planning, divorcing it almost completely from the

---

[14] See Chapter II.

administrative setup, i.e., we shall proceed as if all planning work were undertaken by one single central institute. First, we shall attempt to explain, among other things, the reasoning behind the decisions on basic objectives. Then the planning of the detailed allocation of resources within the aggregates of national product, capital formation, and so forth will be discussed.

Let us start the aggregate analysis on the basis of the following equation:

National income +   capital formation +
deficit on the balance   =   private consumption +
of payments   government consumption.

At a given sum on the left side of this equation, i.e., a given amount of resources, a high capital formation means a correspondingly lower consumption, and vice versa. Thus the equation illustrates the alternative character of the objectives to which a given amount of resources can be allocated. In reality, however, resources are not given. Nor can the planner deliberately choose any constellation of entries on the right side of the equation. Additional relationships are therefore required in order to determine the aggregate amount of resources as well as the allocation of these resources to different uses. These relationships are of two distinct types. In the first place, the planner needs a social preference scale (a social welfare function) regarding the benefits to the community as a whole of each alternative use of resources as well as regarding the sacrifices involved in supplying the resources. In the second place, there may be technical and behavioristic relationships governing supply and demand. If, for example, supply and demand are classified in aggregate variables as in the equation above, private consumption may be related to national income in a particular way: national income or product may be related to the income distribution, and so forth. The planner attempts to attain as high a level as possible on the preference scale, subject to the constraints of these structural relationships. There may be one and only one particular constellation of variables that is optimal, i.e., that represents the highest social welfare under the given constraints. This is, in an extremely simplified form, the essential logic underlying the allocation planning.[15]

In a strict sense the preference scale or social welfare function, upon which the planners base their decisions, is one of their own. In a democratic society of the Scandinavian type, however, there are many channels through which the preferences of the planners are influenced and modified by those of the people: the parliament, the political parties, the trade unions and industrial organizations, economic discussions in the newspapers, personal contact between the top planners and the voters, and so forth. Thus the planners learn whether or not people are satisfied with the objectives stated, and to what extent people want a change in these objectives. For example, is private consumption being restricted more than reconstruction would justify, or should capital formation be speeded up instead, even at the expense of further restrictions on consumption? Should government consumption be higher and private consumption lower, or vice versa? Should equalization of incomes be carried still further even if such a policy by its adverse effect on incentives can be expected to bring about a decline in production? There can be no doubt that the

---

[15] In mathematical terms this logic may be explained as follows: Let $W = W\ (T, C, I, B, N, L)$ be the social welfare function, as it is conceived of by the planners, where W is an index of social welfare, T of government consumption, C of private consumption, I of capital formation, B of import surplus, N of labor input, and L of the inequality of income distribution. Let, further, $R = R\ (N, L)$ be a behavior equation describing the relationship between national income (or product) R, labor input N, and the inequality of income distribution L. We define: $R + B = T + C + I$. This is the equation with which we started out at the beginning of this section. Maximizing the social welfare function under the constraints of the two latter equations, we get the optimum conditions:

$$-\frac{\dfrac{\partial W}{\partial N}}{\dfrac{\partial R}{\partial N}} = -\frac{\dfrac{\partial W}{\partial L}}{\dfrac{\partial R}{\partial L}} = -\frac{\partial W}{\partial B} = \frac{\partial W}{\partial T} = \frac{\partial W}{\partial C} = \frac{\partial W}{\partial I}$$

Together with the definition and the behavior equation this gives seven equations determining the seven unknowns, $T, C, I, B, N, L,$ and R.

preference scale of the planners is strongly influenced by people's attitudes toward these broad questions of economic choice. The fact that the government is judged by the people at the elections intensifies this influence. On the other hand, the influence is also directed the opposite way.

Of course, the planners do not know the exact mathematical form of their social preference scale, just as the housewife does not know her household preference scale when she plans her purchases. But both know fairly well how to make their choice when confronted with a concrete situation.

Regarding the structural relationships a vast amount of information is provided by means of the administrative procedure of Scandinavian planning—information on exogenous variables, technological relationships, and various relationships expressing human behavior. For example, central and local government experts on agriculture, forestry, and fishing have a good first-hand knowledge of the technology of their respective industries, since they are stationed all over the country and are in close contact with the people in their industries. They also have a pretty good insight into behavioristic relationships, which are of significance for planning. Similar knowledge is possessed by government officials related to other industries. Furthermore, valuable information is furnished by the central organizations of the various industries and trades, and, to the extent that persuasion is used as a means of influencing the behavior of labor and entrepreneurs, these organizations constitute natural intermediaries. As already mentioned, the Norwegian trade councils are intended, among other things, to widen these possibilities.

Some of the behavior relationships may be superseded by restrictions imposed by the government, e.g., individual demand functions may be supplanted by the imposition of rationing. Others cannot be set aside within the legal power that the Scandinavian governments possess or want to possess; e.g., the supply functions of labor, as already pointed out. Still other relationships, e.g., many of the technological relationships, may not be set aside by means of any conceivable power. The government may, however, be able to influence economic development by fixing the magnitudes of the government variables that enter into the behavioristic relationships. Furthermore, it may be able to change the form of these structural relations. For example, it may change the form of the labor supply functions by means of persuasion, industrial training courses, and improved general education. All these limitations of and opportunities for government influence must be taken into account by the planners. Later we shall see some examples of how this is actually done.

Among the relationships that have been taken into account in the determination of basic objectives for Norwegian postwar policy can be mentioned the relationship between national product, consumption, and income distribution. At the low level of consumption immediately after the war, it appeared to be obvious that an increase in the supply of consumers' goods would raise the efficiency of labor. This was one of the reasons why consumption was planned to rise rather quickly during the first postwar months. The relationship between national product and income distribution is not so obvious, but there are good reasons for assuming the existence of an optimum law, i.e., an equalization policy will increase national product up to a maximum point, after which a further equalization will lead to lower and lower production. If this is true, it must be taken into account when the extent to which the equalization policy should be carried is determined. Assumptions regarding this relationship have influenced Norwegian decisions on basic objectives.[16] However, no attempts

---

[16] This may be illustrated by the following graph:

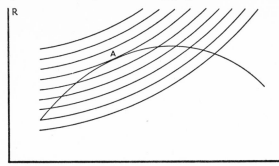

have been made as yet to estimate the form of these relationships by exact econometric methods.

A particular problem that must be watched rather carefully is the exertion of the behavioristic pressure against the restrictions imposed by the government, in particular the pressure against price and rationing restrictions on consumer goods. The technique of this analysis, which has been furthest developed in Sweden, may be described in a simplified way as follows: Capital formation, imports, and government consumption are regarded as government variables, which may be given alternative magnitudes according to the particular policy considered. Independent forecasts are made regarding production, exports, and terms of trade. The supply of consumers' goods is thereby determined for each alternative assumption regarding the government variables just mentioned. The demand for consumers' goods is estimated separately by means of a forecast of the disposable incomes of wage earners, which is based upon the knowledge of prevailing wage agreements and the general status of the labor market, upon definite assumptions regarding the tax and subsidy policy, and so forth. All these estimates are made in the form of increases (positive or negative) from the current year to the next. Finally, all demand increases and supply increases are added up, the sum of the latter is subtracted from the former, and the net increase (positive or negative) in the demand surplus is found.[17]

The obvious purpose of such an analysis is to ascertain to what

---

Here R measures the national product and L is a measure of the inequality of income distribution. The family of curves which are concave upwards are the indifference lines of the welfare function $W = W(R, L)$, where W is the indicator of social welfare. The curve which is convex upwards presents R as a function of L: $R = R(L)$, under the assumption that R is maximized for every L. Under these assumptions welfare is maximized at point A, where $R <$ max. and $L > 0$. This means that the equalization policy should be carried so far, but not farther. The scheme partly illustrates why equalization has not been carried still farther by Scandinavian governments. The use of inefficient means to obtain a given L means that adaptation takes place below the curve for $R = R(L)$. A policy of equalization that leads to an undermaximal R is rational if it does not lead to an adaptation below this curve, and if it leads to the point of tangency A.

[17] In the case of Sweden only a negligible demand surplus has been assumed "carried over" from year to year.

extent alternative policies regarding quantitative restrictions, government consumption, taxes, and so forth will lead to an increase or a decrease of inflationary pressure, and to determine the policy according to the outcome of the investigation. The outcome of such investigations in 1947, together with other indications, actually made the Swedish government increase taxes and, as already mentioned, restrict further building and construction.[18]

Similar investigations have been made in Denmark and Norway, although little has been published about them. Here also they have played a rather important role in quantitative decisions on basic objectives in that they have indicated an upper limit to capital formation above which inflationary pressure might be too difficult to control.

If the social welfare function and all structural relationships determining capital formation, imports and exports, private consumption, government consumption, income distribution, and labor input were known and written down in mathematical form, the values of these variables—i.e., the basic objectives defined in exact quantitative form—might have been found simply with the help of a computing machine. At present this is not feasible, and, as already mentioned, the solution must be found by a process of trial and error or by successive approximations toward optimum welfare. This process is carried out in the form of a balancing of the demand for resources against the estimated supply.

This balancing process is shortened by the fact that it is initiated from the figures of the latest National Account or the current National Budget. The constellation of these figures can be conceived of as the "first tentative solution," which has to be modified to correspond to eventual changes in the social welfare function, in structural relationships, and in exogenous variables, not to mention errors committed in constructing the current budget. Of course, this simplifies the process vastly.

Another simplification, particularly important in short-term

[18] A description in English of an "inflationary gap analysis" is given in a summary of a report by Konjunkturinstitutet, *Översikt över det ekonomiske läget, 1948* (Stockholm, 1948).

planning, stems from the fact that a number of variables can be regarded as predetermined for one reason or another, so that no alternative choice is open. For example, in the last few years the possibilities of obtaining foreign credit have imposed an upper limit on the Norwegian import surplus, and this has restricted the choice in many other respects as well. A second example is the home production of cement, bricks, and lumber, which during the first postwar years could not be quickly increased and consequently restricted the volume of building and construction. One of the first steps taken when commencing the construction of a new National Budget is to investigate to what extent such limitational factors are present.

In order to facilitate the balancing of resources, surveys are undertaken of individual demand-and-supply plans, e.g., of the plans of entrepreneurs for capital formation, production, exports, and the like. In postwar Scandinavia it has often been easy to forecast a demand surplus without the application of plan surveys. Surveys of supply plans have usually been more significant than demand surveys. Nevertheless surveys of, for example, the capital formation being planned by private and government firms have been undertaken in order to furnish a more concrete background for the construction of the capital formation budget. With these plans at hand, the planners can arrive at the final budget by eliminating those individual plans that appear to be of the least social significance.

On the basis of general considerations of the nature described, the decisions on basic objectives are made at the outset of the construction of a new National Budget, but these decisions are only preliminary. Carefully detailed examinations of supply and demand for particular commodity groups and even for single commodities are required in order to ascertain whether the basic objectives can be realized. A final decision on the basic objectives, in other words, cannot be made until the approximation process has been carried through in all its details.

It is impossible, of course, to go into this latter process in all its complexity, but we shall indicate its nature by describing how the detailed estimates are made. At the same time we shall attempt to indicate how the government control system is used in order to influence the allocation of resources. First, the supply of resources will be discussed, and in this connection it is natural to indicate briefly the opportunities for governmental influence on allocation. Next, the allocation planning will be described from the demand side, and in this connection we shall see examples of how the allocation actually is being influenced. Most of the discussion will be limited to Norway.

It has already been pointed out that in all Scandinavian countries a free choice of occupation exists. This of course means that labor has a large degree of autonomy. Apart from training courses and related measures, which may increase the efficiency of labor, various forms of pricing and persuasion are the only means by which labor supply can be modified in amount and direction. A couple of examples from Norwegian production planning may illustrate the nature of this form of control and planning.

During the postwar years it has been clear that foreign currency balances might be increased both quickly and profitably by a larger supply of timber, because timber has limited the production and export of paper and pulp. A comprehensive drive was therefore organized to stimulate lumbering. Forest owners have been given the incentive of substantially higher prices, and, of course, a part of this price increase has been transferred to the lumberers in the form of wage increases. Apart from this, a complex of more specific measures has been undertaken in order to get more work done in the forest: extensive training courses in lumbering technique have been given free by the government; inexperienced lumberers in piecework have been given wage subsidies until they received sufficient training; travel expenses to and from the forests have been partly paid by the government; extra food and clothing rations have been granted to forest workers; government construction works in forest districts have been slowed down during the winter season to release workers for lumbering; unemployed workers fit for forest work are not given unemployment insurance benefits if they refuse to accept forest work; the cabins of the lumberers have been improved and radios have been installed, partly as a result of government initiative and subsidies; a considerable number of motor saws have been bought by the government and either sold at reduced prices or leased to forest owners who cannot afford to buy or do not want to take the risk of buying the saws themselves; conferences have been organized between government officials and forest owners and their organizations in order to explain the importance of an increase in timber production and to stimulate them to greater efforts; production targets have been set for the various forest districts and partly also for individual forest owners, although they are not compulsory. The results of this drive are very encouraging. During the first season (the winter of 1947–1948) the number of workers employed in the forests increased by one third as compared with the preceding year, but because of the heaviest snowfall in many decades timber production increased by only 10 per cent. During the next season the amount of timber was about the largest ever cut in Norway.

The elaboration of production budgets for forestry and for the timber-consuming industries, particularly the building and paper-and-pulp industries, has been based upon definite assumptions regarding the expected effects of the production drive, taking into account the planners' intuitive conception of the supply functions of forest labor and forest owners. Such estimates are made by forestry experts in the Department of Agriculture in co-operation with local forestry officials, the Forest Owners' Association, and the Labor Union for Forestry and Agriculture.

In fishing, another important export industry, the opportunities for influencing production are fewer in the short run. The catch of the main fisheries depends essentially upon the weather, the fish population, and the number of vessels and fishermen taking part. Normal weather conditions are assumed. Oceanographers can forecast the fish population with astounding accuracy. The number of vessels and fishermen taking part in the fisheries is mainly determined by the number of vessels available. Therefore reconstruction of the fishing fleet and its equipment has been allowed to proceed as quickly as technically possible. However, the fish prices also play a role. As soon as these prices are fixed, the expected production of fish is estimated by central and local fishing officials in co-operation with the organizations of fishermen, thus utilizing the latter's special insight.

As long as a demand surplus exists, the volume of production in manufacturing industries can be estimated on the basis of information regarding capital equipment, the supply of fuel and material, and the supply of labor. In the short run the amount of capital equipment cannot be substantially modified by government policy, but over longer periods it may be influenced to a considerable extent, particularly by import licensing. Increases in capital equipment from time to time are ascertained by means of special surveys. For some industries where imported fuel and raw materials are the scarcest input elements, the amount of capital equipment together with the import and allocation policy is the major short-run determinant of the volume of production, prices being fixed only high enough to keep production going. In industries in which labor is the scarcest input element, the prices and wages are of greater importance. Between these two types are industries in which home-produced raw materials are the scarcest input elements. Here the total amount of raw materials may be affected by the price policy, although the allocation policy is the most important factor in the short run. Actually, as already mentioned, the main effort of Norwegian price policy has been to prevent price increase. Only in a limited number of fields have conscious efforts been made to apply price policy as a means of influencing production.

In a number of fields, production cannot be influenced at all, in the short run, by government controls. The production of whale oil by Norwegian whalers in the Antarctic, for example, depends mainly upon the weather conditions, the whale population, the number and quality of the whalers, and the number of their crews, subject to the restriction that the maximum number of whale units permitted to be caught as well as the length of the whaling season is fixed by international agreement. Here also normal weather conditions are assumed. As to the whale population, biological investigations give some indication of the number to be expected. At the time when the estimates are made, all whalers are either on their way to or have already arrived in the Antarctic, so the productive capacity as well as the number of the crews is known. Utilizing these data and their technical knowledge, the whaling companies can furnish the planning authorities with fairly good estimates of the expected production of whale oil.

Another example is the income of the merchant marine, which, when the ships are fully employed, depends mainly upon the tonnage available and the freight rates on the world market. With the help of detailed information about all ships, shipping lines, time charter agreements, and the like, and a special forecast of the freight rates of the world markets, the shipowners' association gives its forecasts of gross freight income, expenditures, and so forth, as well as a breakdown of foreign currency earnings in the main currency types. Since whaling and shipping together produce 10 per cent of Norway's national product and earn 40 per cent of her foreign currency income, it is evident that unmodifiable items in the production and currency budgets play a significant role as fixed points for Norwegian short-term planning. Among other parts of the national product which can be estimated by similar methods may be mentioned the output of hydroelectric power plants, housing services, and a large part of the government product.

Given the amount of foreign disinvestment and borrowing (which has already been discussed), the aggregate imports to be permitted will depend upon expectations of the terms of trade, the volume of production in the export industries, and the possibilities of transferring goods from the home market to foreign markets. The terms of trade are largely determined by the world market. Some rough forecasts of future terms of trade have been attempted, but by and large it has been assumed that these relationships will be the same in the future as at the time of estimation. During the postwar years the volume of production in the export industries in Norway has been largely dependent upon the amount of capital equipment (merchant ships, whalers, fishing boats and equipment, equipment for the war-destroyed mines, the capacity of electrochemical and electrometallurgical plants), and exogenous factors like weather, fish population, and whale population. With the exception of paper and pulp, in which production might have been expanded in case of a larger timber supply, the possibilities of increasing production of export goods by transferring labor to these industries have been very limited. As already mentioned, the possibilities of transferring goods from the home market to foreign markets are also relatively small. Therefore expansion of exports on the scale desired in the long run can be attained only by expanding the equipment in old and new export industries. Consequently, while the possibilities of influencing the aggregate volume of exports over a period of years are great, particularly by means of investment policy, the export budget for a current year has, to a considerable extent, the character of a forecast of what may be expected to be achieved by the various export industries with their existing capital equipment.

All Scandinavian countries plan to expand their exports by 1952–1953, at least to the extent required to pay for the present level of imports. The idea behind this plan, of course, is that up to that point the marginal value productivity will be higher in the export industries than in the branches of production that would have to be expanded in order to replace some of the present imports. The available information on comparative costs in various branches of production seems to sustain this idea. It has been argued that the Scandinavian countries, in order to prevent economic fluctuations originating abroad, should reduce the proportion of foreign trade to national product. However, this point of view does not characterize the present plans.

In the short run also a considerable part of the imports must be regarded as fixed. These are largely goods that are already licensed by the import control and that perhaps have even been purchased by the importers, but they have not yet been delivered. For goods with a long production time particularly there is still a significant lag between licensing and delivery, although it was even longer during the first two postwar years. A large part of Norwegian imports has consisted of such goods, e.g., ships. In 1948 the import of ships alone amounted to almost a fifth of the total imports, and most of these ships were already contracted for when the import plan for 1948 was made. Another part of the imports is stipulated in bilateral trade agreements in force at the time of estimation. These imports regularly find internal buyers and can therefore be regarded as fixed. Finally some import goods have been so scarce on the world market that the deliveries obtainable were smaller than the amounts that otherwise would have been bought. The estimate of such imports has been based on expected deliveries.

To the extent that a choice regarding imports is possible, the composition of the import budget is determined mainly as a derivative of the consumption budget and the capital formation budget, which will be discussed next.

The detailed allocation of the resources allotted for consumption is left to the market mechanism to a large extent, but not entirely. A number of consumers' goods are still rationed, particularly goods that are imported or that require large amounts of imported raw materials in their production. There has been a definite tendency to restrict consumption of a commodity more strongly the more directly it affects the balance of payments. For example, some luxury goods that cannot be produced at home are not imported at all, while others may be available in large quantities simply because they are produced at home. If production of the latter goods requires only labor and raw materials that can be bought freely on the home market, there are no means to restrict such production, except price control, which is not much used for this purpose. If raw materials from abroad are required, production can be restricted more easily; but there has been some reluctance to do so, particularly when the restriction would lead to the laying off of a considerable number of workers. In the Norwegian National Budget for 1949 a change of policy in this respect was announced.

Imports of a number of consumer goods are determined on a compensation basis. For example, in order to sell fox furs to Great Britain, Norway had to agree, in 1948, to import other kinds of furs in return. The furs would not have been imported if the choice had been free. Transactions like this may be preferred to wrecking an export industry that can be expected to yield a relatively high return in the future, but it restricts the possibilities of making a desirable transfer of resources to consumption that has a higher marginal welfare effect.

The fact that parts of consumption can be modified quantitatively while other parts are controlled only by means of taxes, subsidies, and price control calls for two somewhat different techniques when estimating the corresponding types of entries in the consumption budget. While consumption of quantitatively controlled goods may be estimated fairly well by simple methods, consumption of other goods cannot be forecast without taking into account a larger number of behavioristic relationships, in particular the relationship between consumption, prices, and the size and distribution of disposable incomes.

The long-term policy of the Scandinavian countries is to establish a balance on the consumer goods market so that all internal rationing of such goods can be abolished. This will permit individual households to choose quantities freely, subject to the given prices and their disposable incomes, but it does not imply that the market mechanism alone is to allocate resources for consumption purposes. In all Scandinavian countries there is a general consensus that the government even in normal times has the right and the duty to overrule individual household sovereignty in some respects. For example, indirect taxes will surely be used as a means of discouraging consumption of alcoholic beverages and tobacco.

Subsidies will be used to secure a "social housing standard," to stimulate consumption of health-promoting foods, particularly on the part of children, and to provide for a minimum agricultural production at home in order to prevent starvation in case of war and isolation. Consumer goods that now are allocated by the market mechanism may, in the future, be allocated collectively, in one form or another. Unfortunately these questions cannot be discussed here in detail.

The choice between various forms of government consumption may be conceived of as the maximizing of a collective preference function subject to the given amount of resources allocated for this purpose. The National Budget serves as a helpful factual basis for this choice. The method of double-entry bookkeeping forces the administration as well as the parliament to consider in full the consequences of government expenditure for society as a whole. The commodity breakdown supplies the opportunity to compare in a more concrete way the marginal social welfare in government and in private use with respect to each commodity that the government considers using. This is of particular importance in times when a surplus demand exists and when, therefore, people's sense of the marginal utility of income is apt to be erroneous. If under such circumstances government expenditures are decided upon piecemeal without consideration of their effects on the supplies to the private sector, whether in general or for each commodity in particular, it is very likely that they will be too high. If, however, government expenditures are considered as items of a National Budget, such mistakes are less likely to occur. In this respect the National Budget may restore "financial responsibility" and further a rational allocation of resources.

The choice between different forms of capital formation must depend to a large extent upon the composition of future consumption budgets. For certain goods and services, e.g., housing, there is a rather strict technological relationship between the amount to be consumed at home and the amount of a particular type of capital equipment required in order to produce this amount. Scandinavian planning of capital formation relies quite extensively upon this type of data, particularly with regard to reconstruction, the expansion of hydroelectrical power works, housing, and the like. Future consumption estimates, upon which such forecasts are based, are made on the assumption of an unrestricted market for consumers' goods by 1952–1953, a definite development in income distribution, and so forth.

In some fields the formation of capital is limited, not only by the general scarcity of resources, but also by technical bottlenecks that may restrict real investment to an amount smaller than what is deemed to be optimal. For example, such bottlenecks have slowed down considerably Norwegian investment in new ships. Since deliveries of these ships are primarily dependent upon the activity of foreign shipyards, little can be done to speed them up. Another example is the construction of hydroelectrical power plants, which, although proceeding at a high rate, has had to be adjusted to the expected deliveries of dynamos, transformers, and other equipment, part of which must be imported. A large number of other examples might be given.

To the extent that a choice between different categories of capital formation is open, this choice is in part based upon rentability calculations. In such cases external economies are taken into account as far as possible. Such calculations are particularly necessary in regard to the choice between various forms of investment in the export industries. For Norway, rentability calculations indicate clearly that an increase in national productivity may be attained by a further industrialization, particularly in industries that utilize relatively large amounts of extremely cheap hydroelectric power. The industrialization program rests heavily on two cornerstones: expansion of export industries and utilization of the cheap power of the waterfalls. The manpower required for this expanded production in manufacturing industries is expected to come from agriculture and fishing. In order to prevent food production from falling below a safe level in case of isolation, mechanization and rationalization of these industries are stimulated in a number of ways. Among other factors influencing the composition of the capital formation budget are the requirements of defense, the development of backward regions, social viewpoints, and the like.

Besides determining the aggregate capital formation for a given industry, the planners must choose between different entrepreneurs who may want to undertake investment. When a surplus demand exists, the problem is not to find enough investors but to select those who are likely to do the best job. This selection is to some extent based upon cost and rentability comparisons, but existent firms have been in a privileged position. Furthermore, location is taken into account.

The fact that an investment is to be undertaken by a government firm or agency neither raises nor lowers its position on the priority scale. In Denmark, as already mentioned, a restriction of government investment on monetary grounds has taken place, but not in the two other countries. The major criterion for choice among alternative investments is their economic character and rentability (in a wide sense) and not their ownership. Many investments that are regularly undertaken by the government are strictly limited for purely economic reasons, e.g., investments in parks, roads, schools, and hospitals.

In concluding this discussion of allocation planning some attention must be given long-term full employment policy. All Scandinavian National Budgets elaborated so far (up to the summer of 1949) have been based upon the assumption that the aggregate demand will stay high enough to sustain full employment. This assumption is considered realistic inasmuch as no adverse decline in demand originating internally is expected for the next few years. It has been thought likely, however, that a serious decline in demand from abroad might occur. This might eventually affect shipping and other export industries adversely and, if not mitigated, generate a general economic contraction. Comprehensive plans designed to meet such an eventuality have been developed by all three countries; the most comprehensive have been formulated in Sweden.[19]

A characteristic of this antidepression planning is that it does not rely upon single measures but aims at synchronizing economic policy in a number of fields with the purpose of sustaining activity and preventing unemployment. It would carry us too far to discuss all these measures, but one special instrument must be mentioned, the reserve budget. This budget consists of a large number of public works plans that have been elaborated in detail so that the projects can be started at short notice.[20] The projects have also been arranged according to social priorities. Municipalities have been induced to elaborate similar reserve plans. This kind of planning forms a valuable supplement to the kind of planning represented by the current National Budgets.

PLANNING ORGANIZATION AND ADMINISTRATIVE PROCEDURE

Until recently a large part of the economic planning in Scandinavia was carried out by a number of expert committees working more or less independently. During the last couple of years the planning has been more and more co-ordinated within the framework of the National Budget, and a continuously working organization of economic planning has been established. Two of the main characteristics of this organization are (1) that it utilizes the ordinary personnel of the government administration so that relatively few new employees have been required, and (2) that it is highly decentralized, i.e., the planning work is divided among a large number of agencies each being responsible for the prepara-

---

[19] The Committee on Postwar Economic Planning, which was established in 1944 and which continued its work until 1946, has been the major Swedish body for this type of planning. About a dozen comprehensive reports have been presented by this committee.

[20] In Sweden the parliament has already appropriated the funds required for a considerable part of the projects.

tion of a particular subbudget. The planning organization is, of course, closely linked to the organization in charge of economic controls (see pp. 60–73), but in some respects it crosses the control organization so that they are best discussed separately.

In Denmark and Norway the planning is co-ordinated on the top level by a Cabinet Committee for Economic Affairs, headed by the minister for economic co-ordination and the prime minister, respectively. The decisions taken by this committee are promptly communicated to other cabinet members so that, if they desire, they may present proposals for amendments. The cabinet committee is assisted by an advisory committee of civil servants, the National Budget Committee, representing various branches of the central government. The secretariat for this committee is, in Denmark, the Economic Secretariat, attached to the Ministry of Economic Co-ordination and, in Norway, the Division for the National Budget, attached to the Ministry of Trade (which, in Norway, bears the major responsibility for economic co-ordination). In both countries the chief of the planning secretariat is chairman of the committee of civil servants. In Sweden top-level co-ordination is undertaken by the National Budget Delegation, a committee of civil servants headed by the minister of economic co-ordination and assisted technically by the Economic Research Institute of Sweden.

The immediate responsibility for submitting subbudget proposals to the cabinet committee and the National Budget Delegation falls on the various government ministries. The major principle for the division of work among the ministries is that proposals regarding a particular entry in the National Budget are handled by the minstry having the most effective control over that entry, directly or indirectly. Each ministry divides the planning work among its constituent departments and divisions according to the same principle. In many cases these further delegate parts of the work to other branches of the government and sometimes to private organizations, although they retain the right to make changes before the proposals are submitted to their superiors.

The preparation of a number of subbudgets is supervised continually and scrutinized at least once by special committees of experts, on which private organizations are often represented. In Sweden, for example, an Investment Council, with representatives of government, manufacturing industries, agriculture, employers' organization, trade unions, the co-operative movement, and retail and wholesale trades has the object of co-ordinating private investment with public investment. In Norway the Economic Co-ordination Council is in continuous contact with the top-level co-ordination of planning through a subcommittee that eventually submits proposals for amendments directly to the cabinet committee. During the preparation of the National Budget for 1949, a number of such proposals were actually submitted and most of them were accepted. Furthermore, the trade councils will probably be drawn into the planning work in one way or another.

In Norway and Sweden increasing weight has been attached to the regional aspect of planning. Municipalities are induced to prepare investment budgets for their own districts. These budgets are later analyzed and scrutinized both on the county level and on a national level. This part of the planning organization is still in its initial stage, although preparatory work has already started in some districts. The reconstruction planning for the two war-destroyed northern Norwegian provinces has been organized on a regional basis, with a high degree of independence allowed the regional planning authorities.

With this background we shall now describe the administrative planning procedure in Norway. The basic principles are the same in Denmark and to some extent also in Sweden.

Although much preparatory work is done earlier, the actual construction of a calendar year plan for Norway is usually initiated in May by decisions of the cabinet committee on the main outlines to be followed during the planning procedure. Technical decisions are made on the division of the planning work among the ministries (although this does not change much from year to year), on possible special committees to be organized and their mandates, on particular economic and statistical investigations to be undertaken, and so forth. Moreover, a preliminary formulation of the basic objectives is adopted. The wording of this formulation may vary from year to year, but it has always been of the same logical nature as that given on pages 53–60. Finally, in accordance with these objectives more specific directions regarding the allocation of resources are elaborated. Some of these are expressed quantitatively—e.g., the number of housing units to be completed during the year—but most of them are formulated in general terms, indicating priorities. The major purpose of the directions on allocation is to decrease the deviation between the first proposals of the planning units and the final National Budget. The directions regarding the basic objectives and allocation of resources are published together with the National Budget. In the Norwegian publication of the National Budget for 1949, the presentation is organized in two sections: "I, General Directions and Assumptions," stating the basic objectives, and "II, Specific Directions," giving the more specific directions on allocation under the following headings: "Imports and Exports," "Production," "Employment," "Capital Formation," and "Consumption."

As soon as these preliminary directions are prepared, they are transmitted to all ministries, partly as instructions for their particular planning work and partly for information. The ministries pass the instructions and information on to their subordinates, more or less supplemented with additional instructions for their special tasks. When the decisions of the cabinet committee reach the lower levels of the planning organization, supplemented by additional instructions from other superiors, the preparation of the first proposals for subbudgets can commence. By June the work on most subbudgets has commenced. When they are completed they are submitted to superiors, by whom they are often brought together with other subbudgets into a composite plan, which makes it possible to analyze them in a wider context, e.g., the entire import plan is co-ordinated by one division and the export plan by another division of the Ministry of Trade, the plan for the allocation of building materials is co-ordinated by the Housing Directorate of the Ministry of Supply, the manpower budget by the Labor Directorate, and so forth. Finally the various subbudgets reach the National Budget Division, where they are brought together in a preliminary general budget, which, as already pointed out, has the character of a diagnosis budget, at least from the point of view of the cabinet committee. The deadlines for the delivery of proposals to the cabinet committee are set at different times for different subbudgets. The timing is so arranged as to have the basic proposals delivered first. Delivery takes place during August and September. By the beginning of October all subbudgets have been submitted and the preliminary general budget is constructed.

On the various levels of the planning organization, a much larger amount of expert knowledge is utilized than a more centralized planning scheme would permit at the present time. The major weakness of the decentralization is obviously the risk of inconsistency. The same concept may be defined differently by different planning units; an exogenous variable or a relationship that serves as a datum for several planning units may not be estimated similarly by all of them; assumptions concerning government actions may be made in different ways; the objectives may be conceived of differently. Double-entry bookkeeping and the directives attempt to prevent such inconsistencies. Furthermore, thanks to extensive consultations and negotiations among the planning units, the risk of inconsistencies is reduced considerably. Nevertheless, inconsistencies cannot be prevented altogether at the lowest level of planning. This would require that practically every planner continuously consult everybody else. A considerable amount of inconsistency must therefore be rooted out on higher levels. This is done as the subbudgets are brought together in more and more composite plans. But a considerable amount of co-ordination still remains to be done when the budgets reach the National Budget Division for the first time.

The degree to which the various planning units should check for inconsistencies cannot be determined in general terms. The advantage of early co-ordination is that it prevents errors that may later require complicated corrections. The disadvantages are that the checking may force the planning units to wait for each other or may give them an excuse to delay. These advantages and disadvantages must be balanced against each other in each special case.

The cabinet committee, together with its advisory bodies, examines the proposals for subbudgets in order to see whether the preliminary directives have been followed; whether the estimates and assumptions regarding exogenous variables, economic relationships, and government action are consistent; and whether on the basis of the objectives and data the conditions for maximum welfare are satisfied. Moreover, the preliminary decisions on basic objectives and the allocation of resources are reconsidered in the light of the new information that the budget proposals provide. In spite of the co-ordination undertaken on the lower levels, the preliminary budgets have often displayed large demand surpluses. It may be discovered that the preliminary objectives cannot be realized under the given conditions, e.g., because they require too much foreign currency or because the inflationary pressure may be expected to become too large. The possibility of a better testing of the realism of the objectives is one of the advantages of total, as compared with partial, planning. However, while a lack of realism may be discovered at this stage, the presence of realism cannot be proved until a later time.

The co-ordinating activity of the cabinet committee and its advisers results in a number of decisions and suggestions concerning changes in the preliminary subbudget proposals. The planning units must therefore reconsider and revise their first proposals. These revisions require extensive negotiations vertically as well as horizontally within the planning organization, and in some cases the negotiations are even carried as far as to include individual firms. At this stage the trade councils and the Economic Co-ordination Council are intended to play a particularly important role both as promoters and as conciliators of group interests. By their influence it is hoped that these interests may be satisfied to a large extent before the National Budget is presented to the parliament.

Thus the process of successive approximations proceeds until a satisfactory solution is arrived at. This solution may not be the ideal one, if by ideal we mean the mathematically exact solution that might have been found had all data been known and formulated in mathematical terms. The reasons for this are, not only that the data can never be fully known, but also that the advantages of eventual improvements must be weighed against the additional costs incurred by the efforts to achieve them.

The last administrative treatment of the National Budget before it is presented to the parliament takes place in a series of cabinet meetings in which all cabinet members, together with their advisors, are present. These meetings are concluded with the formal adoption of the National Budget as a message to the parliament. The parliament receives the message in the second week of January simultaneously with the government's fiscal budget proposal.

In principle the fiscal budget is prepared as a part of the National Budget. For example, the use of bricks, cement, lumber, and other building materials for government construction of roads, schools, hospitals, military buildings, and administration buildings is determined in the same way and on the same principles as the use of such materials for other purposes, although the selection of the individual projects is to a large degree a matter of negotiation and agreement by the usual fiscal budget procedure.

An obstacle at this point is the fact already mentioned that the National Budget and the fiscal budget are related to different periods of time. This difficulty is partly overcome by agreements

on the timing of certain government expenditures, but full co-
ordination in this respect cannot be achieved. However, as long
as the government cannot buy goods under direct control without having the permission of the various control units, its expenditures will be kept within the limits of the National Budget.

Both budgets are examined simultaneously by a parliamentary
committee and debated later in a plenary meeting of the parliament. This debate, normally occurring in February, ends with the
adoption of a parliamentary observation, which may approve or
disapprove the economic policy implied in the National Budget.
The detailed deliberations on the fiscal budget proceed in the
old form, but in substance the National Budget plays an important role in the outcome. For every proposal involving a change
in the fiscal budget, the party in power insists that the consequences to the National Budget be considered. For example, when
the expenditures for defense were increased in the spring of 1948,
not only did parliament decide upon the fiscal financing, but it
also adopted a recommendation to the cabinet that a proposal for
"national economic financing" should be worked out, i.e., that
the additional expenditures should be introduced into the National Budget and that other entries should be modified correspondingly so as to achieve a balance of resources in the new
situation. However, parliament members still appear to be rather
reluctant to commit themselves to statements on concrete points
in the National Budget. Hitherto the comments of the parliamentary committee, and still more the debates in the plenary
meetings, have been expressed in general and noncommittal terms.

Although the parliament influences the substance of the National Budget by its criticism, the National Budget has in itself
no formal force of law as has the fiscal budget. However, to the
extent that the National Budget is defined as a program for economic policy, it also constitutes definite orders to the control units,
e.g., orders concerning the control of imports and the allocation
of raw materials. Government officials are obliged to follow these
orders just as they are supposed to obey orders in verbal or written

form. One of the advantages of quantitative orders is that they are more precise than other forms of orders.

For private individuals and groups the National Budget has neither the authority of executive orders nor the force of law. To the extent, however, that individuals and groups have agreed upon certain actions or behavior as a part of the plan, the National Budget constitutes a moral obligation. Furthermore, appeals to citizens also have the effect of creating moral obligations. In other words, the National Budget as such does not add anything to the amount of enforced control over the private sector and it does not increase the legal obligations of citizens. These controls and obligations are instituted by special laws. The National Budget only affects the way in which the controls are managed and reminds private individuals and groups of their moral obligations. In the executive sense, it is only a plan for the management of government administration, although it registers the effects of these actions on the entire economy. In a statistical and economic sense, however, it is a national plan.

The fact that the National Budget constitutes a program for economic policy does not imply that it is kept just as it is published in January no matter what happens. Parliamentary revisions of the fiscal budget may require an appropriate revision of the National Budget. And the cabinet itself may also want to revise it for various reasons. Improvements in statistical technique and better information on data relating to the future may well justify such revisions. During the budget period the forecasts of government and private variables are superseded by facts, and to the extent that these facts deviate from the plan they may justify revisions in the figures for the remainder of the period. The reasons for such deviations may be unrealistic assumptions or predictions concerning data, mistakes in deductions from these data, inability or even reluctance to follow up the orders implied in the National Budget, and the like. Changes in the political situation may modify the value judgments of the cabinet and consequently call for revisions; e.g., in the spring of 1948 the growing international tension induced the Norwegian cabinet to propose increased expenditures for defense.

Factors that may justify revisions in the plan are closely watched by all planning units. At regular intervals reports based on ex post facto accounts are submitted to the cabinet committee. These deal with the way the plan is executed, and any important deviations from the policy defined by the plan have to be accepted by the cabinet committee. Thus the superiors can control more efficiently the work of their subordinates. This strengthening of the control is, of course, of particular significance for the cabinet committee and the cabinet itself. Also the parliamentary control is improved in the same way. Another purpose of this reporting system is to inform all planning units about eventual changes in the National Budget as early as possible.

The description above has been related to the one-year National Budget only. But the longer-term planning is more and more being carried on within the framework of the same organization and in a similar way. However, it appears that the procedure for the long-term planning is not yet as well co-ordinated and that the resulting plans are not as consistent as the short-term plans.

CONCLUSION

The weaknesses of a system of direct government control of quantities and prices, as repeatedly pointed out by various authors, are to some extent present in Scandinavia. Some of them are mentioned explicitly in the preceding discussion; the existence of others is implied in the argument at various points. In concluding we shall, however, call attention to this subject once more, and at the same time we shall sum up the major achievements.

First to be mentioned are certain circumstances tending to diminish productivity within particular industries and firms. The tendency of competition to shift production from firms with low efficiency to firms with high efficiency has been mitigated by the price policy and by a policy of allocating fuel and raw materials primarily through the same channels as in the past without vigorously favoring the most efficient producers. Old firms seem to have been unduly favored also by the investment controls, and this form of conservatism has naturally been intensified by the delegation of control activity to the trade associations. Furthermore, the price policy has to some extent discouraged importers from buying as cheaply as possible, and the system of import quotas sometimes has prevented individual importers from taking full advantage of a particularly favorable contract with a foreign exporter. The productivity of individual firms appears to have been adversely affected by the high level and progressive nature of taxation, which, it is claimed, leads to carelessness regarding costs, e.g., expenditures for purposes other than gaining profits appear to have been increased unduly. The tax policy also discourages labor input (including entrepreneurial and professional services) in favor of leisure. The issuance of too many building and material licenses during the first couple of years after the war created temporary shortages of materials, with resulting delays and decreased productivity, particularly in building and construction. A corresponding coupon inflation has taken place for textiles in Norway, and for these goods, as well as for goods that are under price but not rationing control, the consumers have had to stand in lines, search for accidental sales, and so forth. Not only has this been troublesome, but it has absorbed regular working hours and, consequently, has had detrimental effects on productivity. There are, finally, the well-known consequences of an inflationary gap: discouragement of labor input, extraordinarily high labor turnover, and a tendency to hoard labor as well as goods.

Next, adverse effects on the allocation of resources must be pointed to. The rationing of consumers' goods has diminished the possibilities of substitution more than is required by the community's desire to supersede household sovereignty. The subsidy policy, tax policy, and price control have been conducted with the purpose of preventing price increases more than of regulating the allocation of resources, and consequently the supply of highly significant goods has to some extent been discouraged relative to the supply of less significant ones. This has happened partly because of the fact that for goods with heavy weights in the cost-of-living index price increases have not been so easily granted as for goods that weigh less or are not included at all in the index. Partly it is a consequence of the reluctance to admit price increases even on highly significant scarce goods, e.g., timber and certain agricultural goods, the production of which might have been increased faster at higher relative prices. The policy of equalizing wages has further limited the possibility of transferring resources by means of the price and wage policy. In cases where price increases have actually been granted to producers, the corresponding increases in retail prices have been prevented by means of subsidies, and thereby the inflationary pressure has been augmented. Furthermore, resources appear to have been diverted from utilizations that can easily be restricted toward forms of consumption that for administrative or political reasons cannot be effectively controlled, e.g., from the consumption of finished import goods to goods that can be produced with comparatively little or no use of foreign materials. Finally, resources have been absorbed in the activity of control and planning itself, not only within the government but also in the offices of trade associations and in the individual enterprises that have to supply the information required.

Some of these weaknesses are inherent in the control system, others might have been avoided by a better management of the controls, and many have already been or are being overcome. A common characteristic of all of them is the difficulty of measuring their significance quantitatively. They are therefore usually underrated by those who are in favor of the present system and overstated by those who are opposed.

Against the weaknesses a number of achievements may be listed. An uncontrolled and disastrous runaway inflation, which was feared at the end of the war, has been prevented. The level of employment has been extremely high, and practically complete peace on the labor market has been secured. Resources that otherwise would probably have been left idle have been utilized. In Norway and Sweden capital formation has been kept on a high level, and the relative shares of capital formation allotted to the various industries appear to be rational; in particular, external economies are taken advantage of to a larger extent than would probably have been done in a free-market economy. The low costs in the export industries, which the stabilization policy has provided for, will presumably prove to be an important factor in further efforts to improve the balance of payments. Another factor contributing significantly toward this goal is the relatively large capital formation in industries earning foreign currency. Government consumption has been determined in accordance with security and welfare considerations. The private per capita consumption is now well above the prewar level, and income is far more equally distributed than before the war or at the end of the war.

These objectives have been achieved in spite of the deficiencies mentioned above. It is hardly possible to answer definitely the question whether a higher welfare level might not have been attained by means of an entirely different institutional setup, e.g., by leaving the allocation of resources primarily to the market mechanism, with government policy restricted to budgetary and central bank actions only. It would be easier to suggest advantageous minor modifications of the present system or modifications of policy that might have been made within the system, e.g., that a balance between supply and demand for consumers' goods ought to have been established at an earlier time. However, such an analysis would have to take into consideration not only strictly economic, but also political and administrative, problems, and this would lead us too far. Neither can we discuss thoroughly the question of future economic policy in Scandinavia. The control system is gradually being modified in several respects, primarily with the intention of utilizing to a greater extent the market mechanism as a means of allocating resources. How far it will be advantageous to proceed in this direction will depend among other things upon how far international economic co-operation can be extended, how far it proves to be possible to maintain high employment without the effect of a continuous price inflation, and so forth. These are among the burning economic problems that are discussed in Scandinavia at present.

While there may be different views regarding the efficiency of the control systems as well as regarding desirable future modifications, it is more and more being agreed that, given the controls, systematic planning is necessary and advantageous. When a business enterprise prepares budgets or plans for its operations, the purpose is to furnish the management with better information and more efficient tools of analysis, to establish a firmer control and leadership, to extend the possibilities of utilizing special abilities and technical knowledge, to stimulate and enforce a closer co-operation between departments, and to take advantage of the educational value that the activity of preparing plans has for the subordinates as well as for the management itself. The discussion in this chapter has, I hope, made it clear that corresponding advantages can be gained for the nation by means of governmental economic planning. There are yet other advantages to be gained. First, the publication of a National Budget improves the knowledge upon which enterprises and households base their behavior and thus makes them modify their plans in a desirable way. Second, the National Budget provides the government with better opportunities for persuading individuals to act in a particular manner. These two types of benefits are obtained without the imposition of additional government restrictions on the individual. On the contrary, the National Budget rather diminishes the number of enforced restrictions required in order to bring about given behavior. Third, the National Budget widens the democratic influence and control of economic policy. Formerly the quantity and price controls were to a large extent managed independently by the political chiefs and the civil servants of the various ministries, and to some extent by the trade organizations. Thus the administration exerted a much more extensive influence on the allocation of resources than parliament could do by means of its control of the state fiscal budget and the monetary policy. Thanks to the National Budget the distribution of power in this respect is gradually being shifted from subordinate civil servants to their superiors, from these again to the chiefs of the ministries and the entire cabinet, and, finally, from the cabinet to the parliament. So far, however, the parliaments of the Scandinavian countries have not seemed to realize fully the great possibilities provided by the National Budget in this respect.

There are, of course, still many shortcomings in the technique of Scandinavian government economic planning, but improvements are being made on the basis of experience. To the extent that the control system is modified in the future, corresponding changes may be expected in the administrative setup and procedure of planning. Regardless of what changes may be undertaken, the experience that is now being accumulated will be of significant value for future economic policy. It may perhaps be of value for other countries as well.

IV

The Labor Movement and Industrial Relations

By WALTER GALENSON

Assistant Professor of Economics,
Harvard University

T HE highly organized Scandinavian collective bargaining
systems have aroused great interest among students of
industrial relations the world over.[1] It is usually assumed
that Danish, Norwegian, and Swedish developments in this sphere
have been parallel. Actually there are many striking differences,
and in view of the basic cultural unity of Scandinavia these differences and the reasons therefor are worthy of more attention
than they have received. This chapter, while it will attempt to
portray briefly the common characteristics of Scandinavian industrial relations, is also intended as an introduction to the comparative analysis of labor problems in the Scandinavian countries.

TRADE UNIONISM

The roots of the modern trade union movements in Denmark,
Norway, and Sweden reach back to about 1875, when groups of
craftsmen in the printing and building trades began to join together in organizations having as their purpose the protection of
their economic interests. After several decades of preliminary
grouping and regrouping, a central labor federation was formed
in each country just prior to the turn of the century. The Danish
Federation of Labor (De Samvirkende Fagforbund), the Norwegian Federation of Labor (Arbeidernes Faglige Landsorgan-

[1] The interested reader is referred to the following works for particular aspects of the subject: Paul Norgren, *The Swedish Collective Bargaining System*
(Cambridge, Mass., 1941); J. J. Robbins, *The Government of Labor Relations
in Sweden* (Chapel Hill, N.C., 1942); Walter Galenson, *Labor in Norway*
(Cambridge, Mass., 1949); Halvard M. Lange, "Scandinavia," in H. A. Mar-
quand, *Organized Labor in Four Continents* (New York, 1939); *Social Denmark* (Copenhagen, 1945), ch. iv.

isasjon), and the Swedish Federation of Labor (Landsorganisa-sjonen i Sverige), all celebrated their fiftieth anniversaries during the years 1947–1949, the undisputed representatives of organized workers in their respective countries.[2]

Membership. The course of membership growth in the Scandinavian labor federations is shown in Table 11. The Danish federation, profiting from the earlier rise of trade unionism in Denmark,[3] embraced a greater proportion of the eligible workers than its sister federations until recent years.[4] The Swedish federation, after a slow start, made rapid headway until 1907. A depression in the following year and a disastrous general strike in 1909 combined to cancel the early progress, and it was not until the First World War that the losses were recouped. Norwegian trade unionism, partly as a consequence of the tardy industrialization of the country, lagged behind. Not until the nineteen-thirties did it attain a degree of organization and stability comparable with that of its neighbors.

---

[2] In Denmark and Norway all but a handful of the organized workers belong to unions affiliated with these federations (only 26,000 union members were not within the Danish Federation of Labor in 1945). In Sweden, however, successful and well-established organizations of salaried employees (including government employees, Tjänestemännens Centralorganisation), with a membership of 200,000, remain independent. There is also a small syndicalist trade union center, Sveriges Arbetares Centralorganisation, which claimed 22,000 members in 1944. A brief account of the latter organization, one of the few syndicalist labor movements that has been able to establish itself permanently, is contained in Sigfrid Hansson and Olaf Landqvist, *Arbetarrörelsen i Sverige* (Stockholm, 1946), pp. 102–116.

[3] The precise reason for this requires further investigation. Among the contributing factors are the earlier industrialization of Denmark, the small area and relative geographical concentration of industry, and easier access to ideological winds from the Continent.

[4] The extent of organization in Norway and Sweden in the early years is understated by virtue of the failure of important national unions to join the federations immediately. The large Swedish Metalworkers' Union, and other organizations, with a membership of 26,000 in 1900, remained independent of the federation for six years after its establishment. In Norway, the Typographical and Metalworkers' Unions, the two most important national organizations at the time, did not affiliate until 1904. On the other hand, all important Danish national unions joined the federation at the start; in 1899, 75,300 of a total of 89,600 organized workers were within the Danish Federation of Labor.

Table 11. Membership in the Scandinavian federations of labor, 1898–1948.

Year	Denmark	Norway	Sweden
1898	50,959	—	—
1899	75,299	1,600	37,523
1900	77,096	4,800	43,575
1905	68,817	15,600	86,635
1910	101,563	45,900	85,176
1915	131,889	78,000	110,708
1920	279,255	142,600	280,029
1925	239,704	95,900	384,617
1930	259,095	139,600	553,456
1935	381,341	214,600	701,186
1940	515,818	306,500	971,103
1945	604,319	338,600	1,106,917
1948	613,928	447,975	1,211,000

Sources: For Denmark—De Samvirkende Fagforbund, *Under Samvirkets Flag* (Copenhagen, 1948); *Beretning om DsF Virksomhed* (1947); for Norway— Galenson, *Labor in Norway* (Cambridge, Mass., 1941); *Fri Fagbevegelse,* October 15, 1948; for Sweden—*LO Verksamhets Berättelse* (1946); *Fackförenings-Rörelsen,* nos. 33–34, 1948.

Despite differences in the rate of growth, the three federations have attained approximately similar organizational positions within their respective countries. Employing as a rough measure the ratio of trade union membership to total population, an estimated 14.6 per cent of the Danish population, 14.0 per cent of the Norwegian population, and 17.8 per cent of the Swedish population were enrolled in trade unions affiliated with the federations of labor in 1948.[5]

---

[5] Population data are from the 1947 *World Almanac,* adjusted for growth to 1948. It would obviously be more meaningful to relate trade union membership to the labor force than to total population. This would tend to bring Sweden into closer alignment with Denmark and Norway. There is, however, difficulty in defining the perimeters of the organizable labor force, for there are different conceptions of the susceptibility to unionization of white-collar, government, and agricultural workers. If only manufacturing, building, and transportation are considered, then in each country from 85 to 90 per cent of the labor force

Structure and Organization. Broadly speaking, the Scandinavian labor federations are constructed along similar lines. As in the United States, the lowest organizational unit is the local union, which may cover a single plant or a labor market area, depending upon the nature of the activity involved. Local unions are grouped partly along craft and partly along industrial lines into national unions, which in turn are affiliated with the federations. City central trades councils, which preceded the national unions historically, are concerned with local interunion interests, though their importance has declined.

Within this broad outline interesting structural differences appear. In Table 12 are shown the number of national unions and the distribution of membership among them for 1946, separately for each federation of labor. The importance of single or groups

Table 12. Structure of the Scandinavian federations of labor, 1946.

	Denmark	Norway	Sweden
Number of national unions	71	39	45
Average number of workers per national union	8,500	10,200	25,500
Percentage of federation membership in the single largest national union	40	11	18
Percentage of federation membership in the three largest national unions	55	31	33
Percentage of federation membership in the ten largest national unions	73	71	61

Sources: For Denmark—*Under Samvirkets Flag,* pp. 550–560; for Norway—*Fri Fagbevegelse,* March 15, 1947, p. 7; for Sweden—*LO Verksamhets Berättelse* (1946), p. 646.

is organized. See Oluf Bertolt, *Fagforeningskundskab* (Copenhagen, 1946), p. 15; Galenson, *op. cit.,* p. 33; Tage Lindbom, *Sweden's Labor Program* (New York, 1948), p. 11.

of large national unions varies sharply among the three countries. In Denmark the Laborers' Union included within its ranks 40 per cent of the total federation membership, whereas the largest union in Norway had only 11 per cent of the federation membership. When the three largest national unions in each country are considered, Norway and Sweden are at approximately the same level, with Denmark still showing greater membership concentration by virtue of the unique position of the Laborers' Union.

Distribution of membership among the national unions is somewhat more uniform in Sweden than in the other countries, as evidenced by the lesser degree of membership concentration in the ten largest national unions. Swedish national unions are not only larger, on the average, than those of Denmark and Norway —to be expected from the relative sizes of the three countries— but there are fewer craft remnants among them. As many as twenty-six national unions in Denmark had less than one thousand members each, only five Norwegian and two Swedish unions being in that category.

These data reflect a fundamental distinction to be made between the Danish Federation of Labor on the one hand and the Norwegian and Swedish federations on the other. Although all three were initially amalgams of craft unions, the latter two underwent a shift toward the industrial form to an extent that clearly warrants their being categorized as federations of industrial unions at the present time. In Denmark, on the other hand, such tendencies were forestalled by a coalition of the craft unions and the Laborers' Union, an organization of unskilled and semiskilled workers cutting across industrial lines in much the same manner as the British Transport and General Workers' Union. Similar general workers' unions in Norway and Sweden never attained the power of the Danish Laborers' Union and were forced gradually to cede jurisdiction over various fields to newly established industrial unions. But the Danish union made good use of its early organizational strength to fight encroachments upon its jurisdiction.

How can these different lines of development among organizations so closely related be accounted for? Geography was certainly not without influence in this regard. The rural isolation of so many Norwegian and Swedish factories tended to break down barriers between the unskilled and the skilled workers. But in Denmark, particularly in Sjaelland, short distances and easy communication contributed to the preservation of an *esprit de corps* among craftsmen.[6] The relatively small size of the Danish industrial unit of enterprise and the persistence of handicrafts there worked to the same end.

Finally, the earlier foundation of Danish unionism, before the spread of syndicalist doctrine to Scandinavia, may have been a factor in maintaining the craft form of organization. Syndicalism reached its peak in Scandinavia during the decade prior to World War I. The Norwegian trade union movement, experiencing rapid growth during this period, mainly through accretions of new entrants into industry from small farms, was profoundly influenced by the ideals of this philosophy, but the well-established, conservative crafts in Denmark were, with minor exceptions among seamen and building workers, immune to its appeal.[7]

Trade Union Government. In all three federations of labor, the highest legislative authority is the congress, meeting triennially in the case of Denmark and Norway, and quinquennially in Sweden. Between congress sessions important matters are referred to the representative council, a body of about one hun-

---

[6] A unique development of interest grouping in Denmark is the existence of a Women's Labor Union, catering exclusively to unskilled women on an interindustrial basis. Its membership in 1946 was 27,000.

[7] There was some syndicalist sentiment within the Swedish Federation of Labor during the first decade of this century, but the migration of many active syndicalist workers to Norway after the loss of the 1909 general strike and the foundation in 1910 of a separate syndicalist trade union center in Sweden largely purged the federation of its syndicalist elements, although many of the ideas remained.

The Scandinavian experience suggests that the most fertile soil for syndicalism was provided by a combination of rapid industrialization and recruitment of the labor force from among independent farmers rather than agricultural laborers already acclimated to the wage system. This question merits further study.

dred, convening at least once a year and more often if necessary. The executive board is a smaller group that varies in size among the three countries from eleven to fifteen members, including the elected officials of the federation. National union government parallels that of the federations, with some variation.

The most striking governmental divergence among the Scandinavian unions concerns the power of the central federation vis-à-vis the national union. The Danish Federation of Labor, although quite authoritative by American standards, is clearly the least centralized of the three. Originally, it had the power to order sympathetic strikes by affiliated organizations, but it was deprived of this important weapon in 1902 at the insistence of the Laborers' Union. Individual unions are required to notify the Danish federation of prospective contract demands, but they can and do conduct negotiations and determine strategy independently. The federation exercises a degree of negative restraint by virtue of its control over a central strike benefit fund, though this check is minimized by the coexistence of substantial national union strike funds.

Few subjects have been the source of more controversy at Danish federation congresses than the issue of centralization versus decentralization. The decisive, unified bargaining tactics of Danish employers induced periodic attempts to constitute the Federation of Labor a single bargaining spokesman for the workers. The Laborers' Union, however, ranged itself firmly against any invasion of its prerogatives; its commanding position within the federation assured its success in this respect. The history of internal Danish labor politics has been a delicate balancing between the craft unions and the Laborers' Union, neither too willing to subordinate its interests to the whole, but the craft unions readier to sponsor centralization because the method of selecting congress delegates assured them of a majority.

The Norwegian Federation of Labor, in contrast to the Danish, is a highly centralized organization. The federation assumed a great deal of power in its formative years, when it was almost the exclusive repository of strike funds. Although the growth of national union affluence has reduced dependence upon the federation for assistance during work stoppages, the rapid expansion of newly formed industrial unions, the rise of syndicalism, and the strong class consciousness preached by the Norwegian Labor party prevented the dispersion of authority and forestalled extension of the traditional craft separatism that was to be found among the printers, building workers, molders, and locomotive engineers, to mention the most consistent proponents of craft rights. Moreover, there has been no Norwegian national union comparable to the Danish Laborers' Union; the largest single union, the Metalworkers' Union, had only 11 per cent of federation membership in 1946, and could neither impose its will upon the federation nor escape reliance upon federation facilities.

Norwegian national unions are required to submit their economic demands to the executive board of the federation for approval. Failure to heed the advice of the latter may deprive them of federation assistance, financial and otherwise. As a matter of practice, federation representatives either participate in or conduct for the labor side the negotiation of all important collective agreements that are national in scope or concern more than one union. Under its constitution, the federation may assume leadership of a dispute that is likely to affect the interests of more than one affiliate and may order sympathetic strikes.

The Swedish Federation of Labor occupies an intermediate position between the Danish and Norwegian movements. Originally conceived solely as a defensive association, its limited financial resources were reserved for the succor of affiliates against which employers had declared lockouts. Several of the larger unions were unwilling to risk dissipation of their financial and bargaining strength to assist weaker affiliates. The federation was often referred to slightingly as a "statistical office."

Increasingly strong pressure from some of the national unions, particularly the Metalworkers' Union, to establish the sovereignty of the Federation of Labor on a firmer basis, resulted in 1941 in several constitutional changes that greatly expanded the central power. The federation was in effect authorized to co-ordinate wage campaigns involving more than one national union, and its consent was required to any strike affecting more than 3 per cent of an affiliated union's membership. Payment of central benefits was extended to strikes as well as lockouts.

These changes were not effected without strong internal opposition. The proponents of centralization were termed dictators, and some unions threatened to leave the federation in protest. However, by a policy of concession on details, a split was avoided. There is not space to discuss the long history of the Swedish drive toward federation centralism, but labor's rise to political power and the accompanying complexity of the decisions required of the organized labor movement were certainly decisive elements in the 1941 reorganization.[8]

All the Scandinavian trade union movements are characterized by a high degree of internal democracy, the clearest expression of which is reflected in procedure for ratifying collective agreements. In the United States, acceptance of contract terms by union negotiators is tantamount to union ratification, save in exceptional circumstances. In Scandinavia, however, the virtually uniform constitutional requirement of a secret ballot on proposed agreements is the crucial stage in collective bargaining.

It is still not uncommon for agreements reached after days of bargaining to be rejected by the rank and file, in the usually mistaken belief that their leaders have not secured the maximum concessions possible in the existing circumstances. Many union leaders and almost all employers are of the belief that union negotiators should be in a position to make firm commitments, and have urged that steps be taken to limit the frequency of rejection by referendum. The Swedish labor movement in 1941 voted greater power to its negotiators, the referendum becoming more an advisory expression of member opinion. In Denmark legislation has

---

[8] See Jörgen Westerståhl, *Svensk Fackförenings—Rörelse* (Stockholm, 1945), ch. iii.

been enacted to prevent the rejection of agreements by compact minorities in the event of majority apathy.[9] Similar legislation in Norway was repealed one year after its adoption, under strong union pressure, but the executive committees of Norwegian national unions, if they deem participation to be too low, may require new balloting.

The referendum procedure and such other aspects of Scandinavian trade union government as a high rate of turnover in office, low officer salaries, and limited executive authority have created acute problems for the contemporary labor movement. Economic planning requires a degree of trade union responsibility going far beyond the customary preoccupation with wages and other terms of employment. Union leaders are now consulted not only on a broad range of domestic problems but on foreign affairs as well. The necessity for decisive and authoritative response requires greater executive power, and though it is almost inevitable that the trend will be increasingly in this direction, it is certain to meet with strenuous opposition at every step of the way from a rank and file that is exceedingly jealous of its prerogatives.

Political Affiliation. Scandinavian trade unions are strongly oriented toward social democracy in the political field. This half-century-old alliance was threatened only in Norway, where syndicalist doctrine made serious inroads during World War I. Communism, never a serious threat to the social democratic trade union leadership, reached its apogee in 1945 but has declined steadily since then.

Collective affiliation of local trade unions provides the Norwegian Labor party with about 45 per cent of its total membership, and the Swedish Social Democratic party with about 33 per cent. An additional number of trade unionists in each country are enrolled individually. Collective affiliation is not practiced in

---

[9] Section 10 of the Conciliation Act provides that a draft agreement is deemed rejected if more than 50 per cent of the votes are cast against it, provided that 75 per cent of those eligible to vote do so. The percentage necessary for rejection increases by 0.5 per cent for every percentage by which the recorded vote is below 75 per cent.

Denmark, but a majority of the 290,000 Social Democratic party members in 1947 who held individual membership through some 1,350 local clubs were also trade union members.[10]

Except for Sweden, there is statutory machinery for coordinating the policies of the trade unions and the socialist parties. Far more important, however, is the frequent informal consultation between leaders of the parallel movements. While the balance of power between trade union and party varies among the three countries, in none is there domination by either the unions or the party. Rather the two are equals, each with responsibility for a certain sphere, with a mutual recognition of the interdependence of the two branches of the labor movement and strong awareness that division would be disastrous for both.

EMPLOYER ORGANIZATION FOR COLLECTIVE BARGAINING

A distinctive aspect of Scandinavian industrial relations is the prevailing high degree of employer organization. While there is no space for a detailed analysis of the interesting employer movement, a brief résumé of its essential features is in order.

There is in each country a central federated association of employers,[11] with which are affiliated industrial employer associations and individual employers who cannot be grouped within an appropriate association. Recent statistics of membership in the central associations are given in Table 13. Comparison with the trade union membership data in Table 11 indicates that the scope of trade union organization is wider than that of the employers.

However, the membership figures alone understate both the extent of organization and the influence of organized employers in Scandinavia. Thus, in the case of Sweden, the Employers' As-

---

[10] The Norwegian Labor party had 200,000 members in 1947, the Swedish Social Democratic party, 560,000.

[11] Their titles are *Dansk Arbejdsgiverforening, Norsk Arbeidsgiverforening,* and *Svenska Arbetsgivareföreningen.*

sociation is confined to manufacturing and the handicrafts, whereas the Federation of Labor has extended its jurisdiction to all types of economic activity. The Employers' Association embraces a large percentage of the employers within its limited sphere. Moreover, there are in Sweden independent employer associations for agriculture and lumbering, shipping, hotels and restaurants, and other trades. Similarly, in Norway approximately 30 per cent of the organized employers, in terms of workers employed, were outside the Norwegian Employers' Association in 1944.

Table 13. Membership in the Scandinavian central employer associations, 1945 and 1946.

	Number of member associations	Number of member establishments	Number of workers employed by members
Denmark (1945)	246	19,658	212,558
Norway (1946)	16	4,400	160,000
Sweden (1945)	41	7,700	470,000

Sources: For Denmark—Danmarks Statistiske Departement, *Statistisk Aarbog* (Copenhagen, 1946); for Norway—Galenson, *Labor in Norway*, p. 81; for Sweden—Svenska Arbetsgivareföreningen, *A Survey of Social and Labour Conditions in Sweden* (Stockholm, October, 1947).

Of even greater significance is the fact that all the larger manufacturing establishments are within the central employer associations, and that the latter control the key industries in the economy. As the Swedish Employers' Association noted recently, "In collective bargaining . . . the policy of the Swedish Employers' Association is guiding for all employers." [12] The central associations are the obvious spokesmen for the employers in dealing with legislative and administrative agencies.

In each central employer association the highest legislative instance is a general assembly elected by the members, which in

[12] Svenska Arbetsgivareföreningen, *A Survey of Social and Labour Conditions in Sweden* (Stockholm, October, 1947), p. 14 (mimeographed).

turn selects a central board and a small executive committee. The latter body, consisting of fifteen persons in Denmark and Sweden and eight in Norway, is in practice the association's chief policy agency, including within its membership representatives of the important interest groups within the association.

The central employer association normally represents the employer's side in collective bargaining over national agreements. An individual employer member may not conclude an agreement with his workers differing in content from the general agreement without permission of the association. In the event of a conflict an employer may be ordered by the association to institute a sympathetic lockout, a tactic that was quite common before World War II, but which has since become rare. Violation of association rules or the obligations of membership renders an employer liable to substantial fines, which may be collected through the ordinary courts on a straight contract principle.

During a strike or lockout the central association ordinarily pays an affected employer a daily benefit varying between one and two kroner per day for each worker normally employed. This is not intended as full compensation for financial loss suffered from the stoppage, but merely as a source of liquid funds to meet continuing operating expenses. Loans are occasionally made to members who are particularly hard hit by labor disputes.

The association derives its funds from membership dues, which are proportioned to payroll, backed by a subscription bond that each employer must sign upon admission to membership, payable upon demand of the association.[13] Substantial treasuries have been accumulated; the Swedish Employers' Association, for example, reported in 1945 that its funded assets were 62,000,000 kronor, and its guarantee fund was 85,000,000 kronor.

At least since World War I, the Scandinavian employer associations have accepted employee organization and collective

---

[13] The statutes of the Norwegian Employers' Association fix this bond at three times the regular annual dues, while in Sweden it is 200 kronor for each adult male worker and 100 kronor for each female or nonadult male worker

bargaining without reservation. The men who engage in actual negotiation are full-time paid officials, and over the years they have acquired great technical competence and a professional outlook on labor problems. Through constant association with union officials a mutual respect has been engendered that is probably the most important single factor in Scandinavian industrial relations. In Norway, where labor relations have been particularly stormy, a retiring chairman of the Employers' Association recently stated:

I should like to say that the workers' organizations are led by clever men, competent in their trades and devoted to the improvement of labor conditions. . . . Even if we have had differences of opinion, they are always reasonable, and I do not think that I ever participated in negotiation or mediation proceedings where they did not listen to our arguments and give them as much consideration as was consistent with their thousands of mandates. We have no interest in weakening their positions, and when we accord them confidence, we receive confidence in return.[14]

LABOR RELATIONS LEGISLATION

Government regulation of labor relations varies considerably among the Scandinavian countries. It is most complete in Norway and least in Sweden. Danish legislation, although extensive, has largely been enacted on the basis of joint agreement between the central organizations of labor and management, rather than having been imposed upon the bargaining parties from the outside, as in the case of Norway.

Common to all three countries is a well-developed system of government mediation. Upon the failure of employer and trade union negotiators to reach agreement in bargaining over new contracts, a mediator [15] enters the scene in an effort to forestall a work

---

[14] *Arbeidsgiveren* (Norway), Jan. 17, 1947, p. 12.

[15] In Denmark there are three principal mediators, one of whom is designated as chairman, and twelve associate mediators. Norwegian legislation provides for one state mediator with headquarters in Oslo, and for several subordinate mediators in the field. In both countries, however, mediation proceedings are con-

stoppage. Danish and Norwegian law requires both parties to attend mediation proceedings and to postpone direct economic action for a maximum period of one week at the request of the mediator. While there is a similar requirement in Swedish law, no penalties are provided for noncompliance.

If he feels that there is a reasonable possibility of compromise, the mediator may frame a so-called "mediation proposal," which both sides are required to submit to their constituents for acceptance or rejection. While the mediation proposal is not binding in any legal sense, it is of great importance, for to the public it represents a reasonable settlement, in much the same manner as the report of an emergency board under the United States Railway Labor Act. Mediators are understandably reluctant to promulgate proposals that they know will be rejected, and it is rare for a mediation proposal to issue unless at least the immediate negotiators on both sides have given their informal approval.

In the event that mediation fails, the parties are ordinarily free to resort to their economic weapons. Norway, however, adopted compulsory government arbitration during the years 1916–1920, 1922–1923, 1927–1929, and 1945–1949.[16] While this system was in effect, all labor disputes of any significance were subject to final resolution by government boards of arbitration. Denmark resorted to compulsory arbitration during the period of the German occupation, and on several peacetime occasions in the thirties the Danish legislature either averted or ended work stoppages by enacting into law rejected mediation proposals, in order to prevent stoppages that promised to impede the nation's economic recovery.

---

ducted by a single mediator, the chairman or state mediator handling the most important cases. Sweden has seven mediators of equal standing, each with jurisdiction over a particular geographical area; it is the practice of the government, when national agreements are concerned, to appoint an *ad hoc* mediation commission of three to sit with the parties.

[16] During the earlier years, periodic failure of collective bargaining to function led to public pressure for compulsory arbitration. After 1945, however, the Labor government fostered compulsory arbitration as a measure for advancing economic reconstruction.

In Sweden the state has refrained from interfering with the freedom of action of the bargaining parties. Although in all countries both management and labor, except on a few occasions, have firmly opposed government intervention, only in Sweden were they successful in achieving their goal. A joint employer-union Labor Market Board has been established with the function, in part, of acting as a court of last resort in preventing the disruption of vital public services through strikes. It is too early to judge whether this will prove an effective antidote to government intervention, for the damaging 1945 metal trades strike has produced renewed interest in legislation.

No strike or lockout may take place in Scandinavia over disputed interpretations of collective agreements. All controversies of such nature, if they cannot be settled by means of elaborate grievance machinery, must be brought to special tripartite labor courts for final adjudication.[17] Although these courts were opposed originally by the labor movements (except in Denmark, where the Federation of Labor participated in drafting the enabling legislation), they have proved remarkably successful. There is now virtual unanimity that the labor court system is a desirable permanent institution of the labor market.[18]

Norway experimented with legislation designed to regulate the use of the labor boycott. A special Boycott Court was created in 1933 to administer a statute that set forth in detail the conditions under which institution of a boycott was permissible in furtherance of a labor dispute. Labor was uncompromisingly hostile to the Boycott Act, however, and secured its repeal in 1947.[19]

---

[17] The Danish Permanent Court of Arbitration was established in 1910, the Norwegian Labor Court in 1915, and the Swedish Labor Court in 1928.

[18] An English account of the Swedish Labor Court's activities may be found in Robbins, *op. cit.* The principles evolved by the Danish court are set forth in two books: Knud Illum, *Den Kollektive Arbejdsret* (Copenhagen, 1939) and Knud V. Jensen, *Arbejdsretten i Danmark* (Copenhagen, 1946). There is no similar analysis for the Norwegian Labor Court.

[19] This subject is treated in some detail in Galenson, *op. cit.*, ch. vi.

THE RESULTS OF COLLECTIVE BARGAINING

The most mature of the Scandinavian collective bargaining systems is that of Denmark. In 1899 the Danish Federation of Labor and the Danish Employers' Association entered into an agreement, the so-called "September Agreement," which remains the basis of present-day industrial relations with only minor revision.[20] It established uniformity in the rules for terminating agreements and provided procedure for handling grievances and for giving advance notice of work stoppages. The rationale of the agreement was epitomized in the following clause: "It is assumed that the Danish Federation of Labor will be willing to work together with the Danish Employers' Association for peaceful, stable and good relations."

A supplementary agreement reached in 1936 established March 1 as a uniform termination date for all collective agreements and envisioned boards of arbitration for the voluntary submission of disputes on matters other than general wage changes. In addition, there has grown up over the years an elaborate mechanism for handling contract interpretation disputes (the Danish Labor Court does not interpret collective agreements but merely hears complaints based upon alleged contract breaches) as well as disputes over new substantive matters, originally through individual agreement but since 1934 as standard procedure for all members of both the trade unions and the employers' organization.[21]

While there has been direct negotiation between the central

---

[20] An English translation of the September Agreement is available in Socialt Tidsskrift, *Industrial Relations in Denmark* (Copenhagen, 1947).

[21] The 1948 agreement between the Danish Typographical Union and the Paper Goods Employers' Association, typical in this respect, sets forth the following steps in handling such disputes: (1) mediation by a committee consisting of one representative of each party, which shall assemble within three days of the demand therefor; (2) further negotiation by the organizations, upon failure of the mediation commission to settle the dispute; (3) submission of the dispute to arbitration, at the request of either party, the arbitration board to consist of three representatives of each party together with a neutral named jointly by them for periods of one year.

organizations of labor and management in Norway since 1900, the bargaining rules were to be found either in collective agreements restricted to particular unions or in legislation. It was not until 1935 that an agreement comparable to the Danish September Agreement, the so-called "Basic Agreement," was concluded between the Norwegian Employers' Association and the Norwegian Federation of Labor. The principal provisions of this agreement were (1) mutual recognition of the right to organize for collective bargaining; (2) regulations governing the appointment and functions of shop stewards; (3) grievance and disputes procedure; (4) procedure for referenda on proposed agreements; and (5) rules for the imposition of sympathetic work stoppages.[22]

The Swedish Basic Agreement was concluded in 1938, the first of its kind between the two central bargaining organizations. It contained the following stipulations, among others:

1. A bipartite, six-member Labor Market Board was established to deal with specified questions pertaining to the discharge of workers, labor disputes affecting essential public services, and restrictions upon the right to resort to direct action.

2. A fairly detailed procedure for negotiating agreements was provided.

3. Certain restrictions on the right of employers to discharge individual workers were adopted.

4. Certain forms of direct action were prohibited, e.g., strikes or boycotts for purposes of religious, political, or personal persecution.[23]

This agreement arose out of a series of formal conferences between the party organizations that were held at Saltsjöbaden beginning in 1936. The conference has become a permanent feature of Swedish industrial relations in the form of a Labor Market Committee that continues to meet at Saltsjöbaden on occasion. In

---

[22] This agreement was renewed in 1947 with minor changes. For an English translation of the 1947 Basic Agreement, see Galenson, *op. cit.*, Appendix A.

[23] The Swedish Basic Agreement is available in an English translation, published in pamphlet form by the Twentieth Century Fund.

1942 it furthered the creation of a joint Labor Safety Board to work within the field of labor protection, and in 1944 it agreed upon a joint Labor Market Occupational Council to promote vocational training. Thus, although the Swedish collective bargaining system developed relatively late, it has become more complete, and certainly less dependent upon state intervention, than either the Danish or the Norwegian.

As in the United States, Scandinavian conditions of labor are set forth in written collective agreements, which vary in coverage from entire industries to individual establishments. There were in 1940 some 6,200 collective agreements in Norway, covering 392,000 workers; for Sweden the number of agreements (in 1943) reached 14,000 and embraced 1,100,000 workers.[24] These summary figures conceal the degree of centralization that actually exists. In 1942, for example, 107 Swedish collective agreements, nation-wide in scope, covered 423,000 workers, while an additional 154,000 workers were included within 143 district-wide agreements. It was estimated that 50 national agreements in Norway covered a majority of the country's organized workers. Although there are numerous agreements applicable to small units, uniformity of labor conditions is secured through a relatively few key agreements.

With regard to wage content, it may be noted first that the extent to which piecework prevails varies among the three countries. Thus it was found that in 1936 the Swedish ratio of piecework hours to total hours worked in manufacturing and mining was about 60 per cent.[25] The Danish figure for the same year was 41 per cent (46 per cent for skilled workers), falling to 35 per cent in 1944,[26] the corresponding figure for Norway being 36 per cent (1940).[27] These compare with approximately 40 per cent

---

[24] Recent data for Denmark are not available.

[25] Norgren, *op. cit.*, p. 132.

[26] De Samvirkende Fagforbund, *Under Samvirkets Flag* (Copenhagen, 1948), p. 382. This decline can be attributed largely to wartime cessation of construction work, on which piece rates are largely employed.

[27] Galenson, *op. cit.*, p. 216.

for a similar sphere of economic activity in the United States. A peculiar aspect of Scandinavian piece rates is their application to site work in building construction.

There are two major systems of time-wage payment. The "normal wage" system, which establishes a full schedule of occupational wage rates, corresponds to the usual American practice. But in many industries, particularly those in which the work cannot be standardized, collective agreements provide only a minimum rate below which no worker in an establishment may be paid, and actual rates are determined by individual bargaining between the employer and the workers.

The principle of tying wages to a cost-of-living index has had considerable application in Denmark and Norway during the interwar period; it was first introduced in Sweden in 1939. This method of wage fixing was an important determinant of wages during and after the recent war. The scope of the index adjustment has been nation-wide, beginning with 1939, based upon agreement between the central bargaining agencies in all three countries. In Denmark and Norway, the index wage increases were added as a flat öre supplement for all workers (women received less than men), resulting in relative wage advances for the lower-paid groups. Sweden, however, made the adjustment as a uniform percentage addition to wages, thus preserving customary differentials.

Wartime inflation made the cost-of-living supplement an important element in total earnings. In Denmark the nationally negotiated supplement comprised almost 30 per cent of the earnings of male workers, and 40 per cent of the earnings of female workers, in 1947. For Norway about 25 per cent of adult male earnings could be attributed to the cost-of-living allowance in 1946. Sweden abandoned adjustment by the index in 1947, but the bulk of wartime wage increases there were based upon the index agreement. With the stabilization of the price level, it may be anticipated that Danish and Norwegian trade unions will also press for discontinuance of national adjustment by the cost-of-living index.

Real wage comparisons among the Scandinavian countries, though they would be extremely interesting, require elaborate analysis of absolute living standards in the three countries. Comparative indices of real wage trends since World War I do not yield meaningful results, since absolute standards were not similar in Denmark, Norway, and Sweden during any base year. Thus, for example, Danish real wages were 185 in 1939 (1915=100), Norwegian real wages 245, and Swedish real wages 200. Yet Danish employers have always argued that wages in Denmark were relatively higher than those in Norway and Sweden. This seems plausible in view of the fact that Denmark was the first in which organized labor achieved a status of equality in bargaining power with employers.

As for real wage movements in the interwar period, the trend was continuously upward in all three countries, though it was slowed by the depression of 1930. A severe decline in real wages took place during the recent war, particularly in Norway. By 1946, however, Denmark had achieved an 8 per cent real wage increase and Sweden a 7 per cent increase over the 1939 level, while Norwegian real wages stood at 97 per cent of the 1939 level.

INDUSTRIAL DISPUTES

The procedures for the peaceful adjustment of labor disputes have by no means eliminated strikes and lockouts. Table 14 shows the work-stoppage record of the three countries from 1920 to 1939 by five-year periods. The most difficult period came during the post-World War I deflation, when employer efforts to reduce money wages were met by strong union resistance, though in the end the reductions were carried through. The record thereafter was generally much better.

There are striking dissimilarities in the experiences of the three countries. Keeping in mind relative differences in size, it is apparent that Denmark was by far the most successful in averting resort to economic force. Were it not for a general workers' strike in 1925, the worst in Danish labor history, accounting for 95 per cent of the total man-days lost for the entire period 1925–1929, the Danes would have achieved an incredibly low strike level during the decade 1925 to 1934. The only other bad year was 1936, when the refusal of employers to raise wages in the face of increasing prices resulted in a stoppage that cost the country 94 per cent of the total man-days lost during the five-year period 1935 to 1939. During the German occupation stoppages ceased almost entirely, but the rise of Communist influence after 1945 produced labor unrest and resulted in a loss of 1,386,000 man-days in 1946, the most severe strike wave since 1936.

Table 14. Work stoppages in Scandinavia, 1920–1939.

Period	Denmark		Norway		Sweden	
	Number of workers involved	Number of man-days lost	Number of workers involved	Number of man-days lost	Number of workers involved	Number of man-days lost
		in thousands		*in thousands*		*in thousands*
1920–1924	130,670	5,094	276,502	10,822	391,302	22,392
1925–1929	107,760	4,332	100,533	4,807	292,314	10,173
1930–1934	26,835	641	83,206	8,819	157,365	10,937
1935–1939	103,234	3,087	87,642	3,005	82,712	3,530

Source: International Labour Office, *Yearbook of Labour Statistics* (Montreal, 1942).

Norway's labor dispute record, for the twenty-year period as a whole, was the worst of the three. Up to 1931 there were periodic collapses of collective bargaining under the impact of a slow, grinding deflation. After 1931, however, there was a perceptible improvement, due in part to the upward cyclical swing and in part to a strong desire on both sides to avoid further hostilities. During the war there was a cessation of normal industrial relations, but the Labor party victory at the polls in 1945 and consequent trade union acceptance of compulsory government arbitration

eliminated legal strikes entirely and left only a residue of un-
authorized stoppages that in the aggregate amounted to very little.

In Denmark and Norway the bulk of lost time was accumulated
in single "bad" years, as a result of the common employment of
the sympathetic strike and lockout by the highly organized labor
market participants. The Swedish trade unions, however, were
chary of the sympathetic strike as a result of their bitter experience in the general strike of 1909. As a result, bargaining tended
to be more particularistic in Sweden and there is a more uniform
year-to-year distribution of time lost due to work stoppages.

Considering that the Swedish population is about as large as
that of Denmark and Norway combined, the Swedish record of
stoppages from 1935 to 1939, a period that marked the matura-
tion of its national collective bargaining system, is an enviable one.
Work stoppages were held to a very low level during the war,
but the year 1945 brought a protracted strike in the metal trades
that resulted in a more serious loss of working time than in any
previous year of Swedish labor history.[28] Since then, however,
the trend of work stoppages has been on the decline.

Whether over the last few decades industrial relations in Scandinavia have been more peaceful than those in the United States
cannot be answered simply. A comparison of the United States
and Sweden from 1916 to 1937 led to the observation that "the
over-all volume of stoppages in the two countries has been much
the same." [29] But work stoppages are a function not only of the
economic cycle and of employer and labor attitudes toward
collective bargaining, but also of the stage and extent of labor
organization. Until the great organizing drives of the middle
nineteen-thirties, American trade unions were far weaker than
the Scandinavian, and collective bargaining embraced a much
smaller sector of the economy. Moreover, organizational strikes
loomed large in the American record of work stoppages prior to

---

[28] The total time lost for the year 1945 was 11,300,000 man-days.
[29] Norgren, *op. cit.*, p. 166.

the recent war, whereas Scandinavian strikes were almost entirely over economic differences.

For the decade 1930 to 1939 as a whole, the Scandinavian record of work stoppages was worse than that of the United States. Whereas the American labor force in manufacturing, mining, and transport was 18,600,000 against 2,440,000 for Scandinavia (1940), a ratio of 7.6 to 1, the number of man-days lost from work stoppages was 141,900,000 in the United States to 30,000,000 in Scandinavia, a ratio of only 4.7 to 1. However, if only the latter half of the decade, 1935 to 1939, is considered, then United States time lost was 84,800,000 man-days against 9,600,000 for Scandinavia, a ratio of 8.8 to 1. While the absence of recent Scandinavian strike statistics makes postwar comparison impossible, there is no doubt that United States losses of 188,000,000 man-days during the three years 1945 to 1947 far exceed the relative Scandinavian loss of working time.

CONCLUSION

The foregoing pages constitute a very brief and compressed introduction to Scandinavian labor history and practices. No attempt has been made, for example, to describe the interesting recent tendency of organized labor to assume a degree of social responsibility compatible with its political hegemony, taking the form of joint labor-management production committees, jointly sponsored time-study work, and the evolution of national wage planning. Nor has there been any consideration of the far-reaching functional metamorphosis that the trade union movements are undergoing under the impact of labor governments committed to eventual nationalization of industry.

It should be apparent, however, that further analysis of the rich Scandinavian experience can yield much that may be of value in obtaining the alleviation of our own labor strife. While the disparate size of the American and Scandinavian economies militates against literal translation of the Scandinavian experiments in industrial relations, they are at least suggestive of pitfalls to be avoided and of possible fruitful avenues to the goal of labor peace.

v

Social Welfare

By HENNING FRIIS

SINCE the beginning of this century, the system of social welfare legislation developed in Scandinavia has attracted great interest among the experts of other countries because of its broad coverage and its general acceptance among all groups in the community.

The fact that the Lutheran reformation in Scandinavia at the beginning of the sixteenth century placed the state in control of the church and its properties meant that the public authorities very early were forced to take care of people who could not take care of themselves, a task that in the Middle Ages was chiefly in the hands of the Roman Catholic Church. Religious and other private groups have had only a limited part in Scandinavian social welfare during the past centuries. The obligation of municipalities to take care of the poor was recognized long ago. The Swedish poor law of 1763 contains the following passage: "Every parish must provide for its poor." In Denmark the poor laws of 1799 and 1803, which were among the major legislative accomplishments during the period of the absolute monarchy, established the duty of the local authorities to provide necessary assistance in cases of distress. This principle was also included in the Danish constitution of 1849. In Norway the same principle was introduced in the poor laws of 1845.

An important aspect of social welfare in the Scandinavian countries was the establishment of a system of public medicine and public hospitals. District medical officers have functioned in Sweden since 1681; the first Swedish public hospital was opened in 1752. The Danish king erected the first public hospital in Denmark in 1755. In Norway several public hospitals were established in the 1780's and 1790's. In 1806 the Danish king placed the duty of providing general hospitals on the county and city councils, which were called upon to procure and to operate them so that all might receive needed treatment regardless of their pecuniary circumstances. Traditionally it has been the rule for the state or the local authorities to own and operate the hospitals in Scandinavia, and fees have always been very low, not only for the poor but for the population as a whole.

Scandinavian people have therefore grown accustomed to the notion that social welfare is chiefly the responsibility of the state. Nevertheless social welfare legislation before the present century was inadequate, not only according to modern standards but also according to those of earlier times. Beginning in the middle of the nineteenth century the attitude toward the poor became more callous under the impact of a laissez-faire ideology and the growing influence of the taxpayers in local government. In Denmark the poor lost their franchise; in Sweden the obligation to take care of the poor was abolished in 1871. The indoor relief system, well known from the English poor law of 1834, was introduced in both countries in order to discourage people from applying for public relief.

This tendency to degrade the poor had two significant results: (1) Ordinary people with limited means established savings banks, health insurance societies, and other mutual organizations to guard them against coming under the poor law in case of loss of income. This is the system of self-help that later became the foundation of legislation based on the principle of "public help to self-help." (2) Recognition grew that certain cases of distress were so far beyond the control of the individual that loss of the vote could not in fairness be made a condition of receiving assistance.

The need for social security legislation was increased by the new forms of production resulting from industrialization. Agriculture ceased to be the predominant occupation, and within agriculture the number of propertyless workers increased. The cities grew and the factory replaced handicraft, so that a growing part of the population was detached from real property coincidentally with the disappearance of patriarchal working conditions. The guilds, which had formerly taken care of their members during sickness and old age, were abolished.

The demand for social security was voiced by organized labor through its growing economic and political organizations, and also by small farmers and tradesmen who experienced insecurity when the normal income stream ceased. The introduction of the first social security legislation in Scandinavia was therefore a result of collaboration between the Farmers' and Labor parties. The Conservative parties also joined in to some extent, since they considered social legislation a safety valve against revolution.

The era of modern social legislation began in Denmark in the early years of the 1890's. The poor law of 1891 provided that, when distress arose out of specified diseases or out of disability, relief could be given without the imposition of legal disability and particularly without loss of the right to vote.

A law of the same year concerning old-age assistance removed the care of the aged from the operation of the poor law, so that old people over sixty years of age who were unable to provide for themselves no longer had to undergo the humiliations of poor relief. But the amount of old-age benefits, like poor relief, depended upon the judgment of local authorities. This was changed a few years after the First World War when the fundamental principles underlying the present old-age pension legislation in Denmark were adopted.

Another important law was the first health insurance society act of 1892, a measure that authorized state grants to the health insurance societies that had grown up on a voluntary basis in rural districts as well as in the towns. The first industrial accident insurance act was introduced in 1898. Since then liability insurance has been made obligatory for all employers. In 1907 the first act was passed giving state financial support to the unemployment insurance clubs established by the labor unions in many trades. But not until 1922 was a disability insurance act added to Danish social legislation.

By 1930 Danish social legislation had been so expanded as to secure people against the consequences of the most common causes of loss of income, though the system bore the marks of its piecemeal origin and was encumbered by a number of inconsistencies. In 1933, under the leadership of K. K. Steincke, Denmark centralized and rationalized its social security legislation by enacting the so-called "Social Reform," containing the National Insurance Act, which includes regulations governing health insurance, disability insurance, and old-age pensions; the Industrial Accidents Act; the Labor Exchanges and Unemployment Insurance Act; and the Public Assistance Act, including regulations for child welfare, the care of the insane, the crippled, the blind, the deaf, and other special groups, and ordinary public assistance. The social security system has since been improved in many ways. In particular, old-age and disability pensions have been increased since the war.

The development of social security legislation in Sweden came some years later than in Denmark. At the beginning of the present century an act was passed compelling employers to compensate their workers in part for industrial accidents. Voluntary health insurance societies received government support in 1910. In 1913 parliament authorized a national system of compulsory insurance against old age and disability. The grants to the health insurance societies were considerably increased in 1931, and three years later the workers' unemployment insurance clubs were also given national support; but in Sweden neither the health insurance societies nor the unemployment insurance clubs had the same broad coverage on a voluntary basis as in Denmark. In the late 1930's Sweden began its elaborate family welfare legislation.

The period after the Second World War witnessed the greatest expansion in the history of Swedish social welfare measures. It was carried out under the direction of Gustav Möller on the basis of careful committee work. By the health insurance act of 1947 membership in health insurance societies is made compulsory for all adults in 1951. Widows' pensions were introduced in connection with the old-age and disability pension act of 1946. Family allowances were granted for all Swedish children.

The social security legislation of Norway came partly after and partly before that of Sweden. Norway got its first workmen's compensation act in 1894 and its compulsory health insurance act for workers in 1909. In 1915 Norway passed an unemployment insurance act much like that of Denmark in supporting the unemployment insurance clubs of the unions; but it was less successful in attracting the interest of the workers, and a new act in 1938 introduced compulsory unemployment insurance for all wage earners in industry, trade, and shipping. Old-age pension legislation has developed rather slowly in Norway, but in 1936 old-age pensions were provided for persons not well to do.

Norway has no disability pensions, and certain other aspects of the social security system are undeveloped in comparison with those of Denmark and Sweden. Planned expansion of the social services was at the committee stage before World War II, but the German occupation halted all progress. After the war all the benefit rates were adjusted to the new cost-of-living level. In 1949 the Norwegian government published a white paper in which it framed an elaborate social security plan,[1] which, if carried out, will place Norway on a par with Denmark and Sweden in the field of social welfare.

In contrast with the United States, private philanthropy is not very important in Scandinavia. The general view is that social welfare activities are a responsibility of the government and its local agencies. Private efforts have a place, however, in new experiments in the social field. The government steps in when the public is convinced that the new forms of social activity merit support.

In some important spheres of social welfare the government contributes to the support of private welfare projects. This applies, for instance, to most institutions for child welfare and to

---

[1] Joint Committee on International Social Policy, *New Universal Social Security Plan for Norway* (Oslo, 1949), English summary.

institutions for the treatment of cripples and other handicapped individuals. In Denmark maternity aid institutions are semipublic; their administration is financed by the government, but some support comes from special drives, though the government then supplies additional matching grants.

It is characteristic of Scandinavian social legislation that it leaves many areas open to self-government through voluntary societies. In all Scandinavian countries government-subsidized health insurance, for example, is administered by local societies, the leaders of which are chosen by the insured themselves. This applies also to the unemployment insurance clubs in Denmark and Sweden. Within the limits laid down by legislation and the central government, the clubs are competent to determine the amount of premiums paid in and of benefits paid out. The scope of self-government, however, has been reduced as government support has increased, and membership participation in the election of officers is limited at the present time.

By a process of gradual evolution a comprehensive system of social welfare has come into being in the Scandinavian countries. The tendency has been the same in all three countries: public policy has evolved from the negative attitude of the nineteenth-century poor laws, through the system of "public help to self-help" on the basis of insurance clubs, to all-inclusive social security systems with increased grants out of public funds. It has changed from a social policy that punished destitution to one that treats the symptoms of economic insecurity. We are now entering upon a new stage in social legislation in which the public tackles the causes of poverty and thereby identifies social policy with social planning. It is the stage of positive family welfare policy, of new experiments in prophylactic health, of a fight against accidents, and of rehabilitation schemes for disabled persons.

In the following pages the main features of social insurance, medical care, and family welfare in Scandinavia are outlined.

SOCIAL INSURANCE

The social security systems in Denmark and Sweden have never been limited to wage earners or to the lowest income groups, as has been done in many other countries. They are open to small farmers, craftsmen, and tradesmen (except for unemployment and workmen's compensation insurance), and there is a growing tendency to extend the benefits to the whole or the major part of the population in order to avoid class differences.

The health insurance societies in Denmark are open to everyone whose income does not exceed the earnings of a skilled worker in full employment.[2] Even though the insurance is voluntary, 80 per cent of the adult population are members. The Swedish health insurance societies are open to everyone, but they do not include more than 60 per cent of the population. The new health insurance act, which goes into effect in 1951, covers the whole population on a compulsory basis.

The Danish unemployment clubs cover about 95 per cent of all workers in industry and transport and a high percentage of the workers in agriculture and forestry. The percentage is high because the labor unions insist that their members shall be members of the unemployment clubs of their particular trade. The coverage in Sweden has been somewhat more limited. Only in the nineteen-forties have government subsidies to the clubs become large enough for most trades to have clubs. The question of whether the existing voluntary unemployment insurance should be replaced by a compulsory system embracing all workers is now being studied by the Swedish government.

Both the Danish and Swedish old-age and disability pension schemes are open to all social groups; there is, however, the important difference that the Swedish scheme provides for a basic pension to all citizens over sixty-seven years of age regardless of

---

[2] In Copenhagen, 7,800 kroner; in other urban areas, 7,200 kroner; and in rural areas, 6,200 kroner.

their income, whereas the old-age pension in Denmark is paid only to persons of limited means. On the other hand, the minimum age limit is lower in Denmark, sixty-five years for men and married women, sixty years for single women.

Developments in Norway have been somewhat different. Membership in the local health insurance societies is compulsory for all employees with an annual income of less than 9,000 kroner and for all seamen and fishermen, but voluntary for other persons. About 80 per cent of the population are members of the health insurance societies. Compulsory unemployment insurance, which until recently was limited to workers in industry, trade, and shipping, has now been extended to agricultural and forestry workers. The old-age pension scheme is confined to persons of limited means, and the minimum age limit is as high as seventy years. In recent years the philosophy of total coverage has gained ground in Norway, and the new Norwegian social security plan is based on this principle.

One of the characteristics usually included in concepts of a social insurance system is the payment of premiums by the insured covering the cost of the benefits. Usually these premiums are closely related to the size of the compensation to which the insured has a right if loss occurs. This limitation upon the social insurance concept does not fit in very well with the Scandinavian systems, an important feature of which is that an increasing proportion of the cost is paid for out of general taxation, thereby lessening the importance of the insurance premiums. The aim has been to distribute the burden of the social security systems in the same way as other public undertakings. As will be seen from Table 15, not only is a major part of the total of social welfare expenditures paid for by the state and the municipalities (in Denmark 82 per cent, in Sweden 82 per cent, and in Norway 68 per cent), but large proportions of the expenditures of the plans traditionally regarded as insurance schemes are financed by the government as well. Premiums from the insured are to be found in all the schemes except the Danish old-age pension system, in which the costs are borne completely by general taxation. The premium in the old-age and disability insurance in Sweden amounts to 1 per cent of taxable income, and a premium rate of 1.2 is applied in the Norwegian old-age pension scheme.

The division of administrative and financial responsibilities and powers between the central government and the municipalities has been under discussion from the time of the old poor laws. The municipalities want as much administrative freedom as possible, but at the same time they want the central government to share as much of the expense as possible. The central government, on the other hand, is interested in an administration that is relatively uniform throughout the country. It takes the view that the greater the administrative powers that are given to the municipalities, the larger should be the share of the cost that the latter should bear in order to minimize expenditure through good housekeeping. As a matter of fact, there is no stereotyped pattern determining the precise relations between the co-operating agencies of government. There has always been some compromise, but with the extension of services and the growing burden of costs the role of the national government has gained in importance. In Denmark, for instance, the administration of the old-age insurance system is in the hands of the social welfare committees, which are appointed by municipality councils. The cost of the old-age pensions is borne partly by the state, partly by the municipalities of the country as a whole, and to a very small degree by the municipality that pays the pension. The disability pension is granted by the government's disability pension board, but when it has been granted the payment of the pension is administered by local welfare committees. Here the central government bears almost the entire cost.

Contributions from employers except for industrial accident insurance have always been insignificant, since it is believed that the cost will be added to selling prices and thereby will be borne by the population as a whole.

Table 15. Total public expenditures for social welfare in Denmark, Norway, and Sweden, 1947, expressed in millions of Danish, Norwegian, and Swedish kroner, respectively.*

| | Denmark | | | | | Norway | | | | | Sweden | | | | |
| | Expenditures financed by | | | | | Expenditures financed by | | | | | Expenditures financed by | | | | |
	State	Muni-cipalities	Em-ploy-ers	The in-sured	Total	State	Muni-cipalities	Em-ploy-ers	The in-sured	Total	State	Muni-cipalities	Em-ploy-ers	The in-sured	Total
Health insurance, hospitals, and health services	135	194	—	102	431	67	82	27	108	284	184	235	—	90	509
Industrial accident insurance	4	1	14	—	19	1	—	23	1	25	5	—	75	—	80
Unemployment insurance	58	17	10	76	161	—	6	13	13	32	7	—	—	23	30
Old-age and disability insurance	246	167	6	17	436	24	63	—	52	139	235	65	—	72	372
Family welfare, including family allowances and tax rebates for children	119	84	—	4	207	116	85	—	—	201	224	72	—	—	296
Public assistance	4	39	—	—	43	3	38	—	—	41	90	97	—	—	187
Total expenditures	566	502	30	199	1,297	211	274	63	174	722	745	469	75	185	1,474
Distribution in percentages	43.7	38.7	2.3	15.3	100	29.2	37.9	8.8	24.1	100	50.6	31.8	5.1	12.5	100
Expenditures per inhabitant over 18 years of age				65	445				76	313				37	295
Expenditures in percentage of national income					8.3					8.3					7.4

* According to the current rate of exchange 100 Danish kroner correspond to 103.20 Norwegian kroner and 74.78 Swedish kronor. This difference in the rate of exchange does not correspond to the difference in the cost of living, the Swedish currency being somewhat overvalued since the increased valuation of the Swedish krona in 1946. One has, on the other hand, to bear in mind that the choice of the year 1947 (the last year in which statistics were obtainable in all countries) does not do full justice to Sweden. The expenditures for social welfare in Sweden have increased considerably more since 1947 than they have in Denmark and Norway. The expenditures for old-age and disability insurance in Sweden increased to 798,000,000 kronor in 1948 and to 570,000,000 kronor for family welfare.

Table 16. Cash benefits in Scandinavian social insurance schemes, 1949; expressed in Danish, Swedish, and Norwegian kroner, respectively.

	Denmark	Sweden	Norway
Health insurance	Daily allowances up to 6 kr. according to the size of the member's premium	After 1950 (new act): Daily allowance of 1.50 kr. for married women without gainful employment, 2 kr. for pensioners, and 3.50 kr. for all other adult persons. Supplements of 2 kr. for married beneficiaries and 0.50 kr. for each child	Daily allowance up to 6 kr. according to income of the member. Supplements of 0.67 kr. for family supporters and for each child. Total daily allowance must not exceed 9 kr. or 90 % of daily earnings
Unemployment insurance	Maximum daily allowance of 8.60 kr. for single persons, 9.60 kr. for family supporters. Additional housing benefit of 63 kr. in Copenhagen and 42 kr. outside Copenhagen. Supplements of 1.50 kr. for each child	Daily allowance of 2–7 kr. according to the size of the member's premium. Supplements for family supporters of 1.25 kr. and for each child of 1 kr.	Daily allowance as in health insurance
Old-age pension	Pension consists of a basic pension + supplements. Total annual pension to persons without income is: 		Copenh.	Other urban areas	Rural areas
Single	2,160 kr.	1,912 kr.	1,635 kr.
Married couple	3,260 kr.	2,879 kr.	2,444 kr.		Pension consists of a general pension + housing supplements to pensioners of small means. Total annual pension to persons without income is: |	Stockh.	In cheapest communities
	2,230 kr.	1,050 kr.
	3,380 kr.	1,680 kr.		Old-age pension is fixed by local governments. Minimum annual pension to persons without income is: |	Oslo	Urban areas	Rural areas
	1,620 kr.	840 kr.	720 kr.
	2,640 kr.	1,260 kr.	1,080 kr.	

	Denmark	Sweden	Norway

Disability pension	Pension consists of same basic pension and supplements as old-age pension + disability supplement and child allowances. Total annual pension to persons without income:
	
	        Copenh. Other Rural
	                urban areas
	                areas
	
	Single 2,348 kr. 2,128 kr. 1,839 kr.
	Married couple 3,716 kr. 3,311 kr. 2,852 kr.
	Child allowance 504 kr. 444 kr. 372 kr.
		For cases of total disability the amount of pension is same as old-age pension. For other cases it is lower	No disability pension system. (To helpless invalids an allowance may be given of the same amount as the old-age pension)

Industrial accident insurance	Daily allowance is calculated as ¾ of wages; minimum 6.30 kr., maximum 13.10 kr. Disability annuity is calculated as ⅔ of annual wage; minimum 1,680 kr., maximum 3,500 kr. a year	Daily allowances are calculated as about 70% of the wage; minimum 3.50 kr., maximum 14 kr. a day. Supplement for family supporters 1.50 kr. a day. Disability annuity 1⁄12 of annual wage; maximum annuity 7,200 kr.	Daily allowances as in health insurance scheme. Disability annuity is calculated as 60% of annual wage; minimum annuity 1,500 kr., maximum 3,000 kr. + supplement for wife and children of 200 kr. each

The traditional concept of a social insurance system is negated not only by the relatively small importance of premiums in the Scandinavian countries, but also by the tendency in recent Swedish legislation, and in Norwegian plans, to make payment of premiums no longer a prerequisite for obtaining social insurance benefits. In the Swedish old-age and disability system, and in the recently enacted health insurance plan, premiums are retained, but the right to benefits is not conditioned upon actual payment of premiums.

In regard to the size of benefits, there are certain differences among the countries, as shown in Table 16. For a married couple in Copenhagen having no other income, the old-age pension corresponds to about half the average income of unskilled workers. The corresponding figure in Stockholm is a little higher and in Oslo somewhat lower.

In principle the policy is the same: insurance benefits must permit at least a reasonable minimum standard of living so as to obviate the need for supplementary public assistance. There are, however, divergent opinions as to whether it is necessary to graduate the benefits according to the normal income of the insured. Recent Swedish legislation, apart from industrial accident insurance, does not relate benefits to income, the theory being that well-to-do groups should not be favored. The new Swedish health insurance act provides for a flat-rate cash benefit to all, regardless of income. The regular benefits, however, can be increased up to a certain maximum by the payment of extra voluntary premiums. In the Norwegian health and unemployment insurance systems benefits are fixed in relation to the normal income of the insured. The new social security plan continues this provision. Denmark has never had any income classification, but total unemployment insurance benefits must not exceed four fifths of the average daily earnings for persons with children and two thirds of the earnings for other persons.

Whether it is reasonable to reduce benefits if the beneficiaries have other resources has been much discussed, particularly in relation to old-age and disability pensions. In the Danish old-age and disability system, as well as in the Norwegian old-age pension system, deductions are made. Danish old-age pensioners may have an income of up to 50 per cent of the basic pension rate without a reduction of benefits. Income from capital above this limit is deducted in full, whereas only 60 per cent of income derived from work is deducted. As a result of these limitations about half of the population of sixty-five years or more do not receive old-age pensions in Denmark. The disability pension can never be reduced below one third of the basic amount, which is granted without respect to income. The Swedish old-age and disability pension system has a dual character, since a basic pension of 1,000 kronor is granted to all invalids and persons sixty-seven years of age and over regardless of income. In addition to the basic pension, a housing allowance is granted to pensioners of small means except in rural communities with low housing costs. This housing supplement is reduced when there is an outside income by the deduction of 50 per cent of the income above 600 kronor in the case of married couples, and above 400 kronor for single persons. Thus in all three countries the income situation of the pensioner is taken into consideration in fixing the amount of the pension. There is, however, an important difference between these income tests and the means test that is applied in public assistance legislation: the rules for reducing pensions are fixed in the pension laws, whereas public assistance allowances are granted according to the judgment of the social welfare boards on the need in each individual case.

It should be mentioned finally that all cash benefits in Danish social insurance legislation are adjusted annually on the basis of changes in the cost-of-living index, a procedure that safeguards the real value of the benefits.

MEDICAL CARE

In all the Scandinavian countries the public health system has three branches: (1) public health administration, which has general responsibility for the promotion of health and the prevention of disease and general supervision of the medical services, including the hospitals; (2) the hospital setup, which is administered mainly by the counties (which are larger than comparable units in the United States and Great Britain) and the municipalities; and (3) health insurance, which in addition to cash benefits provides low-cost or free medical care to its members.

The directors of the public health administration are doctors, and they serve as advisors to the government departments, which handle the legal and financial aspects of medical care, and as supervisors of local boards of health. The director-general has his special representative in the various counties, the county public health officer, who in turn supervises local representatives concerned with social hygiene in rural areas, the district public health officers.

As noted above, the Scandinavian general hospital system has, from the start, been administered by the local authorities. Certain kinds of hospitals are administered by the central government, for instance, mental hospitals. Privately supported hospitals, which have only 10 to 20 per cent of all hospital beds, are run by religious groups or other voluntary organizations, but no hospitals are operated as private enterprises.

The last twenty years have brought about a reorganization of the hospital system, resulting in the establishment of central hospitals in each county. These have independent medical, surgical, and in most places X-ray departments, in addition to a varying number of special departments. Besides these county hospitals, small local hospitals, each with a surgically trained chief medical officer, are kept for urgent and not too complicated cases. The best possible medical and surgical treatment is thus made available to the population even in rural districts and in remote parts of the country. No serious lack of hospitals exists in any of these countries even though the German occupation of Denmark and Norway delayed the realization of plans for further expansion. The number of hospital beds is shown in Table 17.

Scandinavian hospitals differ from American in that they have

Table 17. Number of hospital beds per 1,000 inhabitants.

	Denmark	Norway	Sweden
	1946	1944	1946
General hospitals	6.5	4.9	4.0
Mental hospitals	2.4	1.9	3.6
Other hospitals	1.1	1.7	4.2
Total	10.0	8.5	11.8
In public hospitals	8.9	6.8	10.0

regular staff doctors who receive a fixed salary and whose entire working day normally is spent in hospital work. Physicians in private practice do not continue to treat patients who are hospitalized. In most cases the chief medical officers of hospitals are also the administrative heads of their departments.

Hospital treatment is free to all members of the health insurance societies. To persons who are not insured the cost of hospital treatment is very low; for instance, in Copenhagen it is 1.20 kroner a day and in most Danish county hospitals 3 to 4 kroner a day, against an average daily cost to the hospitals of 28 kroner per patient. It is not possible by payment of higher fees to obtain such special facilities in public hospitals as single rooms. There are many single hospital rooms, but they are assigned solely on the basis of the needs of the patients. Necessary transportation expenses to and from hospitals are paid by the health insurance.

In addition to free hospitalization, the health insurance societies provide medical attention either free or below actual cost. At the end of the last century Denmark enacted its first law subsidizing the health insurance societies, and since then government subsidies have been conditioned upon the obligation of the societies to grant their members free medical care by general practitioners. Treatment by specialists has been a voluntary matter left to the discretion of the individual local society. Nearly all societies, however, provide for at least some free treatment by specialists. The obligation to grant free medical care kept the Danish health insurance societies from confining their coverage only to a part of the expenses incurred by their members in accordance with a system of refunds, as is the case in Norway and Sweden. There the doctors are paid directly by the patients, and the health insurance system refunds a fixed amount per consultation to the members. The new Swedish scheme increases the refund for medical attention by general practitioners from two thirds to three fourths of a fixed amount per consultation. The refund in Norway now corresponds to about two thirds of the doctor's bill, but the new plan envisions a change from the refund system to one in which the total fee of the doctor is paid directly by the insurance system, as in Denmark. In all these countries the health insurance societies pay the doctor's transportation expenses.

The obligation to grant free medical attention forced the Danish health insurance societies from the beginning to enter into contracts with physicians. Doctors are paid either fixed annual fees per member or fixed fees per consultation. The per capita method is used in most urban areas and includes about two thirds of the health insurance society members, whereas the per-consultation system is used in rural areas. Doctors are permitted to have private practices as well as their health insurance society work.

As the number of members of the health insurance societies grows, the position of the general practitioner has become increasingly important. To some extent this is the result of the numerical superiority of the general practitioner over the specialist, but it is also due to systematic endeavors to organize medical care service on the "family doctor" principle. This principle is accepted by Danish general practitioners and specialists as well as by the health insurance societies.[3]

Under the "family doctor" principle, each family entering a

---

[3] See Barbara N. Armstrong, *The Health Insurance Doctor: His Role in England, Denmark, and France* (Princeton, N.J., 1939), and K. H. Backer, "Medical Organization in Denmark," *British Medical Journal,* Supplement for July 5, 1947, pp. 2–5.

health insurance society chooses its regular doctor, a general practitioner on the panel of the local society. The family may change its doctor, in Copenhagen once a year, but it normally sticks to the same general practitioner through many years. The members of the family always apply first to their general practitioner for medical care. On his advice and reference a specialist may be consulted; when special treatment has been concluded, the patient is sent back to his family doctor with an account of the examination and recommended treatment. The same mode of procedure is adopted in relation to hospitals. This scheme limits care by specialists to what is "necessary," and it results in the family doctor's getting a thorough knowledge of his patients in the course of time, not only of their state of health but also of their social conditions.

Voluntary health insurance in Sweden and Norway developed at a much slower pace than in Denmark, and the societies did not attach importance to the establishment of fixed relationships between families and general practitioners but permitted free choice of doctor for each new case of illness and consultation of a specialist without reference to a general practitioner. In rural districts the system of public district doctors has been the basis of medical care, and here the family doctor arrangement has been introduced by necessity in both countries. In urban areas the public doctors compete with private practitioners, and in Sweden also with polyclinical service established by the municipal hospitals. The polyclinics attached to the hospitals have at their disposal for examination and treatment of patients the X-ray, laboratory, and other facilities of the hospital. This fact, as well as the small fees charged by the clinics in comparison with the rates of private practitioners, has led the Swedish public to turn to the clinics more and more. The result has been that the polyclinics are overcrowded, and this has reduced the possibility of giving personal attention to patients. In recent years both in Norway and Sweden a growing tendency in responsible medical circles has been to emphasize the desirability of the family doctor system.

The number of doctors, including those in hospital service, general practitioners, and specialists, is one per 1,000 inhabitants in Denmark, one per 1,100 in Norway, and one per 1,650 in Sweden. The number of doctors in relation to population is lower than it is in the United States, but the distribution is much more even. There is, however, a need for more doctors, particularly in Sweden, which becomes more pressing as new schemes of preventive medicine are developed.

Medicines are sold below cost under the Danish and Swedish setups. Danish health insurance societies must pay three fourths of the cost of such medicines as insulin and liver preparations. Further, the societies may grant up to three fourths of the cost of certain other essential medicines and up to two thirds of the cost of yet others. All such drugs must be prescribed by the health insurance doctor. In the new Swedish legislation, medicines that are prescribed by the doctor for use in the treatment of certain illnesses may be delivered free, while other medicines are delivered at half the ordinary price, the balance being paid to the pharmacies by the government.

While the issue of whether or not the public should subsidize medicines has been much debated in Scandinavia, free hospitalization and free or below-cost medical attention are unquestioned. It is the general consensus, in the medical profession as well as among the public, that these services are abused to only a very small degree.

FAMILY WELFARE

During the last fifteen years a revolution has taken place in public opinion, and family welfare measures now occupy a central position in Scandinavian social welfare policy. The background for this change in attitude was the downward population trend in the 1920's and the early 1930's. The birth rate, which in the last decade of the nineteenth century had been 27.1 per thousand in Sweden, 30.1 per thousand in Norway, and 30.2 per thousand in Denmark, fell during the period 1921–1930 to 17.5, 20.1, and 20.8

per thousand, respectively. In 1934 it was at its lowest—13.7 per thousand in Sweden, 14.4 per thousand in Norway, and 17.3 per thousand in Denmark. The net reproduction rate fell below 1,000 in all the Scandinavian countries.

In Sweden, particularly, the demographic situation was grave, since the net reproduction rate fell in 1934 to 742, which was even less than that in France. Frightened talk of "the death of the nation" was frequently heard. The most important contribution to the discussion was made by Alva and Gunnar Myrdal in their remarkable essay, *Crisis in the Population Question*, published in 1934.[4] The Myrdals emphasized the fact that population was the very foundation of the social structure and that the problem called for nothing less than a complete social and cultural redirection. They put the problem as follows: How could means be found to enable families to have children without undergoing as a result an unduly depressed level of living? They found the answer in a comprehensive social welfare policy for the benefit of families and children.

The Myrdals' ideas were accepted by both the Swedish and Danish governments, which set up population committees. In an executive order on the appointment of the Danish Government Population Committee in 1935 the secretary of social welfare summarized the new point of view as follows:

A population policy in Denmark which shall be able to unite the nation and overcome the distrust towards population policy, which still exists, must be in accordance with the views of life of a democratic society, and with the cultural and social development of the country, and it therefore has to be an *integrating part of social policy*. This means that in elaborating a Danish population policy the legislation not only has to counteract the tendency towards depopulation, but must also in itself constitute a further step towards a social development in the direction of *better, healthier, and more secure conditions of living for the population as a whole*.

---

[4] Alva Myrdal has published a comprehensive study of population problems in Sweden in *Nation and Family* (New York, 1941; reprinted, London, 1945).

Since the Second World War welfare policies toward families with children have been continued and extended or revised, although the demographic development in Scandinavia is now more favorable.[5] In Sweden a second population committee initiated a new population policy. Whereas the first Swedish population committee was very definitely in favor of giving help by food and rent rebates and so forth rather than in money, the new committee did not advocate any general policy for or against grants of money. It held that for each specific need the most suitable form of service, without any theoretical bias, should be given. A varied system of grants for children was suggested, most of which was enacted into law during the years 1944 to 1947. When these schemes have developed to the extent planned, the money value of the grants and services will amount to about 600 kronor per child per annum for a family with two children of school age. This corresponds to about half the cost of raising children in a working-class family.[6]

Some characteristic features of individual measures in Scandinavian family welfare policies will now be considered.

To encourage the early foundation of families and to counteract uneconomic purchases of furniture and other items on the installment plan, marriage loans were introduced in Sweden in 1938. These loans are advanced through the state bank on a commercial basis, but on easy terms. The interest is 4 per cent and repayment, as a rule, is required within five years. The maximum size of the loan is 2,000 kronor. Marriage loans have increased in importance and are now given to one fourth of all newly married Swedish couples. Direct losses on such loans have been very small.

In 1948 the Danish Government Youth Committee submitted proposals for marriage loans along somewhat different lines. It recommended the lending of amounts up to 3,000 kroner, fixed in relation to the amount of savings and the income of the couple

---

[5] See Appendix, page 353.

[6] H. Gille, "Recent Developments in Swedish Population Policy," *Population Studies*, vol. II, nos. 1–2 (1948).

during the previous two years. The higher the savings are in proportion to income, the higher the loans that will be granted. According to the proposal the couples will have to pay 1 per cent interest; the government will pay the rest of the interest as well as guarantee repayment of the loans. A bill with such provisions is now under consideration in the parliament.

In order to protect working women from dismissal on account of betrothal, marriage, or maternity an interesting law has been put into effect in Sweden. No employer may dismiss a woman employee on account of her betrothal or marriage. Furthermore, women who have worked for an employer for one or more years may not be dismissed because of pregnancy and childbirth and are entitled to a leave of absence for childbirth of a maximum of six months. The most important aspect of these provisions is probably not the purely legal one, but rather the recognition by society that it is morally wrong to subject pregnant women to fear of dismissal. Neither Denmark nor Norway has a similar law.

All the Scandinavian countries give economic assistance during pregnancy and maternity. In Sweden all women receive a lump sum in cash at the birth of a child. All women who belong to a health insurance club receive 125 kronor. Women in the low-income brackets who do not subscribe to an insurance plan receive a grant of 75 kronor, paid through a health insurance club but out of government funds. About 95 per cent of all mothers receive maternity grants in one way or another. Supplementary assistance is given to women who are in evident need of financial help during pregnancy and confinement. This assistance is granted on the basis of appraisal of the individual's requirements, with a maximum of 400 kronor. The grant is usually given in the form of equipment (clothes, beds, and the like) or as food, domestic help, dental care, board and lodging, and so on. More than half of all women receive such assistance during pregnancy and confinement.

The Norwegian health insurance system pays a daily allowance corresponding to sickness benefits to all expectant mothers for a period of twelve weeks. In Denmark female factory workers are entitled to a daily cash benefit of 6 to 7 kroner, which is paid by the state for a period of four to eight weeks. Most of them receive it for six weeks. Furthermore, all expectant mothers who have an income below the income limit for membership in the health insurance clubs [7] receive gratis half a liter of milk a day for six months before childbirth and one liter a day for six months after childbirth.

In the Scandinavian countries as in all other countries induced abortions are a serious problem from a social as well as from a demographic point of view. Abortion is legal in Denmark and Sweden for medical reasons, i.e., when indicated by considerations of heredity (insanity, imbecility, or the like) or when there is danger to the mother's life and health due to exhaustion, chronic malnutrition, attempted suicide, or other acts of despair. Abortions may also be performed if the child was conceived under violence or threat of violence. Abortion for purely social or personal motives is not allowed.[8]

In 1937 when the enactment of the present abortion law was discussed in Denmark, it was argued that it would not suffice merely to prohibit abortion and fix penalties. Above all it would be desirable to introduce social measures giving economic aid and support to women so that they would no longer have economic or practical reasons for interrupting pregnancy. In 1939 a semiofficial case-work agency, the Maternity Aid Institution, was established with branches in all parts of the country. The general purpose of this institution is to give free personal advice as well as social and legal assistance to all married and unmarried pregnant women and to mothers with children. Should an expectant mother who goes to the institution desire to have her pregnancy interrupted, the possibility of getting a legal abortion is investigated. If the conditions that the law requires in this respect are not fulfilled, the institution provides guidance and financial aid to enable the woman to proceed with her confinement. Thus if it is an un-

---

[7] See page 146.

[8] In Norway abortion is legal only for purely medical reasons.

married mother, an order is issued requiring payments by the father, and, if necessary, accommodation before and after the confinement either in private homes or in special maternity homes is obtained. Adoption of the child may also be arranged. Insofar as the agency can afford it, mothers without means are granted assistance in getting baby clothing and in paying for domestic help during the confinement. Courses in cooking, care of infants, and allied subjects are also arranged.

In Sweden a few centers have recently been established to give free advice and help to women seeking to have their pregnancies interrupted. The centers are set up by the counties or county boroughs but financed mainly by the central government.

Confinement costs are extremely low in Scandinavia. In Sweden more than four fifths of all childbirths are institutional confinements. Nearly all such institutions are run by the municipalities and subsidized by the state; they are open to all women. The fee in public wards of the municipality institutions is only 1 krona per day, which should not be considered as a hospital charge but as a sum corresponding to the saving in the expenditure on food in the woman's own home. Women confined at home receive midwives' services free. The midwives who attend women at home are employed and paid by the local authorities, and the equipment required at delivery, including transportable gas and air apparatus for analgesia, are received free by them. Institutional confinements are of lesser importance in Denmark since only about one third of all confinements take place outside the home. Many of the confinement institutions are privately owned. Members of health insurance clubs confined at home have the right to free assistance from a midwife at childbirth and to necessary medical help. For confinement an unmarried woman may go free of charge to one of two maternity hospitals run by the government in Copenhagen and Århus. In Norway the health insurance scheme provides for free midwife services.

Health examinations before and after confinement are important parts of Scandinavian population policy. In Denmark all pregnant women are entitled to three free health examinations by a doctor and seven by a midwife. In Sweden and Norway maternity and pediatric centers all over the country give pregnant women free examinations. In Sweden 60 per cent of all pregnant women attend the centers, which, since 1938, have been run by local authorities with state assistance.

When a child is born, a number of measures are taken to ensure that it grows up under healthful conditions. In 1937 Denmark initiated state grants to municipalities that appoint a public health nurse. Without charge the nurse examines all children at regular intervals during their first year, advises the mother on their care, and, if necessary, urges the mother to see a doctor. About 50 per cent of all newborn children are now examined by a public health nurse, and the service is being extended. In municipalities having health nurses a marked decline in infant mortality has been noted in the course of a very few years. Under a law passed in 1945, parents are entitled to have all children under seven years of age examined free of charge by a doctor three times during the child's first year and later once a year. The costs are met entirely by the state.

In Sweden the maternity and pediatric centers give full medical examinations to 85 per cent of all infants. In most areas the welfare centers have extended their services to children from one to six years of age.

In Scandinavian schools, municipal as well as private, children are generally under health supervision. School doctors and nurses are provided, and regular medical examinations are held. The school doctor's duties are preventive only, and if a child needs medical treatment, he is referred to his family doctor. The school doctor is required to give annual tuberculosis examinations to all pupils, teachers, and staff members of the school under his care. In Norway free dental treatment for everyone between the ages of six to eighteen was introduced by an act passed in 1949. In other Scandinavian countries free dental care is provided for school children in some areas; about 25 per cent of the children participate.

Until recently school meals were provided only for needy children. Opinion has gradually changed on the income limitation requirement, however, since the meals are considered to be of great importance in reducing the burden of the breadwinner in families with children, in facilitating the work of housewives, and in improving the health of the growing generation. In 1937 Dr. Carl Schötz of Oslo proposed replacement of the traditional school meal of porridge or another hot dish by a more healthy diet consisting of bread with butter or margarine and cheese, liver paste, jam, and the like, and a glass of milk, a carrot, an apple, or an orange. This so-called Oslo breakfast has been introduced into many Norwegian schools and also into schools in other countries.

Free school lunches are provided in elementary schools in most Danish cities and in some rural areas throughout the year. Up to 1948 school meals were available only to children of parents in the lower-income groups, but now all children whose parents so desire are entitled to meals.

According to a new plan in Sweden, which took effect in 1947, all children in elementary and high schools may partake of school meals regardless of their family's income. The program is expected to be fully developed in five years. In all three countries the municipalities are responsible for the programs but may ask state subsidies.

Very important in Scandinavian family welfare are the vacation arrangements for mothers and children. For many years Danish farmers have offered free vacations to school children of families having small incomes, especially children from Copenhagen. A considerable number of camps for school and kindergarten children have been established. Free travel to and from the farms and camps is provided by the state.

Swedish children whose parents have an income under a certain level—only 10 per cent of all families with children are excluded—are entitled to one free return ticket a year for a vacation of at least four weeks. The costs are paid by the state according to a law put in force in 1946. Since recreation is of great importance for the health and development of rural as well as urban children, all children regardless of the location of their homes are entitled to assistance. Camps managed by private associations and municipalities receive children in the summertime. In some cases they receive state grants.

Housewives are often in need of a complete separation from housework and the family. To help them obtain this, the Swedish government provides one free journey per year to housewives from both urban and rural areas. Financial considerations have made it necessary to limit eligibility to housewives in families having at least two young children and an income not exceeding a certain amount. Free travel is given to all mothers who want to accompany their children under ten years of age who are entitled to free journeys. Special vacation homes for housewives have been established by private organizations or local authorities aided by public grants.

Home help services have been established to relieve the critical situation that often arises when the mother of small children is temporarily incapacitated. In Sweden the service began in 1944; three thousand home helpers are now available. The service is available to all, but while families with small means obtain it free of charge, well-to-do families pay a fair remuneration according to the number of children and the means of the family. The state pays for the training and the greater part of the wages of the home helpers. The municipalities are responsible for the program and employ the helpers. In Denmark a similar arrangement was instituted in 1949.

In order to provide satisfactory conditions for children both of whose parents are gainfully employed outside the home and to supplement the home upbringing of children whose parents consider it desirable for educational purposes, a considerable number of preschool institutions (day nurseries and kindergartens) have been established in the Scandinavian countries. These institutions are operated by municipalities or by private associations. The demand for such institutions is, however, far from satisfied. In recent years public support of nurseries and kindergartens has been increased. This is particularly true in Denmark, where the state pays 40 per cent and the municipalities 30 per cent of the working expenses of institutions meeting certain minimum requirements. Parents pay a small fee, for children in day nurseries about 4 kroner and in kindergartens 7 to 8 kroner a week.

The classical measure for equalizing the cost of children has been the system of tax rebates and it still remains the most important measure in Denmark. These tax rebates vary in size according to the income of the family as the rates of taxation are progressive. They vary also with the locality, since the deductions are larger for urban areas than for rural. In Copenhagen the deduction in state and municipal taxes for a family with two children and an annual income of 7,000 kroner amounts to about 100 kroner per child.

In Norway and Sweden steps were taken after World War II to introduce children's allowances of considerable amounts. Since 1948 all children in Sweden under sixteen years of age have received a grant of 260 kronor a year. The allowances are paid without regard to the number of children in the family. At the same time tax rebates for children were discontinued. It was considered unreasonable to retain these tax rebates because they are larger for well-to-do families, whereas for families in the lower-income groups there are no allowances at all, because they pay little or no taxes. Rebates for children still exist in municipal taxation, but a bill calling for the discontinuation of these rebates is expected in 1950.

Norwegian children's allowances amount to 180 kroner a year and have been given since 1947 to all children under 16 years of age, except the first child in each family. Widows and unmarried and divorced mothers get the allowances even for the first-born child. Tax rebates for children have been continued in Norway. For example, for a family with three children and an income of about 7,000 kroner the reduction in taxation amounts to about 165 kroner per child in Oslo.

In Denmark children's allowances are now under discussion. Independent of general children's allowances, grants of 370 to 600 kroner per year are given to children of widows and widowers who have an income under a certain amount. Unmarried, separated, or divorced mothers are entitled to payment by the government of the father's contribution to the child's maintenance when the father is slow in paying. The advance payments are granted by the local authorities and are for the same amounts as the grants to children of widows. In Sweden special grants of 250 kronor a child are given to children of invalids, old people, and widows. Unmarried and divorced mothers receive advance payments of the father's contribution.

The object of Scandinavian policy with respect to population has not been primarily to award prizes for childbearing, but rather to reduce differences in the living standards of families with many children on one hand and childless families and families with few children on the other.

Housing

By CHARLES ABRAMS

Visiting Professor, Graduate Faculty of
Political and Social Science, New School
for Social Research; Author, The Future
of Housing

VI

THE postwar world disclosed a remarkable similarity among nations in their symptoms of housing disorder. Whether countries were rich or poor, democratic or monocratic, capitalistic, socialistic, or mixed, all seemed beset by the common problems of housing shortage, by slums and over-crowding, by disrepair of dwellings and spiraling building costs, by an ever-widening spread between the rents of new dwellings and what workers could pay for them.

A postwar survey of sixteen countries showed a housing short-age of more than 12,500,000 dwellings [1] and a building industry unable to meet more than a fraction of the annual need.

War devastation was not the cause of the housing problem; it existed long before hostilities began.[2] It became marked in the great industrial revolution that sent people migrating in droves from the farms to the cities. The impact of that revolution was less upon Scandinavia than on more industrialized nations, but it was serious none the less.

While Sweden's population grew by 43 per cent from 1860 to 1913, its urban population grew by 241 per cent,[3] imposing a demand upon its building industry that the latter was unable to satisfy. Though Denmark possessed no coal, iron, or oil, its quiet countryside too was soon converted into busy fishing villages, rail-road junctions, and city suburbs. Norway responded to a similar impact.

---

[1] Economic Commission for Europe, *Housing Needs and Programmes* (E/ECE/HOU/17).

[2] In the sixteen countries the destruction by war, however, amounted to 4,500,000 dwellings, which turned the shortage into famine.

[3] Leonard Silk, *Sweden Plans for Better Housing* (Durham, N.C., 1948), p. 9.

As mechanization was taking command of many industries and forcing people into the cities, the building industry in Scandinavia, as in the rest of the world, continued to be a handicraft operation, producing its buildings by handicraft methods and with hand tools on the site. Supply was not keeping pace with demand. Overcrowding and slum life were inevitable. They were followed successively by social problems, social awareness of the problems, and, finally, social protest culminating in public intervention.

Social awareness of the housing problem and of the need for improved housing conditions goes back to the cholera epidemic in the middle of the nineteenth century.[4] The city of Stockholm offered loan funds for rental housing, and in Copenhagen, after the Medical Association protested against the slums, some philanthropists put up enough money to build a workingmen's quarter for several hundred families.[5]

But in the world of a hundred years ago, as today, profit, not salvation, was the dominating life theme. The demonstration efforts were never followed by a full-scale program. The movement to supply better housing to workers succumbed under the impact of the speculative and prosperous years that followed 1854. The housing problem has continued in Scandinavia to the present day as it has in the rest of the world.

Scandinavian countries, however, were among the earliest to assume public responsibility for the problem, and the unique ways in which they have assumed their responsibilities have excited the curiosity and inspired the emulation of other nations, particularly

---

[4] See Bryn J. Hovde, *The Scandinavian Countries, 1720–1865* (Ithaca, N.Y., 1948), II, 713. Curiously, in both hemispheres protests against housing were being heard at about the same time—another indication of the simultaneity of housing problems. In 1834, for example, Gerret Forbes, New York City health inspector, inveighed against the "crowded and filthy state in which a great portion of our population live"; four years later Hans Linstow, builder of the Royal Palace, demanded decent housing for workers in Oslo. In 1844 John Griscom in America protested against the immigrant quarters he called "unfit for beasts"; the Thrane labor movement, between 1848 and 1851, demanded public housing, and a group of public-spirited citizens was moved to build Oslo's first low-cost project.

[5] *Ibid.*

America. In 1949 a commission of United States Senators journeyed to Sweden and Denmark, and after studying their housing programs returned convinced that the Scandinavian approach held the answer to the housing problem of America's middle-income group. Curiously, both the supporters of public housing and some of its most unmitigated foes have found common ground in the Scandinavian program. An understanding of Scandinavian attitudes and entrepreneurial patterns is therefore more essential than ever.

The tendency in Scandinavia generally has not veered toward socializing the housing industry but toward meeting the problem with the most efficient agencies at hand. Private enterprise, public agencies, co-operatives, and co-operative-public ventures have all been employed. In Denmark between 1920 and 1929, for example, only 16 per cent of the dwellings in Copenhagen and provincial cities were built by public authorities, 53 per cent by private builders, and 31 per cent by public service societies. In Sweden the ratio between 1919 and 1928 was 10 per cent by public authorities, 13 per cent by public service societies, and 77 per cent by private builders. In Norway after the First World War the amount of public building was far greater because of the virtual cessation of private building, and in 1921 the Oslo municipality built 889 dwellings, while private enterprise with municipal assistance built only 162. But as the years went by the municipality built less and less, so that by 1936 private enterprise was doing the whole job again.[6]

After World War II wider state aid and intervention became essential. *The Post-War Program of Swedish Labor* (1944) recommended the formation of municipal building and real-estate concerns to supplement existing private and nonprofit undertakings, and Sweden has made a start toward controlling some building firms as a means of initiating housing construction.

---

[6] League of Nations, *Urban and Rural Housing* (League of Nations Publications, II, Economic and Financial, 1939, II.A.2 [Geneva, 1939; reprinted 1943]), p. 105.

This may be viewed as a shift toward socialization. Yet in these days of varying mixed economies a limited supplementation of construction through government-owned contracting firms, as is being ventured in Sweden, may not be as much of a challenge to a predominantly private economy as might be thought at first. This is particularly so when the bulk of the materials that go into housing continues to be privately manufactured, when materials industries are stimulated into profitable operation by such intervention, and when government supplementation of construction helps private enterprise to attain the "enduring economic prosperity" at which the labor program admittedly aims.

The labor program also says that "to enable the community to control increase in urban land values, and in particular to prevent rebuilding projects from being impeded by multiple ownership of real estate, all building sites should become municipal property and all apartment houses should gradually be transferred to the ownership of the municipalities." This, if achieved, would represent a more direct step toward socialization.

In Sweden, however, as in Denmark and Norway, the cooperatives rather than the stock corporations seem to be absorbing the investment of the rank and file. They have been growing steadily in strength, and their managers have often emerged as important opponents of government ownership. This is a force to be reckoned with by advocates of all-out socialism. The social and economic complexion of the co-operative therefore cannot be summarily described as either "socialism" or "capitalism" but must be construed in the special light of its own unique development in the whole social and political milieu of each of the three countries.

SLUMS AND OVERCROWDING

It has often been said that Scandinavia has no slums, but this depends on definition. The word "slum" has had a shifting emphasis. It once referred to a room. At the turn of the century

physical deterioration became the dominant factor in the definition. Absence of improvements such as running water then also
began to assume primary importance. The principal index today
should be overcrowding or rents disproportionate to income, the
social by-products of which are far more harmful than the absence
of modern amenities or even physical deterioration. Judged by
physical standards, Scandinavia has few slums, but measured by
the standard of crowding, it is hardly slum free.

Table 18. Number of rooms in Swedish and Danish city dwellings
compared.

Number of rooms	Denmark		Sweden	
	1940	1939–48	1939	1939–46
	per cent		*per cent*	
1 (without kitchen)			16.6 ⎫	
1 (with kitchen)	6.1	8.0	31.8 ⎬ 30.7	
2 (with kitchen)	38.3	38.1	28.5	35.4
3 (with kitchen)	28.9	34.5	12.0	23.4
4 (with kitchen)	14.9	14.8	5.6	6.6
5 (with kitchen)	11.8	4.6	5.5	3.9
Total	100.0	100.0	100.0	100.0

The Housing Census of 1939 showed that 77 per cent of all
Swedish city dwellings had one or two rooms only. In rural areas
almost one third of the population slept in overcrowded rooms or
kitchens tenanted by at least four persons during the night. The
Population Commission found that in 38 per cent of the lodgings
investigated the windows could not be opened in the winter and
the ventilation was "astonishingly bad." In Stockholm in 1935, 5
per cent of the dwellings had more than two persons a room, and
in other towns and urban areas it was 10 per cent in 1933.[7]

In Denmark space standards are somewhat better than in
Sweden, as Table 18 shows. Yet overcrowding was in evidence

---

[7] *Ibid.*, pp. 114–127.

in Denmark as elsewhere with many rooms occupied by two persons a room. In 1940, 4.4 per cent of all urban dwellings were occupied by more than two persons a room.[8]

Norway's position was considerably worse than that of her neighbors. About 6 per cent of Norway's housing was damaged during the conflict. About 25,000 homes were repairable, but 20,000 were beyond salvage. During and after the war, moreover, the number of new marriages increased about 50 per cent, while new dwellings built by private enterprises dwindled to a trickle.[9] Overcrowding, however, existed even before the war, the 1930 census showing that 15 per cent of the urban population, or more than 118,000 persons, lived in overcrowded dwellings.[10]

Norway's housing shortage has retarded her much-needed development of new enterprises, and her postwar budgets have therefore emphasized home building. The housing objective of 1947 called for 18,000 units and an allocation of the necessary wood, bricks, and cement.

THE BUILDING INDUSTRY

The building industry in the three countries is no more advanced in technique than it is in England or America. Hand tools and labor performed on the site characterize this Cinderella of the industrial revolution in Scandinavia as elsewhere. But one important difference that distinguishes Scandinavia from other countries is the growing size and strength of the nonprofit cooperative. Since one of the principal reasons for the inability of the building industry to rise above its handicraft limitations is the small-scale nature of its initiating entrepreneurs, housing cooperatives may yet emerge as the much-needed instruments for rationalizing the industry at the initiating end, instituting the miss-

[8] *Ibid.*, p. 50.

[9] International Congress for Housing and Town Planning, *Financial Aid to Housing: Norway* (Zurich, 1948), p. 5.

[10] League of Nations, *op. cit.*, p. 103.

ing scientific research, and supplying dwellings in volume at low cost in response to mass demand.[11]

Rising costs after the war have complicated the effort to meet the housing situation in the Scandinavian nations. In Norway the cost index showed a rise from July, 1939, to October, 1947, of more than 75 per cent; and in Sweden, though materials prices in March, 1946, were more than 60 per cent over prewar levels, wages rose only slightly. This led to a valiant effort in these countries to develop their prefabrication industries as one means of cutting costs and producing quickly.

The completely packaged house, however, has made no more headway in Scandinavia than it has in highly industrialized America. If an American automobile costing $1,714 were built in 1949 with 1910 tools, as we build our houses, its cost would be around $60,000.[12] Conversely, if mass production of houses were achieved on a parity with automobile production, housing would be available within everybody's means. But we are a long way from the goal.

In Stockholm the standard prefabricated type is a wooden dwelling. Its outward appearance is not too striking, and its standards are not superior to those of hand-built houses, yet production costs are about the same. In Norway prefabricated timber houses were tried after the First World War and again after the Second, but floors have to be laid as in the ordinary house; windows, doors, and other parts are set by hand; site work is reduced by only about 30 per cent; and the savings in wages are said to be more than outweighed by the increase in transportation costs.[13] With the prefabricated house so largely a matter of handicraft, over-all savings are negligible. Norway has also experimented with prefabricated concrete houses, but the total production of prefabricated houses of all kinds in Norway after the war was not over

---

[11] *HSB—Cooperative Housing* (Stockholm, 1948).

[12] National Association of Automobile Manufacturers, *Automobile Facts*, cited in *New York Times*, Jan. 10, 1949, p. 24.

[13] International Congress for Housing and Town Planning, *Housing Progress and Methods Employed to Promote It: Norway* (Zurich, 1948), pp. 5–6.

600 houses annually. In Denmark the total was a little higher but was not over 1,000 houses annually.

Sweden, however, has made more progress here than her two neighbors. While packaged prefabrication still has a distance to go before the industrial revolution can be said to have embraced house assembly, standardization of the wooden elements in Swedish building has been making considerable headway. Forty per cent of all one-family homes in Sweden are made of prefabricated wood elements, and sectional standardization offers hope of some cost cutting in the near future. There is a growing recognition throughout the world, however, that the key to volume production is not prefabrication per se, but mass orders and scientific organization of the building operation. If the job of filling the mass orders is then met efficiently, sizes of doors, plumbing, and other products can be standardized and bought in bulk, materials can be precut, the use of labor can be rationalized, and the house can be produced in volume and at low cost on the site. Prefabrication is the consequence of mass orders rather than its precursor.

Sweden is better able to introduce the prefabricated house at low cost than most countries, for she enjoys the advantages of a big lumber production and of a greater facility for industrial organization of her house-production enterprises. As a small country, she is less beset by conflicting local building codes, heavy differential freight charges, and internal trade barriers, which are so often set up by the multiple groups composing the building industry in the United States. Sweden's production of prefabricated housing for export, moreover, may presage the opening of an important world market and the creation of that mass demand for standardized products which is essential for its success.

An interesting innovation in prefabrication is the small-cottage development, "put together with your own hands," which started in 1927 and has made considerable headway since. The materials are fabricated at the factory; the walls are supplied in sections with door and window frames inserted; everything, including woodwork and inside staircases, is delivered ready for fitting. A special public agency purchases the necessary materials and arranges with contractors to do the more technical work. The house is put up on a plot of about 500 square meters and is leased for 60 years at a ground rent of about 250 kronor a year. Cities lend 90 per cent of the cost to the prospective occupant, and 10 per cent is the occupant's contribution in the form of his work. Priority is given to families with small children.

The experiment has had its difficulties, largely because training an amateur in the techniques of housebuilding is far tougher than turning out a good amateur gardener, and the savings are not commensurate with the time and effort spent. But there is ample personal satisfaction in the thought of helping to put up one's own home which strengthens the personal attachment to the product and yields a dividend more lucrative than money. This phase of her enterprise is reminiscent of the self-help housing efforts of the Quakers in Philadelphia, which have as yet not gone beyond the demonstration phase but which have aroused considerable interest.

The most notable respects in which Scandinavia has forged ahead in housing are (1) housing co-operatives, (2) planning and house design, (3) housing of the elderly, (4) aid to large families, and (5) land policies. These policies have had international influence and hold important interest for America in particular.

CO-OPERATIVES

Housing co-operatives have developed and expanded in all three Scandinavian countries.[14] Sweden's co-operative movement was born in the 1880's, but it really became an important force after World War I. The first major effort was the Co-operative Housing Society of Stockholm, which was founded in 1924. By

---

[14] See Chapter VII. See also *Cooperative Housing in Europe*, A Report of the Banking and Currency Subcommittee Investigating European Housing Programs, January 31, 1950 (Washington, 1950), and *Cooperative Housing Abroad*, Final Report of Subcommittee no. 1 of the Committee on Banking and Currency, House of Representatives, Pursuant to H. Res. 331 (approved October 13, 1949), February 10, 1950 (Washington, 1950).

1945 it had built 2,500 apartments. It was, however, limited in capital and too localized in its operations. In an effort to meet mounting shelter costs, the Tenants' Union in Stockholm set up a new Tenants' Savings and Building Society called HSB (Hyres-gästernas Sparkasse- och Byggnadsförening). The guiding hand of HSB is Sven Wallander, who was inspired by some of the speculative co-operative developments in America, most of which ironically have since failed. HSB today carries on its work in virtually every town in Sweden and is responsible for 11 to 13 per cent of Swedish housing construction. In 1945 there were 42,000 members in HSB, with an investment of 628,000,000 kronor, and there were 120 local societies. By 1947 it was functioning in 130 communities.

HSB is a savings bank as well as a building society, and in 1947 it held deposits of 23,000,000 kronor. It paid interest of 2.75 per cent to depositors in 1946; building-fund certificates pay 3.5 per cent. HSB functions as the "national office" but might better be called a "grandmother society." It inspires the formation of "mother societies" in various areas, which build the projects and then turn them over to a "daughter society" composed of the tenants who finally own and operate the projects. HSB does the financing and the architectural and engineering work. Each daughter society is represented on the board of the mother society, and the mother society, in turn, is represented on the board of each daughter society. The mother societies also elect delegates who set up the administrative board of HSB.

Co-operators make payments that include interest and amortization on the mortgage loan, repair costs, management charges, fuel, and reserves. If the tenant dies, title passes to his heirs. A tenant may sell, subject to the approval of the corporation, but at no profit, although he receives credit for his amortization. He may sublet at a price fixed by the society, but the society may elect to name the sublessee.

HSB builds not only co-operatives but municipal projects for large families of low income, subsidies for which are advanced by the state. The city and HSB control the venture, though the city retains majority control.

For its various projects a co-operative may get a variety of aids —third mortgage loans up to 95 per cent of cost, a government guarantee against a rise in interest rates so as to keep charges steady, cheap land, interest-free additional loans to take care of rising postwar costs, and priorities in allocations of material and labor. Finally, a subsidy is paid to larger families of low income on the basis of the number of children.

There are also some smaller co-operatives in Sweden, the largest of which, Svenska Riksbyggen (SR), started operations in 1941. By 1949 it had built more than 15,000 dwelling units. HSB, SR, and other co-operatives account for about 20 per cent of Sweden's annual house production.

A recent innovation that is expected to set the pattern for a good part of Sweden's future housing construction is a joint venture between SR and the city under which a quasi-public corporation has been organized, on the board of which the city of Stockholm, SR, and other special designees act as directors. This agency builds housing for low-income families with 100 per cent government loans, thus meeting the needs of those who cannot afford down payments.

In Denmark the first housing co-operatives started as early as 1865, but the important societies were really founded just before World War I, when the housing shortage had become particularly acute. Wild speculation in housing had marked the beginning of the century and led to overproduction and a crash. Banks grew wary, showed reluctance to lend and, indeed, were unable to continue financing speculative building. Soon there was unemployment in the building trades and a housing shortage. The leaders of the co-operative movement and the trade unions then began to weigh the potentialities of housing co-operation as a cure both for the housing shortage and for unemployment. The initial venture was small but encouraging, and in 1912 the Workers' Co-operative Housing Society—largest of all the co-operative housing societies—was founded. It was followed the ensuing year by another large association, the Workers' Co-operative Building Society.

The Workers' Co-operative Housing Societies, the most common form of associations, admit to membership any person of good reputation. Every member pays a membership fee of 25 to 30 kroner ($3.75 to $4.50), which goes into the reserve funds. The society is managed by elected representatives of the members. Its object, as laid down in the rules, is to build good cheap housing for members, which is provided to them according to priority of membership in the society. The member also has to buy shares in an amount geared to the size of his dwelling unit (generally equaling about 3 per cent of his equity investment). The right to occupy a dwelling is inheritable, but it may not be sold for speculative profit.

A second type of Danish building society is the self-owning association, or Social Housing Society, which differs from the workers' co-operative housing societies in that the board of managers is not elected by the occupants but functions in association with the local public authority in the particular area. Admission of member occupants is subject to the approval of the local authority, and only persons with an income below a fixed level may qualify for membership. Property of the social housing societies may be taken over by the local authorities after a fixed period, and profits, if any, become public property. Occupants continue to pay the same charges in social housing units even when costs are reduced as the result of retirement loans. The accumulated surpluses are then used to help supply additional building.

The Workers' Co-operative Building Society is a third variety of co-operative. It is a nonprofit company whose shares are held mainly by the building societies, supported for the most part by the trade unions. The occupants of the flats built by the society are not required to be members of the society as in the case of the workers' co-operative and social housing societies. The rules of the society provide that the property may not be transferred to private ownership, and in the event of liquidation the property reverts to the public.

Of particular importance was the founding in 1941 of a special national society called Arbejderbo. It was established on the joint initiative of the Urban Co-operative Union, the Federation of Housing Societies, the Confederation of Danish Trade Unions, and the Labor Movement Economic Council. The purposes of this society are to assist in the establishment of new housing societies, advise on technical, economic, legal, and administrative problems, and if necessary give financial aid.

In Norway before World War II there was only one co-operative building society, but such societies have expanded rapidly since the war's end and have formed a national union. More than 10 per cent of current home construction is now done for these societies.[15]

EXTERIOR PLANNING AND DESIGN

The past holds a restraining hand over replanning in Scandinavia as elsewhere. City planning in democratic countries is more than the plotting of housing, streets, and parks on an architect's blueprint but must operate within a complex of vested rights and strive to improve the living patterns of the greater number without confiscating the established rights of the smaller. It is within the democratic context that city planning in Scandinavia proceeds.

Take the case of Copenhagen, once a fortress. With the influx of population it could not easily expand beyond its circumscribed boundaries to take over its neighboring communities, so that as immigrants flowed in from the rural areas in response to industrialization, new stories were simply built upon the old ones; side

---

[15] *Ibid.*, p. 7. For an interesting discussion of postwar planning and housing problems in Norway see also article by Erik Rolfsen in International Federation for Housing and Town Planning, *News Sheet VIII* (London, March, 1948), p. 10.

houses and rear houses cropped up wherever there was a bit of open space or garden; lofts and cellars were turned into dwellings. Fire and health hazards were the consequence, but each legislative act thereafter, while it aimed to improve conditions, only laid down minimum standards, which reduced the hazards but continued the interior and exterior space standards at low levels. The opening of the Frederiksborggade district in the last century released more space to dwelling use, but produced only another host of dreary tenements with small rooms that still plague the area today. Though the building legislation of 1889 did prescribe minimum dimensions for rooms and represented some improvements over the old, it was really not until the turn of the century that a healthy reaction against the bleakness and the crowding of the past set in. Open spaces and squares with trees and fountains appeared on the urban scene, and though interior standards were not revolutionized, bays and balconies, red-tiled gabled roofs and plain brick surfaces began to appear and give life to the urban landscape. The brick tradition has been the Danish tradition since medieval times; after 1900 it was reinstated.

Copenhagen's building law of 1939 allowed for more freedom in planning and facilitated the building of balconies; dwellings soon began to be erected with living rooms adjusted toward the sun instead of facing upon the street; and the smaller-scale ventures of the past began to give way to well-planned projects of whole blocks, with their more generous opportunities for original layouts and design.

The rigid patterns of the past restrained Sweden's redevelopment as it did Denmark's. The influx of population into the cities after the industrial revolution brought it tenement houses, too. The houses were put up on densely built blocks and hardly blended with the old medieval structures, which still retained their quaint and romantic attractiveness. By the time of World War I more than 93 per cent of the families of Stockholm, Gothenburg, and Malmö lived in multiple-family dwellings.

Industries in Sweden are scattered throughout the land in small and medium-sized towns, and their labor supply is being continuously fed by a flight from the rural districts, which together with the high marriage rate has heightened the demand for dwellings.

In contrast to Sweden and Denmark, Norway's commonest type of dwelling is the one- or two-story house built of wood. A few of the large towns, however, do have brick houses, and in Oslo more than a third of the houses before the last war were four stories or more in height. Many of the smaller dwellings are owner-occupied, with one of the apartments rented out by the owner to help pay his upkeep charges. Like her sister nations Norway suffered from intense overcrowding. Dwellings composed of one and two rooms (in addition to a kitchen) equaled nearly three fifths of the total, whereas those of one room and a kitchen amounted to about one fourth of the total. The war destruction, which occurred mostly in the towns of 15,000 to 20,000 population and in the smaller villages, intensified the need for immediate rebuilding and threatened to scuttle the plans for rationalized reconstruction.

Against this difficult background the three countries have succeeded in making long strides toward reorienting their dwelling and outer space standards. The task is by no means free of difficulties, and each country has its own unique problems. In Denmark it is not easy to win co-operation from communities adjoining Copenhagen to effect a regional replanning. Opinion, moreover, differs on the wisdom of having a swelling Copenhagen in so small a country. The Copenhagen region today holds more than a quarter of the country's four million inhabitants. It is expected to grow to a million and a half inhabitants, and defense considerations, as well as the general advantages of decentralization, suggest that it might be better to shift some of the population to smaller units. One suggestion is to build some long ribbon developments up to the city of Elsinore on the north coast. Another plan is to build a series of satellite towns around the great city. It is agreed that the development of the city in rings as in the past is best avoided, and instead of concentric layers there will be ribbon or "finger" communities reaching out of the palm of a hand, represented by the present Copenhagen district.

A newly developed system of electric railways will service the new communities. Shops and institutions will be built at the stations. Ample greenbelts will be provided between the fingers. Access to the big city will be made quicker and more comfortable. Industries will be located in designated portions at the ends of the new developments. Well-planned flats will be supplemented by little summer cottages near the city to which the city dwellers may repair for recreation. An effort will also be made to rationalize administrative problems in the region by setting up a regional council.

Sweden, too, has made remarkable progress toward the beautification and general improvement of her cities and towns. A town-planning law that has been in effect since 1931 requires each town to file a comprehensive plan showing the proposed residential districts, the proposed means of transportation, and provision for greenbelts, utilities, and other essentials. Buildings of historical or aesthetic significance are required to be preserved wherever possible.

Rigid local regulations lay down rules for maximum heights, the types of structure that may be erected, their physical arrangement in the over-all plan, and the kinds of materials that are to be used in the building.

No structures may be erected which do not conform to the over-all plan. The Swedish land developer must therefore first investigate its permissible uses. A developer may even be prevented from building for a limited period during the promulgation of plans. Every building application must first run the gauntlet of departmental investigations. Projects requiring governmental aid are scrupulously checked to make sure they conform to the best interests of the general development for the area. Large building operations by the co-operatives have facilitated the layout of comprehensive developments containing civic centers, shopping places, recreation centers, and schools. HSB's plans for Arstaterrassen in Stockholm and Örby, a Stockholm suburb, are good recent examples of comprehensive neighborhood planning.

Norway's planning program has been beset with exceptional difficulties. In some districts, particularly in the north, the buildings were so completely destroyed that considerations of city planning had to give way to the more imperative need for winter shelter. Buildings erected during the occupation placed heavy burdens on the local communities, were erected hastily and in makeshift fashion, and presented serious problems of replanning and reconstruction.

Norway has sought to meet her difficult replanning problem by setting up a reconstruction department in the Ministry of Supply and Reconstruction and a central planning bureau to help the local communities with their plans. Statistics have been gathered, professional assistance has been furnished the communities, and public information has been disseminated to the local population to obtain their sympathy and co-operation. Norway's war damage provided an impetus for extensive planning operations, and by late 1946 all major plans were ready for promulgation. Local wishes are scrupulously respected in Norway, and decisions are made only after careful consultation with the mayor of the locality affected, the municipal engineer, and the local planning authorities. Community centers have been agreed to in a number of areas and work has gone ahead. Sites have been provided by the cities, and the state has been making the necessary loan funds and subsidies to build them.

A major problem has been the matter of reallotment of sites in devastated areas. Arduous negotiations have been needed to plot the new boundaries. Difficulties have been experienced, particularly with the small businessmen in the area, each of whom is anxious to retain his old site and fearful that the new one offered him in exchange may not be as strategically located.

One thing appears certain to the visitor. In all three countries city and neighborhood planning is a paramount national consideration, natural advantages are being utilized or restored, and a new landscape is already appearing that represents a break with the bleakness that was the by-product of the past.

INTERIOR SPACE STANDARDS

Though interior space standards have been low in Scandinavia, there have been many encouraging signs, one of which is the recognition of the importance of open outdoor space as an amenity of the dwelling unit. In America even some of the newer private projects often cover most of the plot so that the occupant gets only a view of a grim yard, a glimpse of a neighbor's family life, or a smell of his cooking. Parks and open play space are rarely planned as an amenity of the project save in public housing undertakings, and even a large development like Stuyvesant Town in New York City, with a population of 25,000, is planned without a school.

In Scandinavia, however, the tendency has been to plan dwelling units, playgrounds, and private and public open space all as part of the project. The location of the buildings is not dependent upon the old street patterns but is oriented to the sun.

Particularly important is the private balcony, which has become a characteristic of Scandinavian housing. In Denmark it was first introduced to perform the functions of a fire escape, but it gradually took on new utility and today it has become part of the city landscape. It is really an "outside room," having multiple functions: sunning the baby, relaxing in the open, storage, airing linen, serving tea or breakfast in the sun. Few amenities could accomplish so much in emancipating the urban American mother from some of her parental chores as the Scandinavian balcony. For in the metropolis of today giving the baby an airing means (1) dressing it for the outdoors, (2) preparing the carriage and maneuvering it from apartment or storage cellar to the street, (3) wheeling the baby five to twenty blocks to a park, (4) watching the baby while it plays in its carriage or on the ground, (5) feeding the baby or caring for its other needs and functions along the route, (6) wheeling the baby five to twenty blocks back to the apartment, (7) returning the carriage to its storage place and emptying it, (8) undressing the baby and preparing it for the new temperature.

With a simple balcony the mother can perform many household tasks while the baby is sunning near by, and the number of carriage trips can be reduced to a minimum. In America balconies are provided for a few wealthier folk, who may have a country place in summer and do not need them, but they are not provided for the poor to whom balconies are as essential as the cookstove. Few factors in the ensuing decades are more capable of making the American apartment house obsolete than is the absence of the balcony.

Since one of the more serious by-products of the last war has been the contraction of space and the sacrifice of standards in the effort to offset the rise in building costs, it is heartening to see Sweden and Denmark enforcing improvements of their space standards despite the spiraling of their building costs. About 38 per cent of all Danish dwellings before the war had two rooms and a kitchen; 30 per cent had three rooms and a kitchen. Of all houses and flats built in 1948, 45 per cent had three rooms and a kitchen.

To be eligible for grants, a Swedish dwelling in a block of flats must be not less than two rooms with a kitchen and have an area of at least 50 square meters. In urban communities the standard is three rooms and a kitchen with an area of 70 square meters. In detached rural houses, the minimum space standard is 60 square meters. Grants are also linked to adequate standards such as water supply, drains, central heating, water closets, and separate bathrooms. Projects are required to be suitable for families with children and to have good facilities for recreation.[16] In the Swedish developments, it is not uncommon to see carpentry shops, play-

---

[16] *Ibid.,* p. 15.

rooms, and nurseries. HSB has even provided a "children's hotel" where the children can stay when parents go away for a vacation.

The houses built by co-operatives and public agencies in Scandinavia reflect in their workmanship and use of materials an investment for use rather than for speculation, and both site selection and site planning have built up an immunity against early blight.

THE "MISCELLANEOUS WAY"

What is most impressive is the refreshing variety of forms and formulas that impels one to refer to the Scandinavian approach as the "miscellaneous way" (rather than the "middle way"). In America one can roam from coast to coast and note a sameness in the architecture of towns, i.e., the chain-store grocery built from office specifications, the slightly rehabilitated relics of the beard-and-sideburn period, the latest design in gas-station pumps, a sprinkling of brand new Federal Housing Administration specimens of unremitting uniformity, or a public housing project that looks exactly like a public housing project. The emerging Scandinavian landscape is an inspiring contrast in form and spirit.

In contradistinction to Stuyvesant Town in New York City, one recalls HSB's Reimersholme in Sweden, set up on an island with a beautiful view of the surrounding country and an architecture that utilizes rather than conceals the natural scene. There is the streamlined Marmon, with one continuous and forthright-looking balcony on each floor decked with flowers. There are the houses designed for families in which both husband and wife work, with the necessary conveniences incorporated into the architecture to lessen the tensions of the working mother: community dining rooms where families may take their meals; community kitchens where meals are prepared and served in individual apartments; nursery schools for children; day nurseries for infants; special after-school activities for older boys and girls.

One should not get the impression that Scandinavia has solved all its problems. But housing in the world of today is still in its demonstration phase, and in Scandinavia may be found the most varied and interesting examples. In the suburbs of Copenhagen, one recalls the Grundtvig Church and the apartment development built around it in medieval tradition, the modest, sane, and simple architecture, and, above all, the high quality of Danish interiors with their expert use of color, fittings, ceramics, and wallpapers.

But variety is present not only in architecture; it exists also in the financial and social approaches to the problem. On the outskirts of Copenhagen, for example, the writer came upon an artists' colony of small houses, built in the simplest style by a co-operative housing society and combining in the most practical manner both living space and excellent working conditions for the artist or sculptor. There are large studios lit by ample window space and having more than 350 square feet of floor area. These dwelling studios were financed by artists who put up their works as down payments.

In Sweden there are not only public building agencies, building co-operatives, and private builders, but in one of the smaller cities the writer found a large development made possible through a joint venture between the industries in the area and the municipality, each of the interests holding shares in the owning corporation and each being represented on the board of directors. Housing for the elderly, little week-end cottages, summer developments where one does his own gardening, the incidental but essential facilities for the care of children of working parents—these are a few examples in Scandinavia's catalogue of varied housing demonstrations.

GOVERNMENT AID

The types of aid to home construction differ in Scandinavia from those in other parts of the world. In America, for example, federal aid to housing has been induced largely by emergency considerations—economic pump priming, experimental slum clearance, defense and war housing, and the rehousing of veterans.

There is as yet no unified, over-all purpose, no recognition that housing is a long-range problem requiring long-term treatment. In Scandinavia the obligation to house the people decently is accepted as a political fact, enabling a coherent and not a sporadic approach. The aims are not only to encourage family expansion but to hold down rentals, ease housing credits, stabilize the interest rate, rationalize mortgage financing, and guide the quality and livability of the houses. These aims are achieved more or less by the type of subsidy and credit controls.

There is no governmental aversion to second and third mortgages such as developed in America after the great depression. Governmental insurance of a single mortgage for 90 per cent of value became the postdepression American policy because of excessive charges exacted by private lenders for second and third mortgage loans. In Scandinavia, however, savings banks, insurance companies, and quasi-public institutions make the first and second loans, while the third mortgage loans are taken by the state. Sweden and Denmark may also make loans on first and second mortgages through one of their own institutions, but rarely is the third mortgage privately financed. By state ownership of the junior liens, the government has influenced the flow of private money, reduced the amount of money required for building, achieved low interest rates, and controlled the character of the developments.

The amount of the advance varies with the character of the recipient. The first and second mortgages in Sweden to private builders generally totaled about 60 per cent. Private builders today will get advances from the government which will bring the total loans to 85 or 90 per cent of cost. Co-operatives are aided more liberally, with loans up to 95 per cent of cost. Municipalities and joint-venture agencies composed of co-operatives and municipalities are lent third mortgages, which bring the loans up to 100 per cent of cost.

Another important form of aid is the government guarantee against a fluctuating interest rate. This means that if interest rates rise above 3 per cent, the Swedish government will reimburse the borrower for the excess. This makes it possible to keep the rents constant.

Recently extra loans have been made available to take care of increased building costs. These are free of interest for ten years.

Grants are also given to families with a minimum of two chil-dren. These amount to 130 kronor a child a year in the new apartment buildings, and to 20 per cent of the original capital cost in detached houses. Eligible families can have an annual net taxable income of not more than 4,000 kronor for those with two children and up to 7,000 kronor for those with five children. This policy was influenced by Gunnar and Alva Myrdal, who, seeing a declining population threatening their country, pressed for a housing policy that would stimulate the bearing of more children.[17]

Denmark's support of housing through government loans goes back to 1887, but it was really after 1933 that the government interceded on a substantial scale. The aid extended follows the Swedish pattern. Danish legislation prior to World War II also authorized secondary loans. Interest rates were about equal to government rates. Postwar rises in building costs have also necessitated government long-term loans at low rates. As a further aid, new buildings, residential or business, are given an exemption from taxes.

As in Sweden, the subsidies in Denmark vary with the type of builder. Private builders, local authorities, and co-operatives are all eligible for aid. Interest rates are higher for the private builder and lower for buildings erected by co-operatives and local authorities to whom loans may be made at rates as little as 1.5 to 2 per cent. Table 19 shows the type of aid given in Denmark and the terms.

Public aid to housing in Denmark does not stem from a desire to socialize the housing industry. "The importance Denmark at-

---

[17] Gunnar Myrdal, "Population Problems and Policies," *Annals of the American Academy of Political and Social Science*, CXCVII (May, 1938), 201.

Table 19. Subsidies granted to various types of housing and housing agencies in Denmark.

	Loan limit (with guarantee from the local authority)	Annual amortization	Interest rate
	%	%	%
Multifamily dwelling erected by co-operatives	97	2.2	2.0
Single-family and row houses erected by co-operatives	97	1.7	1.5
Housing erected by the local authority	95	2.2	2.0
Owner-occupied homes (persons of modest means)	90	3.2	2.2
Other owner-occupied housing	85	3.2	2.2
Tenement houses built by private persons	80	3.2	2.5

taches to building undertaken by co-operatives," says Einer Engberg of the Danish Ministry of Housing,

is due on the one hand to the growing recognition that private building, despite rigid restrictions upon its operations, must be supplemented by other forms of enterprise more directly motivated by the community's social needs. Yet simultaneously there is a great hesitancy about allowing building activity to be undertaken by the government or by local authorities directly. The co-operatives afford a compromise through a form of organization which respects the social and financial interests of the community in house building while not neglecting the benefits of private initiative and of competition between the different entrepreneurs.

A special subsidy is given to large families in co-operative or municipal projects. The subsidy is geared to the number of children in the family: it amounts to 30 per cent of the rent for families with three children, 40 per cent for those with four children,

50 per cent to those with five or more. Families with 6 children living in cottages or houses having at least three rooms in addition to the kitchen may get subsidies up to 60 per cent.

In Norway a dearth of mortgage money and high interest rates were responsible for retarding home building before World War II. Although loans were available at from 4.5 to 6 per cent, no more than 60 per cent of the cost would be advanced. All too often, therefore, Norwegians were faced with having to put up prohibitive amounts of equity money to finance their home purchases. The central government had left home financing to local authorities, which supplied some local tax subventions, but this proved hardly enough to inspire dwelling production at reasonable cost. Rents in Oslo's houses built in the late 1930's without state subsidies exceeded 27 per cent of income for more than half of the tenants in one-room flats; in two-room flats, even with maximum support from the city, rents still remained at 22 per cent.[18]

Wartime destruction focused attention on Norway's housing problem more than ever before, and in 1946 a housing bank was established with a capital of 20,000,000 kroner. The capital was supplied by state and local authorities, supplemented by public subscriptions. Mortgage loans were made up to 75 per cent of estimated value on houses built for profit, and up to 95 per cent in other cases. Co-operatives could borrow 90 per cent of value, and owner occupants of one- to four-family houses 85 per cent.[19] Because interest rates eased in Norway after the war, the housing bank has been able to grant loans on first mortgages at 2.5 per cent, which is the postwar rate of interest on state bonds.

HOUSING FOR THE ELDERLY

Few social reforms are as inspiring and as important for America as the program for the housing of the elderly in Scandinavia. The

---

[18] International Congress for Housing and Town Planning, *op. cit.*, *Norway*, pp. 5–6.
[19] *Ibid.*

movement started in Denmark in 1891, when European poor laws were putting all public charges, old and young alike, into public workhouses. The shift in attitude toward the elderly is a milestone in European social history. That the program received its greatest impetus in Scandinavia is a tribute to the latter's progressiveness.

In Denmark today about 500 comfortable homes accommodate nearly 13,000 old people in what are known as old people's homes, while private institutions make provision for more than 4,000.

No stigma is attached to living in these houses, for the Danish approach is noninstitutional. Outwardly these houses look like those of other families. Current policy aims to give the pensioner a private room for himself or two rooms for couples. About 250 homes have separate hospital departments or wards. Almost all of the homes are equipped with electricity, water mains, and water closets. About nine out of ten units have central heating and baths, and about 88 per cent—more in rural areas—have gardens.

In 1937 government grants were made for the housing of pensioners who are able to care for themselves. The houses are usually not over three stories high and consist of one-room apartments with an alcove and kitchen for single pensioners. Married couples may have either a one-room apartment with a kitchen or a two-room apartment with a kitchen. In most of the houses there are common bathing facilities and a meeting room, which may be used for family parties. In Copenhagen single old-age pensioners pay a monthly rent of 28 kroner, and married couples pay 34 kroner. In the communal flats, the average is 23 kroner and 28 kroner, respectively.[20]

Sweden, too, has made strides in housing its elderly.[21] Dwellings are available both to pensioners and to elderly people enjoying independent incomes. Applications are accepted in rotation. Swedish houses have one-room apartments opening onto a large corridor, with common meeting rooms for concerts, meetings, and entertainments. Men and women are housed on the same floor.

---

[20] *Social Denmark* (Copenhagen, 1945), pp. 70–72.
[21] Elizabeth Denby, *Europe Re-housed* (New York, 1938), pp. 86–89.

Common kitchens serve food through a lift opening to each floor, but tenants may also do their own light cooking in small kitchens. Medical care is on hand and a careful watch is kept over the general health of the occupants who need attention. When a tenant is no longer able to care for himself, he is moved to a dormitory. Maximum rents were fixed before World War II at from 120 to 240 kronor per annum for one-person apartments. The subsidy varies too from community to community, ranging from 25 to 80 per cent of the building cost.

In Norway also the housing program for the elderly has made considerable progress. By 1943, 350 homes for old people were scattered throughout the country: Oslo had 24, Bergen 35, Trondheim 9, and Stavanger 16. Pension aid extended in 1936 helped to pay the low rent. An innovation in the Norwegian program was the provision of some small cottages with gardens for the use of couples. The program is administered from the central headquarters in Oslo by designated representatives of the city, the church, and the taxpayer.[22]

Scandinavian experiences have had much to do with inspiring the recent British National Assistance Act. In America there should be growing interest in the housing of the elderly because of the aging of the population and because America's cities and its houses are being designed for the younger generation and the average family. Space has become precious because of rising building costs, and the extra room once occupied by the elderly parent has been eliminated in the interest of economy. Many old people have therefore drifted to the furnished rooming house or little hotel, where their needs are not attended to and where their happiness all too often depends upon the temperament of the landlady or the hotel manager. No governmental program has as yet been undertaken for housing America's elderly, and in 1949 none was even under consideration. The approach in America is still insti-

---

[22] This information was derived from the Norwegian Information Services in New York City and the *Norwegian Konversasjons Leksikon* (Norway, 1943).

tutional. The elderly in 1940 composed one third of those earning $500 to $1,000 a year in America and more than one half of those earning under $500.

LAND RESERVES

Scandinavian countries have pursued a systematic policy of increasing their land holdings both within and outside their city limits. The land is then released for private, co-operative, or public development as construction is ripe. Stockholm holds 32,500 acres of vacant land within the city and considerable land outside. This land was acquired with the help of the state and is leased for agricultural use until building projects are ready. The five next largest Swedish cities own from half to as much as 80 per cent of their administrative areas.[23] Copenhagen owns more than one third of the total area available for building within its city limits, and Oslo owns a suburb that is twice the area of the city.[24]

By owning reserve land, these cities have been able to control the direction of their future growth far more realistically than zoning can ever do. Zoning ordinances in America are gradual in their approach, and, while they may prevent unwholesome intrusions in newly developing sections, cannot effectively control the future developments. Only actual ownership of the land can realistically control the type of developments and bring to them the planned neighborhood with its own environment as well as the proper location of parks and recreational centers. New York state's laws that permit the acquisition of excess land were influenced by Scandinavian policy.

---

[23] Donald Monson and Astrid Monson, "Ideas from Sweden," *American City*, LXIV (May, 1949), 140–142.

[24] George J. Stigler, *Some Economic Aspects of Municipal Land Policies of American Cities* (New York, 1932); National Resources Board, Urban Planning and Land Policies, *Supplementary Report of the Urbanism Committee* (Washington, 1939), II, 228.

LESSONS FOR AMERICA

There are many lessons to be derived from Scandinavian housing policy. They are not all applicable to the American scene. Scandinavian subsidy policies based on the number of children are not adaptable to the American program. Leasing land owned by municipalities might be very desirable indeed from the standpoint of the city, but American cities might face refusal by mortgage lenders to make loans on leased land. Self-help cottage erection may represent an interesting experiment but is hardly a solution to our housing problem or even to a substantial part of it. Scandinavia too has little to add to our own limited knowledge of prefabrication techniques.

Yet a number of policies are worth study and adaptation. Accumulation of reserve land as a method of controlling future development, housing for the elderly, housing co-operatives, Scandinavian planning techniques, junior financing in place of the full guarantee of mortgages, balconies for low-rent housing, and Scandinavian architectural innovations [25] are all deserving of emulation. Although Scandinavia has not found the magic key to the world's housing problems, she is an important laboratory with a host of interesting demonstrations—some fresh in approach, many of them tested by experience, and all of them worthy of sober study by those who seek a method of satisfying pressing social needs within the framework of the democratic process.

---

[25] *Denmark*, a special number of *The Architectural Review* (London, November, 1948); Catherine Bauer, *Modern Housing* (New York, 1934).

VII

Producer and Consumer Co-operatives

By EDITH J. HIRSCH
Lecturer, New School for Social Research

VOLUNTARY co-operation between producers and consumers is deeply rooted in Scandinavia. It is of the greatest economic and social importance for these Northern countries, and in Denmark, Sweden, and Norway it covers nearly all farmers in their farm activities and between one quarter and one half of all consumers.

Voluntary co-operation among the many small farms has been found to be the most efficient way of processing, trading, and exporting the products of agriculture. Through voluntary co-operation livestock production has become Denmark's most important export industry, paying for most of the raw materials and manufactured goods that the country has to import. Consumer co-operatives have been instrumental in all Scandinavian countries in raising the standard of living of the working population through reducing costs and improving methods of distribution. At the same time co-operative societies have played a highly important role in the culture of the Scandinavian countries.

The question has often been raised whether the success of this movement in Scandinavia is due to a special capability on the part of these Northern people for economic co-operation. It is quite evident that voluntary economic co-operation has taken deep root among the populations of the Northern and Central European countries, such as the English, the Scandinavians, the Germans, the Swiss, and the Scandinavians of the American Middle West, whereas the Latin and Slavic nations have been much slower in developing producers' and consumers' co-operatives, to the detriment of production and distribution. In the development of co-operation in Scandinavia, however, education and economic necessity have undoubtedly been more significant factors than has any possible inherent trait in the population. The good general education of Danish farmers, which provides leaders as well as understanding members, has been the precondition for the enormous success of the Danish farm co-operatives, the pioneers in Scandinavia. To this, one other element should be added: There are probably no other nations as genuinely democratic in their social attitude as are the Scandinavian countries.

As in other countries, Scandinavian co-operatives and private enterprise have clashed very seriously in the past. The consumer co-operatives have grown up in a steady fight with private business. They are still making inroads into new fields of production and starting new economic enterprises, mainly where they feel that a private monopoly prevails that should be broken. Although there is no social discrimination against the co-operatives as has been the case in many other European countries, there are differences of opinion regarding taxation. The consumer co-operatives feel that the "dividends" or patronage, which they distribute among their members, constitute savings of these members rather than profits. Private business disagrees. On the whole, however, co-operative societies and private enterprise are now living together in relative peace, and today the co-operatives are a firmly entrenched form of Scandinavian business, a very important sector of its economy, which is expanding into new fields rather than defending old ones.

Officially the Scandinavian co-operatives are nonpolitical. Their membership, however, is mostly made up of farmers and industrial workers, and the influence of the farmers' and the consumers' co-operatives in public life is considerable. A breakdown of the membership of the Swedish consumer co-operatives, which have expanded into the middle classes more than the Danish and Norwegian, shows the following percentages: farmers and agricultural workers, 20; industrial workers, 36; unskilled workers, 20; professional people, 15; and tradesmen and shopkeepers, 9.

The famous British beginnings of consumer co-operatives were inspired by the highly ideological aims of Robert Owen. The pioneers of Rochdale, who founded the first successful store, while much more down to earth in their actual enterprise than Owen, included in the constitution that they drew up in the winter of 1844 the statement that they were going "to settle education and government." Similar idealistic attempts were made in Denmark, Norway, and Sweden from 1850 on, but unlike their German contemporaries, many of which survived, they either failed or did not grow to any real importance.

Success came with the first Danish dairy co-operatives about thirty years later. Born out of sheer economic necessity, with no idealistic strings attached, these producers' co-operatives showed clearly the enormous value of joint economic efforts. They were not only imitated by farmers in other districts of Denmark, but gave new incentive to the consumer co-operatives in the rural districts, which from then on continued to grow. It thus came about that, unlike those of Western Europe, consumer co-operatives in Denmark in the nineteenth century were mainly located in the rural areas. In Sweden and also in Norway, the co-operative idea was chiefly limited to dairies and occasional consumer stores in rural districts. The later great development of Swedish consumer co-operatives, which carried them into the towns and cities and made them the largest retail and wholesale businesses in the country, began only shortly before the First World War.

The differences in the development of Scandinavian co-operatives from those of England and Western and Central Europe is easily explained by the former's origin in the rural districts and by the difference in the economies. Industrialization in the Scandinavian countries had started much later than it had in Western and Central Europe. Large-scale industry and large industrial centers did not develop before the last quarter of the nineteenth century. Even then they remained small for a long time, as compared with Western Europe. The economic activity had its center in the rural districts and in the small towns that supplied the countryside. The industrial workers were for the most part employed in small-scale enterprises, and most of them had their roots on the farms. This has changed to a large degree in the past decades, and since then consumer co-operatives have moved into the cities.

At present about 42 per cent of all Danish, more than one quarter of all Norwegian, and nearly one half of all Swedish families belong to consumers' co-operatives. About 10 per cent of all retail sales and 20 to 25 per cent of all grocery and food store sales go over the co-operatives' counters. Consumer co-operatives have a large share in the wholesale business, especially in food, and own a number of flour mills, bakeries, slaughterhouses, and other industrial plants for the needs of their members in each country. The development of consumer co-operatives can be seen from Table 20.

Table 20. Membership in consumers' co-operatives and number of local societies, 1947.

	Denmark	Norway	Sweden
Number of local societies	1,971	1,081	677
Membership in local societies	420,300	257,000	877,186
Percentage of families in local societies	42	25–28	50
Number of shops		1,234	7,177

The farmers' co-operatives consist of co-operative dairies, co-operative bacon factories, butter export societies, cattle export associations, and so forth. They have made large-scale business out of a large number of very small enterprises. They sell their products in the wholesale market and have taken over at least part of all farm exports through a number of different co-operatives, each of which serves one purpose only. They produce, import, and distribute food, seed, fertilizer, and agricultural machinery and equipment. Their factories take care of the needs of their members, and some of them export as well. Their central organizations are of great importance in the economic policies that affect their members.

Table 21. Turnover of local societies, wholesale organizations, and own production, 1947; expressed in thousands of kroner.

	Denmark	Norway	Sweden
Sales of local societies	450,000	421,384	1,279,000
Sales of wholesale organizations	289,467	99,500	657,000
Own production	84,717	35,500	329,000

Sources: Review of International Cooperation, July, 1948, and government statistics.

The national consumer co-operatives' wholesale organizations of Denmark, Norway, Sweden, and Finland founded in 1918 a joint importing agency, Nordisk Andelsforbundet, with headquarters in Copenhagen and London. These four countries also formed the first international co-operative industrial enterprise with the building in 1931 of an electrical bulb factory in Stockholm, which was meant to break the world monopoly. In 1939 the idea of international collaboration on a co-operative basis was carried still further in the foundation of the International Trading Agency with headquarters in London.

Two developments are outstanding: the Danish farmers' co-operatives, after which the Swedish and Norwegian were patterned, and the Swedish consumer co-operatives, a magnificent achievement of the twentieth century.

THE DANISH FARM CO-OPERATIVES

The history of Denmark, long before the beginning of the farmers' co-operatives, had been favorable to the co-operative

Table 22. Turnover and membership in Danish farm co-operative societies.

	Turnover		Members
	1945	1923	1945
Agricultural productive and sales societies			
Dairies	1,059.0	665.0	185,659
Butter export societies	209.5	187.9	733
Sale of offal by bacon factories	514.5	433.1	197,714
Special activities of bacon factories	66.8	—	—
Egg exports by bacon factories	8.6	13.1	—
Co-operative egg exports	23.1	19.2	41,000
Cattle export societies	54.8	15.9	33,378
Cattle sales association	72.2	—	81,300
Poultry-killing stations	8.2	—	66,304
Seed supply association	26.8	4.5	6,049
Agricultural purchasing societies			
Feedstuff societies	79.7	107.1	96,868
Fertilizer society	25.4	21.1	61,718
Danish dairies' joint purchasing and engineering works	14.5	6.3	1,636
Cement factory	4.7	7.0	1,173
Coal supply society	4.1	4.6	1,212
Funen coal-purchasing society	3.1	—	233
Other societies			
Tryg insurance society (income from premiums)	10.8	3.8	249,426
Dairy and farm accident insurance society (income from premiums)	5.9	2.0	206,000
Association of parish councils' accident insurance society (income from premiums)	0.3	0.2	23,910
Co-operative pensions society (income from premiums)	2.9	0.3	4,960
Sanatorium association	1.1	0.5	360,246

Source: Danmarks Statistiske Departement, *Statistisk Aarbog* (Copenhagen, 1925 and 1947).

idea.[1] As in other European countries, co-operation had existed for centuries in small agricultural communities, where cultivation was established by the farmers in common. In the second half of the eighteenth century, as the money economy was becoming increasingly important, the system of a feudal economy had become unprofitable. Under the influence of the new eighteenth-century ideas, the whole manorial system was abolished in 1788. Though free to move wherever they chose, most of the farmers stayed on their holdings, paying rent to the estate owners. At the same time the common fields were broken up and reallotted. In a relatively short time the farmers were able to buy their farms from the estate owners. From the moment of the peasants' liberation enormous progress was made in the agricultural sector. Thirty years after the farmer had been freed, the crops had increased by 100 per cent.

Danish agriculture up to the middle of the nineteenth century was based on the production of cereals. Grain was the main export commodity, but grain growing became less and less profitable in the second half of that century because of the overexploitation of the soil and the competition of wheat from overseas. Slowly Danish agriculture shifted its weight from grain production to livestock holding.

Of greater importance still for the rapid growth of co-operative organizations was the high level of rural education. Compulsory education in elementary schools had been introduced as early as 1814. But much more was accomplished later through the folk schools that were founded in 1844 and that expanded over the country in the seventies. They laid the groundwork for the co-operative movement in that they provided it with the many leaders it needed, as well as a membership conscious of the value of joint democratic efforts.[2]

The co-operative way of doing individual farm business in

---

[1] For the Danish producers' co-operatives see Einar Jensen, *Danish Agriculture* (Copenhagen, 1937); also *Social Denmark* (Copenhagen, 1947); Henning Ravnholt, *The Danish Cooperative Movement* (Copenhagen, 1947).

[2] For a description of the folk school, see pages 235–240.

Denmark did not start with any philosophical idea about co-operatives. As early as 1852, when grain growing started to become less and less profitable, the Royal Agricultural Society of Denmark issued a circular recommending the establishment of joint dairies. When the need for new export commodities became more imperative from about 1863 or 1864 on, some attempts were made to establish "joint dairies," the first one in Marslev, near Odense. The quality of the milk, however, suffered when it was transported from the farms to the dairies for churning, and no real success was achieved. Butter making remained efficient only on the estates, where enough milk was produced to manufacture it into butter on the spot.

A new incentive for joint butter production was given to the farmers in 1879 when L. C. Nielsen succeeded in constructing the first workable milk separator. This invention made it possible to collect the milk daily from the various farms in a neighborhood and to have it made into butter, without loss of quality, in a dairy large enough to support a specialized dairyman. The result was that even the small farmers with a few cows could now produce butter of the same quality as that of the big estates.

Hjedding, in Western Jutland, is considered the mother of all Danish farm co-operatives. Its constitution and organization became the pattern for all dairy co-operatives. These were its rules: (1) Membership should be open to all farmers in the neighborhood. (2) The farmers were to be jointly liable (they should deal "all as one and one as all"). (3) The profits were to be distributed in proportion to the quantity of milk delivered. (4) Each farmer was to have one vote, regardless of the amount of milk he delivered. (5) Each farmer was to deliver all his milk to the dairy, with the exception of that used on the farm.

The founding of this first co-operative took place in the winter of 1882–1883 when a traveling dairyman suggested that the quality of butter could be improved if the farmers would churn their milk jointly. A meeting of the farmers in the village was called, and the majority agreed to the venture. Because of the joint and unlimited liability of the members, enough money could be secured at low interest to start the building. An organization meeting was called, the co-operative procedure of the new dairy was agreed upon, and a committee and a manager were elected. One of the assembled farmers was charged with the drafting of the rules. Working together with two other farmers all night, he emerged at five o'clock in the morning with the above-mentioned rules, which soon became the backbone of the whole new agricultural movement, a model "constitution." The Hjedding farmers had made history.

The first co-operative creamery proved successful. Four years after the idea was conceived, as many as 176 local creameries, each with its own co-operative and its own constitution, were actively at work in the same part of Western Jutland. From then on the movement snowballed. In 1900 there were 942 dairy co-operatives. In 1923 there were 1,335 co-operative creameries, which processed 86.2 per cent of all the butter in Denmark. At present, about 91 per cent of all the milk is processed in nearly 1,400 co-operative dairies.

In competition with the co-operative system, private dairies could no longer succeed; the economic odds were against them. Dairy co-operatives, therefore, have developed without any hard fights with private enterprise. The struggle came when the co-operatives abandoned their habit of selling their produce to private dealers and formed their own wholesaling organizations.

As the number of dairy co-operatives rose and dairy farming grew, co-operation among the local societies became advisable. In 1901 the co-operating Danish dairy societies were established, and in 1912 the Federation of Danish Dairy Societies was founded, to which belonged all local dairy societies and the regional associations they had formed. This over-all society, though it has no production or selling functions, has done much to further the interests of Danish dairying.

Because of bad roads and difficulties of transportation, the creameries had to remain neighborhood enterprises. With the great improvement that has taken place in the roads in recent years and the general introduction of automobiles and trucks, the trend is now toward larger creameries, which receive their milk from larger districts. It is, therefore, probable that the number of dairy co-operatives will decrease in the near future, while the percentage of butter produced in creameries will remain the same or increase.

Co-operatives have now taken over a large part of the marketing of butter, and at present ten co-operative butter export societies account for 55 per cent of the total Danish exports of butter. Some of them are dealing directly with British co-operative wholesale societies.

The dairy co-operatives have been responsible for the high quality of Danish food exports. They were the first to pay for butter according to its butterfat content and the cleanliness of the milk. They were eager to improve the dairy herds through better breeds, scientific feeding, and improved hygienic conditions. The Danish co-operatives were the first to develop these scientific methods and to make them available to all farmers, irrespective of the size of their holdings. They achieved all this without any government help.

As a result of the co-operative creameries, the Danish hog industry was greatly extended. The farmers who delivered the milk to the co-operatives got back the skim milk. In order to use it, they started raising hogs on a commercial basis. As dairy production increased, hog raising became a recognized business. The English market was there to take the surplus that could not be used at home. From being a by-product of butter production, hog raising soon became more important to the Danish economy than the production of butter, and before the war hogs were the most valuable export item.

The first co-operative slaughterhouse was founded at Horsens in 1887. The prices offered to the farmer by the wholesalers were very poor, and, after trying in vain to improve them, the chairman of the local agricultural society issued an appeal for the establishment of a co-operative packing plant. The realization of this project, however, was much more difficult than the establishment of the first dairy. Bacon production was a much riskier business than dairying because there was a less certain demand. Also, the amount of capital needed was much larger, and there was opposition from wholesale buyers and private slaughtering firms. After a series of meetings in the district, however, 1,200 producers agreed to join and promised to deliver 10,500 hogs per year; 1,100 guarantors put up security up to 107,000 kroner. Opposition to the whole project was strong and difficulties appeared from everywhere. The plant survived, however, and in the next few years many more bacon factories were established. In 1890 there were ten, with a membership of 15,648. Just prior to World War II there were sixty-one co-operatives with nearly 200,000 members; they processed 85 per cent of all Danish hogs and had a turnover of nearly half a billion Danish kroner. At present, the same number of co-operative bacon factories handle 89 per cent of all the hogs killed.

Unlike the dairies, the slaughterhouses were not neighborhood businesses. They served a much larger community and were concentrated in the main towns. This meant that the co-operative idea had to have a much stronger hold on its members than in the case of the neighborhood dairies where the members had known each other practically all their lives and were working together in an enterprise that could be easily controlled and, if necessary, managed by the participants. Co-operative slaughterhouses were big business and needed professional management.

The Danish co-operative packing houses were for a long time the only ones in Europe fully comparable to the large-scale mechanized American packing plants. Like the co-operative dairies, they are providing the advantages of large-scale enterprise to all farmers, regardless of the size of their farms.

The educational influence of the packing co-operatives is perhaps more conspicuous than that of any other co-operatives. The farmer gets the full price per pound for his hog only if it measures up to the demand of the English customer for lean bacon, which means hogs of a special breed and a live weight of between 200 to 220 pounds. If this weight is not reached or if it is exceeded, the discounts made by the co-operatives are very sharp. This has standardized the Danish hog, which is now just right to produce the bacon for the British breakfast table.

Right from the start the co-operative bacon factories did their own marketing. This was another reason for opposition. In 1890 the Joint Bureau of Co-operative Bacon Factories was established, and in 1897 a national federation of all co-operative bacon factories was created. As in the case of the over-all dairy organization, the federation is not a business organization, but it has done much to further the efficiency of hog production and marketing. In 1902 some co-operative bacon factories set up their own agency, the Danish Bacon Company, in London. Its aim was to eliminate the commission paid to agents and to counteract any monopoly agreements on the part of British importers, thereby assuring the individual farmers the best possible price.

To increase further the profits of their members, the various bacon factories in turn established factories to make use of the by-products. Several of these factories are manufacturing serum and other medical preparations, of which Denmark is a leading producer in Europe.

After the first dairy and bacon co-operatives were founded, the co-operative way of doing business took hold of nearly all the activities of the farmers. Local co-operatives, joined together in national organizations, are handling egg exports, cattle sales, cattle exports, poultry killing, and poultry exporting. Of great importance are the various farmers' purchasing co-operatives, the first of which was founded in 1898. They include co-operatives for the buying of feed, fertilizer, and coal and cement. Sometimes they have their own plants. The cement plant, which was intended to break a monopoly, was for many years the object of some of the most bitter fights between the co-operative movement and private interests. It cost the co-operatives a good deal of money to see the plant through its first years.

Apart from these co-operative societies, there are farmers' associations of a more educational or scientific nature, such as the various breeding and cow-testing associations. In addition, a great number of the farmers belong to the consumer co-operatives, through which they buy food, household goods, small farm implements, and gasoline. A farmer may easily belong to ten or twelve different producers' co-operatives as well as a consumers' co-operative.

Of course the paragraphs of a constitution alone do not create a co-operative society or a co-operative spirit. The Danish farmer considers the co-operatives part of his own farm business. He attends the meetings of his co-operatives, makes proposals, and subjects himself to the rules passed by the majority. He agrees to the fines that the manager of the co-operative may impose upon him for deficiencies in the quality of his deliveries, expecting his neighbors and fellow members to be treated in exactly the same way.

THE SWEDISH FARM CO-OPERATIVES

Co-operation among Swedish farmers on a really large scale did not begin until 1929, and it was achieved only with government guidance and financial assistance. Co-operative creameries had existed since the 1880's and 1890's, but they remained local enterprises and did not contribute greatly to the efficiency of dairy farming as did the Danish dairy co-operatives with the help of their national organization. Hog production increased in Sweden also, as a by-product of the dairies, and starting in 1899 co-operative slaughterhouses were built after the Danish model. They developed slowly, however, and up to 1932 they produced only 40 per cent of all the pork and only 3.5 per cent of all other meat. Since 1880 there have also been some egg-marketing associations as well as feed- and fertilizer-purchasing associations, shaped according to the Danish and German patterns. Yet the only large-scale organization before 1930 remained the Stockholm Milk Central, which was founded in 1915. In 1935 it had 160 operating points and processed 88.4 per cent of all the liquid milk used in Stockholm. The Swedish farmer produced mainly for the home market, and efficiency and the quality of the products were, therefore, not of the same importance as in Denmark, where agriculture was for a long time the only sizable export industry.

From 1929 on, the Agricultural Society of Sweden, founded in 1917, assumed a more influential position in regulating farmers' marketing and purchasing. It had come to consider that co-operation among farmers according to the Danish model was a necessity for the improvement of farm production, processing, and marketing, especially since the depression of the early thirties hit Sweden just as hard as it did most other countries. The government, with the help of the Agricultural Society, offered financial support to secure the organization of farm co-operatives all over the country but delegated to the farmers' organizations the execution of the necessary measures. Directions for organizing co-operatives were drawn up centrally by the Swedish Agricultural Society. Once begun, the process of organization took hold rapidly, but from the top down. Co-operative farming in Sweden, except in its early beginnings, was thus not a spontaneous movement. However, it must be said that the system could not have been established so quickly if the farmers had not been willing and able to go along.

In 1932 the Agricultural Society succeeded in creating the Swedish National Creamery Association, the first Swedish organization of farm co-operatives on a national scale. This national organization in turn was active in organizing new local dairy co-operatives. National organization of other local farm co-operatives and a subsequent quick growth in their number followed. At the beginning of the Second World War, of 290,000 farm owners, 260,000 were members of dairy co-operatives and

280,000 members of co-operative slaughterhouses. Altogether the Swedish co-operatives then had a turnover of two billion kronor.

World War II forced Sweden to rely almost entirely on its own resources of food and feed; previously she had imported up to 10 per cent of what she needed. When the war broke out, the co-operative organization of the farmers had already been carried through and had proved to be of enormous value in keeping the Swedish population adequately supplied. In spite of scarcities the farmers sold through their organizations at official prices and black markets were insignificant.

At present 95 per cent of all milk, 96 per cent of all butter, and 87 per cent of all cheese are processed co-operatively. The farmer sells his grain and potatoes through marketing co-operatives and buys feed, farm equipment and machinery, gasoline, and building material through purchasing co-operatives. If he owns woodland, he sells his lumber through the forest owners' organization.

CONSUMER CO-OPERATIVES

Denmark. The first successful Rochdale store in Denmark was opened in 1866 in Thisted, Jutland, after some earlier attempts had failed. It was founded by Pastor Hans Christian Sonne, the "provisions parson," who was strongly influenced by the ideas of the welfare organizations to which he belonged and by the model of the first English societies. In the towns as well as in the rural districts the earlier co-operative ventures had had a strong philanthropic character, and the number of actual workers participating had not been large, but Sonne succeeded in arousing the workers' interest. The initial opposition to the new venture was considerable, but sales rose nevertheless. In accordance with the aim of "raising the socially lower, depressed, and dependent section of the population to a higher moral, intellectual, and social level and thereby to a more honorable place in the community," the society opened a library and reading room, started a health and unemployment scheme, and laid out allotment gardens. In

1867 the "Randers Workers' Society" was founded. After some years the movement grew rather quickly, although chiefly in the rural districts where it was carried along by the success of the dairy co-operatives. In 1872 there were 62 societies; in 1874, 92; and in 1890, 545, of which all but five were in rural districts.

Laborers in the towns and the few cities again became interested in the movement after 1910, and since that time co-operatives have been organized in nearly all urban districts. In 1945, 42 per cent of all Danish families were members of consumer co-operatives, and 10 to 12 per cent of all retail sales were made through them. For many members of the Social Democratic party and the labor unions it is a matter of course to belong to a consumer co-operative. Yet the rural districts have remained the stronghold of the movement, as the whole existence of the farmer is closely connected with the co-operative movement. It is the farmer who buys the largest part of his total purchases, both for farm and personal needs, through the co-operative stores. Urban members are much more loosely affiliated. In the villages the co-operative store is often the social and cultural center of the community; the farmer is more likely to serve in some capacity in his small co-operative store than is the urban worker, who necessarily belongs to a much larger co-operative and in addition has many other opportunities for diversion. The importance of the rural co-operative is expressed in the fact that in 1947 Denmark had as many as 1,971 local consumer co-operatives with an average membership of only 200.

In their price policy the Danish consumer co-operatives have mainly followed the English example of selling at current prices and distributing as high a dividend or patronage as possible. This dividend is distributed once a year, around Christmas time. Only in recent years, after the Swedish co-operatives had made a success of it, have the Danish co-operatives tried to sell at lower than current prices in order to influence the price level.

As in other countries, the growth of the consumer co-operatives into a real movement started with the formation of the Co-operative Wholesale Society in 1896. The wholesale organization has helped the locals to improve all aspects of their business. While the various co-operatives remain independent and are governed, as formerly, by their members, they have received invaluable help in buying, organizing, and accounting, and in the training of their personnel from the Wholesale Society, the board and officers of which are elected by the delegates of the 1,971 locals.

Although in all countries the co-operatives represent the multitude of anonymous citizens, yet in each country one man has given the impetus to the movement and stamped its development with his character. The Swedish people have their Albin Johansson, the Norwegians had their Advokat Dehli, and the Danes had their Severin Jørgensen. It was Jørgensen who conceived the idea of a co-operative wholesale organization in the eighties, when nothing similar existed in any other Scandinavian country, and forced the individual co-operatives first into regional and later into national co-operation. He became the first chairman of the national organization in 1896 and remained at the helm until 1913; even after retiring at the age of seventy-one he remained on the board, which he left only at the time of his death in 1926. The consumer co-operatives, incidentally, were only one of his interests in the co-operative movement. He was also one of the founders of the Central Co-operative Committee, the Farmers' Co-operative Egg Export Association, and the Co-operative Bank. He favored collaboration among the co-operatives of the Scandinavian countries and between them and co-operatives outside Scandinavia.[3]

The Danish Co-operative Wholesale Society, like its sister organizations in other countries, has founded a number of industrial enterprises that are supplying the local organizations. Industrial plants are also owned by some large local co-operatives, such as the Copenhagen society. In every case, the idea was to supply the membership more cheaply than could be done through buy-

------

[3] See Ravnholt, *op. cit.*, p. 38.

ing from private industry, and thus to give the greatest benefit to the individual member.

Sweden.[4] The Swedish Co-operative Union (Kooperativa Förbundet, usually called KF) announces with pride in its report for 1948 that approximately half of the Swedish population, 877,000 families of on the average 3.6 persons each, belong to its network of local co-operatives. This percentage is higher than that of the first nation to develop modern co-operative organization, Great Britain. The report also proudly points out that the Stockholm Co-operative Society (Konsum Stockholm) is the second largest in the world, with 129,000 members and a turnover in 1947 of 238,000,000 kronor. It has approximately 800 stores and restaurants and one department store, the second largest in Sweden.

Nowhere has the relative economic and political importance of consumer co-operatives reached the peak that it has in Sweden. Whether in the cities or in the rural districts, the most efficient and most modern food stores belong to the co-operatives. Twenty-five per cent of the food and grocery sales and twelve per cent of all retail sales go over the co-operatives' counters. Being the largest retail organization in the country, the co-operatives have steadily used their economic superiority to force prices downward to give all consumers the maximum benefit. They have compelled the other retailers to follow their lead in rationalizing and reducing costs. Thus, before the war, retail as well as wholesale margins in Sweden were considerably lower than in this country, Denmark, or Norway.[5]

KF, besides being the union of all local co-operatives, is by far the largest wholesale organization in the country, buying directly from factories as well as importing from abroad. In 1947 its turnover was 657,000,000 kronor, two thirds of which was sold

---

[4] See Anders Hedberg, *Consumer Cooperatives in Sweden* (Stockholm, 1948); G. R. Ytterboom, "Agriculture Cooperation," *Annals of the American Academy of Political and Social Science*, CXCVII (1938), 185–199.

[5] See Julius Hirsch, *Den Skandinaviske Kolonial-Engroshandels Normtal* (Copenhagen, 1942).

to the local co-operatives and one third to private business and government agencies. Buying is concentrated in thirty different sections organized on a commodity basis. This makes for an enormous buying power, which has assured KF of the lowest possible prices.

KF's own industrial production, initiated in 1920 to force down oleomargarine prices, is becoming increasingly important year by year. Without any financial help from outside, financed only by the profits of its wholesale activities and later by the profits from its already established plants, KF has invaded a large number of industries in fields where it felt that an existing cartel should be broken and prices drastically reduced. After its margarine plant had been established and prices reduced, KF went into the flour-milling business, which was concentrated in the hands of a few big concerns located in the main ports. Tre Kronor, KF's first flour mill, situated on the now co-operatively owned island of Kvarnholmen at the entry to the port of Stockholm, is one of the most modern and best equipped in the world. Together with Tre Lejon in the port of Gothenborg and with the bakeries that were added, it is now producing everything from oatmeal and cornflakes to macaroni and Sweden's national bread, rye-crisp. Incidentally, while many of the larger local co-operatives have their own bakeries, all the rye-crisp sold by the co-operatives is made by KF at the lowest possible cost.

After having acquired a shoe factory in 1925, KF in 1926 bought a galoshes factory, galoshes being an essential item in Sweden. Within a few years the price of galoshes, which had sold uniformly over the country for 8.5 or 7.5 kronor per pair, dropped to 3.5 kronor, and the total number of pairs sold increased.[6] Besides making galoshes, KF's rubber plant is also manufacturing tubes and tires. The oilseed needed for the margarine factory is crushed in KF's own plant. Cash registers, previously imported

---

[6] See Mauritz Bonow, "The Consumer Cooperative Movement in Sweden," *Annals of the American Academy of Political and Social Science*, CXCVII (1938), 171–184.

from the United States, and sewing machines are manufactured for the domestic market and for export. KF has acquired the oldest and largest household china factory in Sweden and is producing dinnerware and decorative china in addition to plumbing fixtures and ceramic high-frequency material. KF has a cannery and garment factories manufacturing women's and girls' dresses and men's clothing, shirts, and overalls. From its forest resources KF supplies sulphite and sulphate pulp, which serves as raw material for its paper mill and its war-born staple fiber plant. Two KF plants are making farm machinery and equipment, and two others are producing superphosphate and nitrogen fertilizer.

A story quite of its own concerns the electric bulb factory "Luma," which belongs to the wholesale organizations of the four Scandinavian countries, and was the first international co-operative industrial undertaking. KF built the factory and asked the co-operatives of Denmark, Norway, and Finland to join since bulb prices in all Scandinavian countries were extremely high because of the world monopoly. Shortly after Luma had begun to produce, bulb prices dropped by 40 per cent, a saving to the Swedish consumer of 6,000,000 kronor a year or one kronor per inhabitant. There is now a Luma plant in Oslo, Norway. In addition, in 1936 the Swedish-Scottish-British Luma Co-operative Lamp Society was organized with a plant in Glasgow.

KF has its own book-publishing department, which, among other things, is the leading publisher of economic literature. Among its educational activities are a correspondence school and a co-operative college, a special instruction center for the co-operative movement. In line with its effort to encourage thrift, KF is acting through the local societies as a savings bank for the 877,000 individual members and has organized a fire insurance, as well as a life insurance, society. KF has interested itself in some of the most beautiful housing projects for low- and middle-income groups. Each project, to be sure, has as its main shopping center one large or several smaller co-operative food stores, some of them the first self-service stores in Sweden. Each store is equipped with the most modern apparatus, especially in the meat, fish, and dairy departments.

KF rather than the local organizations has been described at length because the consumer co-operative movement in Sweden, which was inactive until the beginning of this century, has been built, not from the bottom up, but from the top down through this wholesale organization. Founded in 1899 as a central organization for the local consumer co-operatives, it began to be of real importance only in 1904 when it took over the function of a wholesaler for the local co-operatives. Shortly afterwards it began to advise and control the latter in many of their activities. At the present time no local co-operative can be admitted that does not comply with KF's rules as to financial stability and accounting and auditing procedures.

In spite of the valuable co-operation and efforts of nearly a million local members, the Swedish consumer movement in its present form is largely the creation of a single man with a most unusual gift for organization and for choosing his associates, Albin Johansson. An employee of KF at the time it took over whole-saling functions, he organized the first really big co-operative society, the Stockholm Konsum, with a membership that now numbers 129,000. He was back in KF when the first factory was started in 1920 and has been the most important member of KF's Board of Executives ever since. In American terminology he combines the functions of president, chairman of the board, and managing director of a company that, through its branches, comprises 877,000 stockholders.

A tremendous power is vested in the small Board of Executives comprising KF's chief officials. The board's functions are analogous to those of the president and vice-president of an American corporation, except that on certain major issues the approval of the Administrative Council is required. This is a body of twenty-two members, which meets eight to ten times a year and appoints and supervises the Board of Executives. Half of its members are managers of local co-operatives and completely versed in all problems of co-operative business. They are therefore in a much better position to supervise the Executive Board than are many directors of American corporations; thus they provide a guarantee of sound business conduct. The Administrative Council is elected, not by the individual local co-operatives, but by the district meetings of the eighteen districts into which the present 677 local co-operatives are organized. Thus the individual co-operative has little to say about who is actually to govern its central organization. In a sense, this puts still more power in the hands of the Board of Executives and its leader. In contrast to a private corporation, there cannot be a majority of stockholders strong enough to influence major issues or to decide questions of personality.

Though Swedish co-operatives have 877,000 members, they are organized in only 677 local organizations, whereas Danish co-operatives, with half as many members, have nearly 2,000 co-operatives. The Swedish co-operatives firmly believe that in most cases large local co-operatives can operate more efficiently than small ones, and in recent years, therefore, the trend has been in the direction of merging small local societies. There are still co-operatives with as few as 200 members, but they are rare and exist in very thinly settled areas. Co-operatives with several stores are now the rule. Often they own a plant with neighboring co-operatives or, if they are very large, own a plant of their own. Stockholm, however, with its 119,000 members and 800 outlets is an exception as much as the very small rural co-operatives. The organization of the large co-operatives is, of course, very different from that of the small, but the basic regulations are the same: sound finances and no extension of credit; profits to pay interest on the shares of each member first, then 15 per cent of the profits to the co-operative's reserve fund, and the remainder as dividends to the members; and one vote to each member.

While this shift to large local co-operatives may ensure maximum efficiency, it has the disadvantage of militating against close connections between the co-operative and its members. Eventually the member of a co-operative may become a registered customer rather than an active member. The leaders of the movement are fully cognizant of this danger and are doing everything they can to combat it through their educational facilities, group meetings, and other such activities. Long ago the movement concentrated all its energy on the single aim of improving the standard of living of its members and of the lower- and middle-income groups in general. Through a first-class organization it is resolved to eliminate inefficiency in marketing and to break cartels where they exist to the detriment of the consumer. This aim cannot be attained on the level of small-scale business; it requires a powerful organization strictly controlled from above and far-sighted leaders who are in a position to make their own decisions.

The co-operatives are by far Sweden's most important chain-store system. They have revolutionized both retailing and wholesaling, thereby bringing enormous benefits to the entire population. That they have nevertheless remained a democratic organization is to their very great credit, even though they have had to give up some of their original goals.

Norway. Consumer co-operatives existed in Norway after about 1850, but by 1880 most of them had disappeared. The present movement can be traced to 1894 when, under the leadership of Advokat O. Dehli, the first successful consumer co-operative was founded along Rochdale lines. In spite of Dehli's efforts the growth of the movement was relatively slow. It began to grow more vigorously after Dehli had succeeded, in 1906, in establishing the National Co-operative Association of Norway, which was to have the dual purpose of acting as the union of the local co-operatives and as their wholesale organization. At the outset there was not much interest in the union, and only eleven of the existing co-operatives joined. In 1910, when Danish consumer co-operatives had 35,000 individual members comprising 26 per cent of the families, Norway had only 66 local societies with 3,750 members, or 3 per cent of Norwegian families.

From the beginning the central organization included production, banking, and insurance co-operatives, since the farmers' co-operatives had no central organization of their own. The movement was largely rural until the German occupation. One reason for the slow development may have been the opposition of private enterprise, to which the government yielded.

Norwegian co-operatives are different from the Swedish and the Danish in that they deal to a greater extent in materials, machinery, and implements for farmers and fishermen and in that they play an important part in the marketing not only of farm, but of fishery, products. The farm co-operatives are not nearly so highly developed as in other Scandinavian countries, although farm purchasing associations, co-operative dairies, slaughterhouses, mills, and even a co-operative farmers' bank do exist.

Unlike Swedish and Danish co-operatives, the Norwegian societies are engaged in small local industries. Thus in 1947 there were 223 such businesses with a total of 600 employed workers, or not quite three per workshop. Apart from such enterprises the central organization runs a number of plants. There are, for example, three oleomargarine plants, a mill, a candy factory, a radio assembly plant, a garment factory, and the bulb plant belonging to Luma. Total production of the central organization's plant amounted to 35,500,000 kroner in 1937. During the occupation the Germans tried to suppress the co-operatives. The members did not dare to meet and the sales turnover declined rapidly. As soon as the war was over, however, the development was reversed and the number of local co-operatives, which had been 875 in 1939, increased to 1,081 in 1947, and it is still growing.

VIII

Adult Education

BY PER G. STENSLAND

Associate Professor of Education,
Kansas State College

W E SHALL probably always debate what role particular educational efforts have played in the history of social change. A sociologist or political scientist may record and analyze a set of unmistakable changes and find among them the sudden growth of educational movements and institutions. Were these educational phenomena a result of social and economic disturbances and new arrangements or did they enter the picture so early that they may have had causal effect on the changes in society? An educator may easily be carried away by a spectacular coincidence between certain educational developments and changes in the environment. It seems tempting to trace social progress to new ventures in education.

These reflections are inescapable when the discussion turns to adult education in modern Scandinavia. Educators and social scientists alike have shown puzzled interest in the social and political changes in the Scandinavian countries. They have noted the apparent coincidence between the growth of social democracy and the expansion of strong, popular movements. They have marked the role of voluntary and free, organized efforts to spread education in these popular movements. At times, enthusiasm or need for an argument in a discussion has led observers to suggest that a strong causal relationship existed between sociopolitical democracy and widespread education for such democracy.

The Scandinavian may, to a degree, have been "master of his destiny" through education; undoubtedly there came "light from the North" to many educators watching the Scandinavian scene;

many of the study groups and schools for adults were "laboratories of democracy"; the folk schools of Denmark may be "a way out" offered to modern community educators; much of "the middle way" in Sweden may have been built on work in study circles.[1] Nevertheless, we have to view with caution any general conclusion that social democracy in Scandinavia sprang from social education, or that popular social movements grew efficient and mature because of popular adult education in these movements. The reason is threefold. First, education like any other factor in a society both affects and is affected by other factors; thus it is difficult, indeed, to isolate cause and effect in a historical sense of the word. Second, there is no proof that other educational developments would not have had as strong an effect as the adult education efforts that were made. How can we now tell whether a democratizing secondary school development in the North would not have been accompanied by sociopolitical changes very much the same as those we now combine with adult education? Third, while the practical development of adult education has been spectacular in Scandinavia, analytical research in the field has been weak, nay, nonexistent; thus very few data can be mustered to substantiate reliable conclusions on the efficacy of adult education.

When, nevertheless, an attempt is made here to assess modern adult education, the aim is to analyze it as one of many outward signs of social change, without regard to its role in the causal chain of events. The author starts with the suggestion that adult education, like any other fair-sized social arrangement, has shown certain traits unique to Scandinavia. Thus it reflects the particular combination of social forces that arose in that society. At times it may also reflect the perplexities and potentialities of any modern democratic society.

---

[1] See Moses M. Coady, *Masters of Their Own Destiny* (New York, 1939); Joseph Hart, *Light from the North* (New York, 1927); Peter Manniche, *Denmark, a Social Laboratory* (London, 1939); Marquis W. Childs, *Sweden, the Middle Way* (New York, 1948); and Sir Richard Livingstone, "The Way Out," in *The Future in Education* (Cambridge, Eng., 1944).

ROOTS IN LIBERALISM, HUMANISM,
AND NATIONALISM

Several ideological strands work themselves into modern adult education in Scandinavia. It was inspired not from one but from many of the social and economic ideas that stirred the nineteenth century.

Seen as a voluntary effort to increase the opportunities for organized and self-directed learning, adult education germinated in the soil of liberalistic reform ideas. Using a pat phrase, one could say that the movement was "a child of nineteenth-century liberalism." It was related to the new radical and unsettling forces that had sprouted in the American and French revolutions, and that later found voice in the political reforms and revolutions around 1830 and 1848. Political and social liberalism allied itself with a form of cultural liberalism.

In the struggle for political change there were efforts to give to the challengers the intellectual and cultural tools to compete with those in power. It is no surprise to find the first Danish folk schools in the wake of the constitutional reforms of the 1840's in that country, nor the first Swedish in the years after the parliamentary reforms of the 1860's. Obviously the education of citizens was justified in a society where new political rights and responsibilities were enunciated.

Likewise, the liberalistic reform movements in the religious field were linked to a series of attempts to spread education among adults. Early Scandinavian folk schools were as unmistakably expressions of religious liberalism as was the more subtle advocacy of widespread reading of the Bible.

New cultural experiments naturally thrived on the dissolution of traditional economic and social structures in the old society. A sharp increase in population in the first decades of the century had enlarged those groups in the rural communities who had no, or little, land. The old trade guilds were being broken up in the cities, around 1840 and 1850; economic classes were replacing traditional social estates. The new groups of this society in the making had no strong ties with the traditional pattern of formal education. The stage was set unwittingly by both land reformers and free traders for nontraditional education experiments. Thus, the political parties or groups who sought political liberalism worked not only for the first compulsory public education for children (e.g., in Denmark in 1814, Sweden in 1842, Norway in 1827), but also for increased cultural opportunities among grown-up citizens.

In the latter half of the nineteenth century, when movements grew that sought to extend political liberalism, parallel efforts were made to increase popular political education in these movements. Study circles, lectures, and schools inside the Swedish temperance movement and all the Scandinavian labor movements are convincing samples of this combination of political reform action and adult education.

Seen as a cultural movement, adult education also had deep roots in Western humanism. The attempts to clarify and to further idealist-humanist philosophy that were made in the early 1800's, and later in the middle of the century, had their distinct effect on early Scandinavian adult education. If any Northerner be selected as "the father of modern adult education," it should be Denmark's Nicholaj Frederik Severin Grundtvig. Several signs point to the profound influence Grundtvig had felt from German idealist philosophers like Fichte.[2] Grundtvig was a spokesman for the romantic-historicist movements swelling during and after the Napoleonic wars.

The humanist tradition of Western Europe with such men as Fichte took one course, with men like Grundtvig another; while Fichte ended up advocating education of the elite, Grundtvig came forth with the call for a broad folk education. This naturally put him in sharp conflict with those who spoke for humanist traditions in classical and scholastic terms. An outspoken classicist in

---

[2] See for example F. Skrubbeltrang, *The Danish Folk High Schools* (Copenhagen, 1947), pp. 9 ff.

Sweden like Esaias Tegnér, a contemporary of Grundtvig, spoke for esoteric and ultraconservative education and doubted that education among "the working classes" should be anything but religious. "Any other knowledge is deemed not only unnecessary, but actually harmful," he said.

The trend took a different turn. Efforts were pushed to establish libraries for the people and "societies for the dissemination of knowledge through reading." In these ventures church leaders took an early interest; parish libraries sprang up, often adding a taint of philanthropy to the concern for education. The printed book more than any other means of communication represented Western cultural-humanist traditions. Obviously the new era of the press had to do with organized "dissemination of knowledge." When the Swedish publicist F. A. Ewerlof in 1831 returned from England, he brought with him fresh ideas on the education of the people. Lord Henry Peter Brougham's *Practical Observations upon the Education of the People* was translated into Swedish and published one year before the first public library bill was presented to the Swedish parliament (1833). In the years to follow societies were formed for "the dissemination of useful knowledge" and series of booklets were published offering "useful reading for the people."

Liberalist-humanist philosophy was based on an assumption that people could be helped to help themselves. Humanism fused with a philanthropic concern for the people, blossomed into countless self-aid societies and organizations that marked the decades around the middle of the century. This happened through both economic and cultural association. The 1840's and 1850's saw a great number of "education circles" formed in Sweden "to bring the members of craft and industry groups together in edifying and constructive contact with one another and with people from the educated classes." [3] All this was in close accordance with the principle of voluntary mutual aid.

---

[3] Statens Offentliga Utredningar 1946:68, *Det fria och frivilliga folkbildningsarbetet* ("The Swedish Adult Education Commission Report"), (Stockholm, 1946).

The same air of beneficial work for the people some decades later hovered around the first adult education work done by university-trained leaders. When scientists and university professors in the 1880's took the initiative to start labor institutes and adult education courses for the people, they did so driven by a conviction that liberalism carried with it the duty to help people educationally to help themselves.

The third thread in the fabric of Scandinavian adult education was nationalism. In many ways European nationalism during and in the wake of the Napoleonic wars had its influence on cultural movements. Romantic search of historic records for old Nordic heritage and myths was part of that trend. (Grundtvig himself was a poet and historian in search of the folk traditions of Denmark.) Denmark had been defeated in the wars, Sweden had lost Finland, Norway had been born as a modern nation and joined in an uneasy and unequal union with Sweden. These facts decades later were to play an important role in the movement for an educated citizenry. In many variations a theme was repeated that had been voiced by the Swedish poet Tegnér: the task was to regain the lost Finland "within the borders of Sweden," to offset the material loss with cultural growth and expansion.

The connection between the predicaments of a nation and a growing interest in adult education was clear in Denmark in the period 1848 to 1864. The country was threatened and brought to defeat by Prussia. The fairly liberal 1849 constitution was challenged and finally changed in 1866. Folk schools grew up as bulwarks for a nation and a democracy, not only as idealistic colleges for the common people.[4]

Sweden faced a less immediate and concentrated but none the less serious change. It was painfully rebuilding its representative government structure. It was adjusting to a deep-going agricultural change. It was slowly preparing for an industrial revolution. Among other forces for adjustment entered the folk schools. Finland under tsarist Russia experienced comparative freedom up

---

[4] The first Danish school was established at Rödding in 1844.

until the last two decades of the century. Later this freedom was threatened. Part of Finland's "inner defense" against Russian oppression was the folk schools. There is little doubt that the Norwegian folk schools had a close connection with the nationalist-romanticist forces that increasingly criticized the unhappy union with Sweden.[5] Many years later the Scandinavian folk schools were to be centers for romantic-patriotic youth movements around the turn of the century. They had always aimed at inter-Scandinavian understanding.[6] Lately this new Scandinavian spirit materialized in plans for a joint Northern folk school.

A fourth environmental circumstance that underlay the growth of adult education in Scandinavia was the inadequacy of the traditional educational system. The liberal trends early had given birth to compulsory school laws in Denmark, Norway, and Sweden. Gradually illiteracy was being wiped out. However, the slowness with which postprimary education facilities were changing spurred organized efforts to offer opportunities outside the public schools. Sweden's secondary schools may be given as an example, devoted as they were until the late 1870's to either scholastic studies or to training for public service. Only in rare instances did these secondary schools (after 1878 called public secondary schools) receive students from outside the professional families or the economically well-situated groups of the people. Not until 1904 were municipal secondary schools authorized and girls admitted to public secondary schools. A strong focus on training for university studies dominated Scandinavian schools not only at the time when the first folk schools were founded but later when a wider, more inclusive adult education movement arose.

It is thus far from wise to state bluntly that adult education as a social phenomenon was made the cultural force of liberalistic

---

[5] The first Norwegian folk school was founded at Sagatun in 1864. In Sweden three schools opened in 1868; Finland got its first school, at Borgå, in 1889.

[6] See Karl Hedlund, "Folkhögskolans nordiska sammanhang," in *Svensk folkhögskola under 75 år* (Stockholm, 1943).

movements, or that it was a natural outgrowth of the great humanist cultural tradition, or that a peculiar Scandinavian political crisis created it, or that it came about because other educational opportunities were closed. Rather, a combination of all these factors worked the result.

The decades in which the first fumbling attempts were made to spread knowledge among the people, the 1830's and 1840's, were years of deep ideological unsettlement, of brewing social changes, of the breaking down of old group barriers. While little was foreshadowed of the industrial revolution or the coming urbanization in the North, the peoples there were on the move. That fact was made clear by the challenge of new "free church movements," the introduction of organized temperance efforts, the regrouping of economic forces through free trade acts, the increased communications with the Continent, Great Britain, and the United States, the first signs of emigration from the old countries to a new world.

All these tendencies were to increase in strength during the 1860's and 1870's. When the unsettlement and disturbance later found expression in growing popular movements, adult education received a strong and lasting new impetus. The ferment of social change created not only movements for direct action (trade unions, co-operatives, political parties, temperance lodges), but for ideological support of that action. Such support came from well-organized, free, and voluntary adult education groups.

One obvious reason for efforts to educate people outside the regular school system lay in the lack of trained lay leadership for the social movements that came about. Much of the initial leadership in labor, free church, temperance, and farm organizations had come from outside (from other countries and other social groups). The future life of popular movements depended, though, on a steady rejuvenation and recruitment from the ranks. Second-level leadership was needed, especially as the new social movements were in conflict with power groups that had had greater opportunities for training, schooling, and educative experiences.

In a sense, the characteristic of a vital adult education movement is its capacity to support or challenge power.[7] It may focus on "transferring culture" that has sustained groups in power; such was often the mark of the early British workers' education movement that concentrated on spreading university culture to workers. It may be occupied with extending to the unprivileged educational opportunities denied them earlier in life; such was often the mark of American attempts to extend public education through night schools and university extension. It may construct defenses for and interpret the policies and actions taken by special interest movements, build the basis for intelligent leadership and understanding followership; such was the mark of Scandinavian adult education once the industrial revolution set in.

The tools for adult education that gradually were hammered out in Scandinavia show marks of both old sociocultural traditions and new forms for social change.

Traditional education institutions, like universities, public schools, libraries, furnished some, but by no means all, of the leadership. While some university leaders, carried by the wave-of-progress optimism, left their college careers for folk schools or started to offer lectures outside the campuses in the 1890's, the old institutions as a whole did not extend their regular courses to people in the communities, and the contempt for "popular science and culture" was unmistakable in academic halls. Nor did the public schools play any vital role in adult education. Except for references to school library responsibilities, little was said about what the public schools might do for adults. The libraries only slowly changed from depositories of learned culture to community centers. Thus, the new educational needs called for new forms and institutions. The picture of present Scandinavian adult

---

[7] In a crude fashion adult education may be used to "diminish and smooth over" disturbances. This happened when the Swedish industrialist, Dickson, donated a library to keep workers in Gothenburg occupied with useful, and innocuous, reading. In a less crude fashion it may be advocated as "an alternative to revolution," as no doubt happened in many early labor institutes run by philanthropists and intellectuals.

education still shows the marks of this initial drive away from traditional learning.

THE FIRST NEW TOOL

The first uniquely Scandinavian pattern was created by the folk schools, envisioned by Grundtvig.[8] Young adults were drawn together for winter terms of five to six months and summer terms of three or four months in the folk schools to live and learn in an atmosphere of free inquiry and friendship.

Grundtvig had called for a break with the Latin-school traditions, so the schools first centered their works on an inspirational awakening of the students. "To awaken, cherish and enlighten that human life which should and must be expected of the young of Denmark" was his intention with the people's high school, whose aim in more modern times, but in concord with that first principle, has been expressed thus: "Not to impart real knowledge first and foremost, but to educate the human being, give him a proper attitude towards life, not in the form of a cut-and-dried philosophy, but by helping the pupils to think for themselves and to distinguish between real and false values." In Denmark and Norway this trait was more apparent than in Sweden, where community studies and practical subjects early crept into the teachings. In all the countries the schools shunned the school-master or the university professor approach to method. "The living word" dominated the scene, later combined with group discussions.

The schools were run either by the principal himself (usually the case in Denmark and Norway) or by an association of community leaders (the case in Sweden). They were, indeed, as free from the fetters of public school curricula and administrative laws

---

[8] In Denmark the idea was put into practice by men like Christen Kold, Ludvig Schroeder, and Jens Appel; in Norway by theologians like Christopher Bruun, Herman Anker, and Ole Arveson; in Sweden by academicians like Leonard Holmström, Theodor Holmberg, and Herman Odhner.

as they were remote from the theories and ideas of the academic universities. Only gradually did public authorities consent to assume part of the financial responsibilities. In Sweden this happened earlier than in Denmark and suggests a reason for the greater stability and longer life expectancy of the Swedish schools.

Most of the early traits of the folk schools have been modified. Still one can recognize the original idea in the modern institutions that call themselves people's colleges, whether in Denmark, Sweden, or Norway. The schools are mainly intended for young adults who have had no educational opportunities beyond the elementary school. They are residential schools, the courses running for five to six months in the winter for young men and three to four in the summer for young women. The school day usually starts at 8 o'clock in the morning and ends at 5:30 in the afternoon, six days a week. The curriculum, though broadly outlined in the present laws, is largely decided by the individual faculty. The content of a course mostly is for the instructor to decide. Community and group circumstances matter far more than set standards for what a five-month course "should contain." [9] A people's college is run with little interference from public authorities. It is administered by a principal, who often sets the personal atmosphere for the school but who works with regents or boards that represent the interests of the community rather than the interest of distant Royal Boards of Education in Oslo, Copenhagen, or Stockholm.

Life in the schools is marked by the fact that most students live in a co-operative social environment for several months. In close contact with the teachers and the principal, they create for themselves a living community. Incidentally, this community life has apparent positive value, but also negative risks: while informal discussion and social gatherings are many, formalized study re-

---

[9] The principal subjects in the folk schools are (1) language and literature and (2) sociocultural studies. In a Danish school, courses in the Danish language and literature take up 10 to 12 hours of the 50- to 55-hour total weekly schedule; in a Swedish school, 5 of 42 to 45 hours a week. Sociocultural subjects in an average Swedish folk school curriculum take up 11 of 42 hours.

quirements and social patterns few, the school may itself become an artificial, semi-ideal world painfully far removed from the life that the students will live when the course is over.

The folk schools are small. Few of them have more than a hundred students in their courses. The 59 Danish schools attract annually around 7,500 students, the 70 Swedish schools slightly more than 7,000, and the 29 schools in Norway close to 2,500. The number of students limits the direct influence of these centers, but they exert a strong influence on the local population, which is admitted to lectures in the schools and for which special meetings are arranged. Their size, however, permits everybody to know everybody else on the campus, which unquestionably strengthens the individual community education effect.

In the early years the ties between folk schools and agricultural schools were strong. This connection weakened in Denmark as early as 1870. In Sweden, where there have been several decades of joint administration, the drive for wholly separate farm schools did not succeed until the end of the 1930's. This severance brought the folk schools to a position where they could concentrate on general education while the vocational needs of the farmers were met by farm schools. Meanwhile a movement had been increasing in strength to link folk schools to organizations with special interests, like the labor unions, the free churches, the temperance groups, the young farmers, the political parties. Not geographical proximity but commonness of interest was the basis for this new adult education venture in Scandinavia.

The idea that social movements should have schools of their own grew to a conviction: an education center was a spiritual home; it widened the discussion of aims; it provided the organizations with leadership. The first folk school for labor in the North was founded at Brunnsvik in Sweden in 1906, the second in Esbjerg in Denmark in 1910. Other special interest groups were to follow the lead of labor, creating their own centers. The Danish co-operatives founded a school on a semi-Grundtvigian base in 1910. Their Swedish colleagues seven years later took over a regular folk school near Stockholm. In one form or other the political parties created schools that they patterned after the Grundtvigian folk school, though curriculum and bias excluded these schools from public financial support. The Danish gymnastics movement shortly after the First World War started its regular folk school (Ollerup); the Swedes followed fifteen years later with their school (Lillsved). During the First World War a group of liberal young Lutherans in Sweden organized a folk school (Sigtuna), and the Baptist and Missions churches later founded their leader headquarters in similar schools (Sjövik and Ljungskile). In Norway, as in Denmark, the Missions churches made schools of their own; pietist and strongly religious educational efforts were offered as challenges to "dangerous" tendencies of the Grundtvigian folk schools.

This trend itself was a sign that folk schools no longer turned solely to farm people for support. Students increasingly came from wider geographical areas and wider sections of the people. Some schools were established in cities, like the International People's College in Elsinore, the urban schools in Esbjerg, Roskilde, Copenhagen, and Stockholm. Most schools began to show lower percentages of students from the farm sections of the population.[10]

In a more subtle way, though, the folk schools have changed during the years. The Swedish schools early had given much attention to social and economic subjects, the Norwegian and Danish more to literature and history, but all of the early school leaders had been conditioned by the Grundtvigian "folk school atmosphere." These traditions from the great Swedish, Norwegian, and Danish leaders were forceful enough to make many schools appear somewhat romantic and idealistic, once the crisis of the First World War had come and passed. Some change was

---

[10] In Denmark the farmer-student figure sank from 75 per cent during the First World War to 43 per cent just before the Second; in Sweden, from over 80 per cent to 56 per cent.

called for. Young leaders and new adult education organizations demanded new subjects and new methods. Such a change in the original scheme also was signaled by the competition with new secondary schools that finally entered the social scene of Scandinavia. When the modern high school and junior college grew in importance, especially in nonurban areas, the inevitable result might have been a drop in attendance in the folk schools. The answer was an imperceptible change in the folk school character to include more vocational subjects.

Traditions of book culture and formal schooling always had influenced the folk schools. While Grundtvig and Kold in Denmark had stormed against the dead words in books and advocated "the living word," most of the later leaders in the movement borrowed the practice of textbooks and formal class techniques from the regular schools. While the folk schools were originally thought of as centers for a deep and realistic rejuvenation of society, much of the curriculum was devoted to the same tool subjects and basic content offered in high schools. Once public authorities granted regular support, they set down regulations in laws, which, even though they were extremely liberal, left the folk school less complete freedom. The present Swedish folk school (where the legal regulations have gone further than in Denmark and Norway) thus has definite standards set for number of class hours, students, type of subjects, and qualifications of teachers.[11] Yet the Swedish minister of education in 1943 ventured to speak for all Scandinavia at the seventy-fifth anniversary of Sweden's folk schools, in these words:

---

[11] Denmark got its latest law bearing on the schools in 1942 (the High School Act). Public grants were thereby increased and greater allowances made for scholarships to students. (The total grant to students in 1948 was two million kroner, covering close to two thirds of the student body.) The 1942 law also improved the position of the instructors. Sweden's folk schools had been supported by state funds as early as the 1870's, but not until 1919 was there a written folk school law. The 1919 act has been amended several times. (At present, grants under this law amount to over two million kronor, with additional grants for scholarships to students.) In Norway the schools have become part of the regular school system.

The folk schools always were pioneer schools. They have been given their full freedom to carry on experiments in teaching and cultural education. Liberalism and Scandinavian orientation have always been their sign. From the beginning free from public control they have preserved their independence throughout the years. They should be maintained as educational laboratories, necessary in our times, when so much is marked by bureaucracy and regimentation.

The words of this conservative political leader have a ring of confidence in the educational freedom that the schools had fought for and successfully sustained even with state laws forcing certain limitations upon them. The same testimonies were given with even greater justification in Denmark at the centennial in 1944. Here was, after all, a school to which thousands of leaders in the Danish farm and co-operative movements had gone not for specific training but for general education. Here was a volunteer youth school that so persistently had held certain progressive education ideas that even in the year 1944 the original refusal to hold examinations and give grades was upheld. Here was a school that had done much to prove that public grants from the state did not mean control from national authorities. Here was a school whose indirect cultural influence had been pervasive.

Even if the number of students has been limited,[12] and the schools in spite of the new trends have stayed largely rural, their impact is unmistakable. Among their students are a great many who have taken up roles as leaders in popular movements, government, and political parties. The community influence of these centers is visible in counsel, advice, and service of their instructors. However intangible and unprecise such an assertion is, the very fact that new educational means and methods have been tried out, and a new approach to education control has been demonstrated, has made the schools a ferment in the intricate process of social change during the last hundred years.

---

[12] In the four Scandinavian countries a maximum of 22,000 students a year attend folk schools.

OLD CARDS RESHUFFLED

"The living word" of Grundtvig and his followers was taken up in the public lecture movements born in the late 1870's. University leaders and men of letters had become convinced that science and philosophy should be popularized and thus made the resource of others than intellectuals.

In both Denmark and Sweden the birth of a labor movement coincided with the appearance of adult education efforts carried out by representatives of what have been called "cultural-radicals." There were attempts to create urban parallels to the rural folk schools. In 1879 Denmark got its first reading club for workers. The year 1880 marked the opening in Stockholm of the still existing Labor Institute.[13] A few years later the government granted support to "lecture courses for the working class." In both countries the liberals among university professors and students were enthusiastic about efforts in Great Britain and the United States to extend university teaching to the people. Thus a Scandinavian variation of university extension was born, starting in the early 1890's. It built on, and in Sweden still builds on, lecture societies in the local communities. From central organizations specialists and experts would go on tours to the towns and villages for local "community lecture nights." It was, as one of the leading Swedish university men said, the duty of a university "to participate in the present efforts to strengthen popular education with all personal and institutional resources." Norwegian equivalents to the Swedish lecture societies are the so-called "folk academies."

The hundreds of popular lectures in the countryside and in the city centers were the movies of those days—the sparkling evenings of contact with a strange outside world. The very times in which

---

[13] Norwegian liberal educators and worker societies founded a Workers' Academy in Oslo in 1885. The first of a group of "workmen's institutes" in Finland was opened at Tammerfors in 1899.

the lecture movement started were saturated with a profound respect for natural sciences; many of the early lecture leaders were scientists. Much of the content of these lectures centered on world problems as seen from the college quarters. The lectures never left the formal concept of "the living word." There were few if any attempts to "invite questions from the audience," or to stimulate discussion in informal ways. All in all, it is not surprising that the movement stayed within the ranks of the middle class, offering what an American educator has called "an orchestra ticket to the social theatre."

Many years later the public lecture movement in Scandinavia was to be revived and strengthened through new devices suggested by the popular movements. The emphasis of the lectures was to shift slowly from natural science or semientertainment to social and political science.[14] More lectures were to be offered in series, and in close relation to other adult education activities going on in the communities. The present strong trend in Sweden is toward lecture series of four sessions in two days, supported jointly from public grants and aid from the organizations in the community. This trend and the evidences of decreasing numbers of single lectures and of local lecture societies indicate waning public interest in what was once a spectacular education movement among adults.[15]

A starting signal for change on the local public lecture scene came from Finland. Folk school leaders in the four Northern countries had taken part in the public lecture movement and still do, but their interest would naturally turn toward more significant and long-lasting contributions to the communities. Influenced by the temperance movement in Scandinavia, Finnish adult educators in 1905 tried a variation on the community college idea,

---

[14] As late as 1945 more than 50 per cent of the tax-supported public lectures in Sweden were given in the fields of geography, natural sciences, and mathematics.

[15] Though an aggregate total of some 700,000 persons attended public lectures in Sweden in 1945, only a fourth of all parishes had societies. In Norway the 200 folk academies drew audiences of about 140,000 annually.

a "moving folk school course." As these courses now operate, they offer a combination of lecture series, classes, discussions, and social evenings. A staff of instructors or specialists work out a community institute in collaboration with the local organizations. In Sweden, where the number of three-week folk school courses in the last fifteen years has increased from 80 to 200, district adult education councils are responsible for the program planning, state and local public authorities give support from taxes, and all organizations of importance collaborate in publicity campaigns and local arrangements. Some sessions in these courses are devoted to "tool subjects"; most center on issues and problems that concern the people in the communities.

The old public lecture thus has changed. In the wake of the university-fired enthusiasm of the 1890's came insistent attempts to bring the formal lecture closer to what the people wanted in form and content on the local scene.

Like the lecture, the library was among the traditional tools of education. The public library could no more stay unchanged once it had been introduced as adult education than could the public lecture. Once it had left the first stage of being a branch of the public school, i.e., often the state church, it had to change. The modern public library movement grew faster in Denmark and Norway than in Sweden and Finland.[16] The march of this new trend was first new city libraries, later modernized parish libraries, and last a system of regional "central libraries" servicing the communities in larger districts.

Still, the book was far away from the people. The people needed books in their own organizations. Books had to be easy to get and easy to read to be of any help in the ever-spreading adult education movement. Take Sweden as an example once more: the labor, temperance, farmer, and church groups pushed for and

---

[16] American and Danish impulses gave Sweden its first formula for tax support of public libraries in 1912, though Denmark itself did not have a state law until 1920. As early as 1902 the Norwegian parliament had approved a plan to modernize the library system. An office was established in the State Church Ministry to advise and service communities.

obtained tax support from district and national bodies for small book holdings in their study circles. While the public library movement was slowly adjusting to the new social climate, the organizations created "public libraries" of their own, or small library stations, run by the people in the organizations. Thus Sweden now has over 6,500 tax-supported library units, with a total of over one million customers. Of these units, 1,500 are regular public libraries, serviced by a number of central libraries; 5,000 of them are study circle libraries.

THE SECOND NEW TOOL

Neither the university and the lecture nor the library and the book were destined to widen the work that was only begun with the folk schools. That role was to be played by the popular movements and the study circle, the second Scandinavian contribution to world adult education. In a strange way it combines the folk school idea with the lecture and the book, the university class and the library. "The study circle is first of all a library club," said Oscar Olsson, the founder of the first study circle in Sweden. "But it is also a reading club, a lecture society, and a group of friends. It can without any difficulty be combined with regular classes. It is the idea of mutual aid adapted to adult education."

The home for this new tool of adult education was the many people's movements. In the wake of industrialism and urbanism and in response to new ideas from abroad, industrial workers, city folks, and farmers organized on the economic front, in labor unions, and in co-operatives for consumers and producers. Good Templars pushed their efforts on the social front. Social-Democrats and Liberals forged modern political parties for advance on the political front. "Free churches" attracted those unwilling to follow the state church. The two decades preceding 1900 are dotted with data on the founding of trade unions, parties, church organizations, lodges, and co-operatives.

There was little place for all these organizations, now entering the local communities, in the existing programs of adult education. The lectures were too few, the libraries too forbidding, the folk schools too far apart and too much geared to rural youth. Leaders were needed, well-trained and schooled in the new ideas. Group morale and loyalty had to be strengthened, knowledge and understanding of the new goals extended beyond the first-line leaders. The answer was some form of flexible, personal tool for learning close to where the people worked, lived, and strove in their organizations. That new tool was the study circle first tried out by a temperance lodge in Sweden in 1902, under the leadership of Oscar Olsson. The aim of the study circle was to create the "we feeling" necessary in a popular movement, to provide for "wholesome reading," and to promote discussion of vital issues. This could best happen in the informal atmosphere of a small group of like-minded people. Circles were formed to study elementary subjects, literature and history, social and political science, philosophy, art, and music. For leaders, the circles used people in the ranks more often than professionals. "The living word" was combined with discussion, the reading of books with preparation through manuals and study guides. The seriousness of a traditional school class was mellowed, but not softened, by a spirit of friendship and fraternity. Most of all, the modest bits of learning to the early leaders were weapons in the long struggle for a stronger and more intelligent democracy.[17]

The idea of a new study form for common people caught on. In 1912 a young teacher in the new labor school at Brunnsvik in Sweden formed the Workers' Education Association (ABF) intended to encourage study circles, libraries, and lectures among members of the Labor party and the trade unions. In Finland a Workers' Education Union was started in 1919; five years later the Danish labor movement followed suit; the Norwegians started

---

[17] See for example Marquis W. Childs, *This Is Democracy* (New Haven, Conn., 1938); Ragnar Lund, *Swedish Adult Education* (New York, 1939); Gunnar Hirdman, *Adult Education in Sweden* (Stockholm, 1947); Johannes Novrup, "Adult Education in Denmark," and Jon Mathisen, "Adult Education in Norway," in Ragnar Lund, ed., *Scandinavian Adult Education* (Copenhagen, 1949).

a correspondence school in 1918 and got their first labor education organization in 1927. The Good Templars, who had started the new trend, no doubt gave the idea to other temperance organizations; in Sweden the National Templars formed their study circle organization in 1917; in Norway the young leaders of the Temperance Society started study circles and lectures in 1923 and formed their adult education organization ten years later.

Others than workers and temperance people grasped the challenge of this innovation. Influenced by British mission summer camps, Norwegian church leaders organized mission circles in 1910, Swedish rural youth leaders formed their study circle societies in 1917, and Norwegian colleagues followed in 1922. White-collar unions began organized adult education work along the same lines in the middle of the thirties. At the same time, revitalized farmer organizations took up study work in special units for adult education; in Sweden the new adult education societies were connected with the Farmers' party, in Norway with community life associations. Concerned from its inception in education work among members, the consumer co-operative movement in Scandinavia early had encouraged discussion-and-conversation groups; these co-operative study groups, simultaneously with the study circles, increased in number and importance, especially after the First World War.[18]

Apparently the study circle lent itself best to already organized groups.[19] Oscar Olsson once had said that the basis for the study circle was "the social unit," the close-knit, homogeneous group. Decidedly, the initial tendency to look on these adult education groups as "the brain and conscience" of the movements determined the later developments. The assumption was that if the

[18] For a discussion of the special problems of co-operative study groups, see Herman Stolpe, *Cog or Collaborator, Democracy in Cooperative Education* (Stockholm, 1946).

[19] Early efforts to copy the Swedish temperance study circle in Norway failed, "for lack of financial support and organizational aid," according to Arent Midtbø. Once the Norwegians tied the circles to organized groups, they succeeded (Midtbø, *Handbok for studieringer* ["Handbook for Study Circles"], [Oslo, 1946]).

organized group took care of more than the immediate and initial needs of the members, it would grow stronger. In this respect the popular movements of Scandinavia followed the same sociological pattern as the American churches. As a church in this country grew stronger socially the more diversified its activities became, so a labor union or temperance lodge in Scandinavia grew stronger the wider its appeal was.[20]

So far, the study circle has been more popular in its homeland, Sweden, than in other Northern countries.[21] In 1946–1947 over 250,000 Swedes were enrolled in close to 23,000 circles; an additional 45,000 met in co-operative discussion groups. The largest enrollment by far was registered in the labor movement, where the ABF enrolled over 125,000 members in close to 10,000 circles. Church organizations followed with close to 35,000 members in 2,500 circles. Young farmers had organized over 3,000 circles with 27,000 enrolled, and the Good Templars had sent more than 22,000 members to their 1,900 circles.[22]

However impressive such figures may be, the reach of the program in the Swedish community still is limited. A generous esti-

---

[20] The following paragraphs largely refer to the study circles in Sweden. More extensive material is available from that country than from Denmark and Norway.

Accredited study circle associations, which are entitled to state aid under the 1947 formula, include the Workers' Education Association (ABF), the Farm Youth Association (JUF), the Rural Adult Education Association (SLS), the International Order of Good Templars (IOGT), the National Order of Templars (NTO), the White Collar Union Study Association (TBV), and the Adult Education Association of Swedish Churches (SKB). Lately the extension organizations led by students at the four universities (Stockholm, Uppsala, Lund, and Gothenburg) have been added to the list.

[21] The Danish Workers' Education Union, formed in 1924 "to spread enlightenment among the working population," recently estimated its total attendance at study circles as about 10,000, while evening schools drew up to 18,000, and free lectures some 40,000 in rural areas and a maximum of 100,000 in cities (*Social Denmark* [Copenhagen, 1947], pp. 369 ff.).

[22] The Swedish study circle organizations also arranged over 500 lecture series with more than 45,000 enrolled. They also ran close to 5,000 libraries with more than 2,500,000 book loans per year. At the four universities the students ran what now amount to evening colleges. Enrollment figures during the last years in the student-run university extension courses have increased rapidly.

mate of participation in labor education groups stays around 10 per cent of the membership in the trade unions. The temperance lodges show a slightly higher proportion of participants. Farm youth participation may climb as high as to 20 per cent of the membership of the mother organization. In percentage of the total adult population, the quoted figures are shorn down still lower: an average of 3 per cent of the adults in Sweden participated in study circle work in the early 1940's. The response is rather unevenly distributed over Sweden, the greatest number of groups being found in rural areas.[23] Though cities like Stockholm show inspiring enrollment figures, less than 5 per cent of the adults took part in study circle work in 1943–1944.

The great majority of the Swedish study circles are short-lived. The most recent study showed that half of the rural youth circles in 1943–1944 had existed less than three years; in 1936 the average age of a labor education circle was one year.[24] This puts a new light on the original idea of the circle as a "group of friends." The very fact that the group rarely lives long makes it more a study class than an informal friendly circle. The choice of study subject, the method of work, the pattern of standardization—all have made the study circle of 1949 look different from its ancestor of the early 1900's.

In a 1936–1937 study A. Wallentheim said that "the early study circles used more irrational, but therefore also more lively, flexible, and personal methods" than did the circles of the middle thirties.[25] Regularization and mechanization had crept in. One of the signs of growing regularization was the strong tendency to

---

[23] In 1943–1944, 61 per cent of the study circles were registered in rural areas; 64 per cent of their membership was male. Indications are strong that the average age in the rural circles is rather low: in 1943–1944 the largest adult education organization (SLS) gave 22.9 years as the average age for the members.

[24] Statens Offentliga Utredningar 1946:68, *Betänkande om Det fria och frivilliga folkbildningsarbetet avgivet av 1944 års Folkbildningsutredning* ("The Report of the 1944 Adult Education Commission in the Swedish Department of Education"), (Stockholm, 1946).

[25] "Studiecirklarna," *Folklig Kultur*, August, 1940. *Folklig Kultur* is a journal published jointly by the study circle organizations in Sweden.

use fixed and set methods. The 1944 commission report confirms this tendency with data from 1943–1944. While 63 per cent of the circles in 1936–1937 used "a free combination of methods," less than 3 per cent followed such liberal practices in 1943–1944. The use of nationally distributed correspondence texts and manuals had increased from 26 per cent to 40 per cent during those ten years. This indicates that methods were increasingly bent toward a question-and-answer relationship between the group and an impersonal "instructor." In 1936 close to 70 per cent of the study circles declared that they used textbooks and over 50 per cent depended on homework by members; there are no indications that these practices decreased during the following years, but there are many indications that the first informal "groups of friends" some two decades ago looked less like school classes.

If the choice of methods strengthens the "regularization" trend, still the selection of leaders and instructors may counteract the effect. Few leaders in the study circles are professional teachers. Most of them have grammar school or folk school diplomas, a few have college or junior college degrees.[26] Only about a third are termed "specialists." In other words, the instructor in a study circle still is a lay person, close to the group. He often is relieved of administrational responsibilities; a leader is the chief functionary of the circle, and in most cases this leader is a member of the mother organization (the union, the lodge, the church unit, or the party). Another factor that may preserve the nonschool atmosphere of the study circles is the housing arrangements: close to 50 per cent of all the circles in 1943–1944 were housed in study rooms of unions, lodges, churches and societies, or community centers, while less than 25 per cent met in schools, libraries, or public institutions.

Leaders like Gunnar Hirdman of the Workers' Education Association fear that the circles have come to deal too heavily with tool subjects that should be given in schools. Such subjects, he

---

[26] Out of a total of 3,600, 2,900 instructors had grammar school, folk school, or junior high school diplomas.

said recently, "have played a much larger role in adult education than the leaders of the movement would wish." In the future, he thinks, less time will need to be spent on courses "that simply remedy a lack of grade-school fundamentals." [27] A further examination of what the study circles offer makes clear, however, that their role is to complement rather than copy, on a higher age level, a traditional school scheme. Half of the circles in the Workers' Education Association in 1946–1947 dealt with organization problems, parliamentary law, and social and political science. Of all the circles in Sweden that year one in four had studied social and political subjects.[28] Intimate contact with the mother organizations would work as an additional brake to any wholesale shift from "friendly group" to school class. In the early years this organizational support had been rather narrow; the trend today is an ever-growing co-ordination among various organized groups on the top national level, and among district organizations in the regions. Since 1936 Sweden has had a co-ordinating adult education council in which all the large study circle associations participate. Here plans are laid for joint leadership training, publications, and appeals for public support; here much of the initiative to regional and local co-operation has originated. This co-ordination trend no doubt has halted any listless drifting of the study circle from the original purpose of free, voluntary, and democratic inquiry and discussion.[29]

The chief financial support has come from the organizations that sponsored the study circles; many received their biggest contributions from compulsory and collective membership fees, paid through the mother organizations. By the middle of the 1930's, when the first survey was made, surprisingly few leaders indicated that finances were of crucial importance to the success

---

[27] *Op. cit.,* p. 12.

[28] Of a total of 14,000 circles, 3,500 had chosen social and political subjects, 1,800 languages, 2,500 arts and crafts, 1,800 various trade subjects, 1,500 religious topics.

[29] Since the Second World War the co-ordination trend has been even stronger in Norway, where a great number of local adult education councils have been established (Mathisen, *op. cit.,* pp. 184 f.).

of the circles. General interest from the public and the method followed in the studies were rated far more important as encouraging factors. Lack of housing facilities and a constant worry about adequate study material, however, were important enough to suggest support from public sources. So the study circles entered the field of public adult education.

The first important push for support was directed at local and regional boards and councils, from which the study circles asked for grants to buy books and set up small library stations. Swelling enrollment figures and spreading responsibilities (for example in the emergencies around 1942–1944) were strong justifications for demands on national resources. In 1944 a representative commission was appointed to study the over-all problem of public support for adult education. On the basis of the commission report a law was passed in 1947 granting state support, matching local funds, to all accredited circles. In all the other Northern countries plans for state support are either completed or under way.

The new legislation sets specific qualification standards. Local supervisory boards and central study circle associations have to approve the leaders and the textbooks used. Study circles to qualify for state support have to be either foundation circles (in elementary and skill subjects), education circles (social, civic, cultural subjects), or youth circles. In all three cases, the number of hours per session and sessions per semester is set. In foundation and education circles the law specifies the minimum number of circle members. For all practical purposes the Swedish study circle has devised a public adult education formula very much like some of the states in this country. The only difference is that, while public support here has been tied to public institutions, in Scandinavia it has been given to voluntary popular movements.

It is too early to suggest that Scandinavian adult education has indicated a way of combining public support from tax sources with free and largely unfettered private education.[30] It is safe,

---

[30] This observation should be considered against the background of the general school picture in Scandinavia. The schools are national and the official church

however, to say that these new movements have shown that spending public money does not have to be combined with strict public control, nor with such publicly owned institutions as schools or libraries. Coming from countries with strong social-democratic and public ownership traditions this suggestion is something of a treat!

SUMMARY

Among the Scandinavian countries there are few significant differences in the adult education programs. Gunnar Hirdman has said, "In all of them adult education has the same purpose: to encourage social, moral and intellectual responsibility among members of the popular movements, and to educate men and women for a higher standard of national and world citizenship." [31]

Today we face a multiform crisis in organized social life. Much of this crisis is bursting out in flashy conflicts—strikes, party dissension, pressures, war. Much of it is hidden in indifference, the slow withering of formerly vital organizations, or in bitter competition and brazen intolerance among groups. In most of its manifestations the adult education movement in Scandinavia has tried to offer cures for this crisis. Three aspects of this attempt stand out as significant.

First, the social and cultural change desired could be made a reality only through sound deliberation on the change—through widespread and popular analysis of the possible solutions. This could be done through educational efforts that were close to the people on the scene, largely controlled by them, even devised by them and their organized groups. Part of man's mastery of his destiny lay in self-directed civic, cultural, and moral education. A "school for life" thus became more than a phrase in Scandinavia.

---

is organizationally tied to these schools; although local school boards and units have much to say, the national pattern of elementary and secondary school curriculum and organization is unmistakable.

[31] Page 16. Hirdman is the present Director of the Workers' Education Association of Sweden.

Second, the inevitable distance between leaders and their followers in democratic society somehow had to be bridged. This could best happen in small, voluntary groups where members of action organizations scrutinized the policies and programs. Thus, Scandinavian adult education in many forms offered the people a vehicle for communication with the leaders. At the same time it gave a chance for the ordinary members of the groups and communities to "feel at home" with far-off ideas and distant directions. The folk school was literally "a home"; the study circle figuratively became "the home" of many movements.

Third, action itself was not sufficient, nor was education of leaders and members. Somehow adult education had to be suggested and promoted as a public responsibility. The dilemma was how a democratic education movement among adults could be combined with necessary public legislation, how freedom and self-direction could be preserved under state support rules. The Scandinavian movements, strongly anchored in voluntary groups and originally born out of protest against existing social arrangements, through persistent experimentation succeeded in effecting a compromise. Government was, they argued, responsible for supporting democratic organs for self-analysis and free criticism. Outside traditional means of evaluation and criticism, the adult education groups would bring the ordinary man back to the scene for decision.

Adult education in Scandinavia has aimed less at filling in gaps than at building a basis for intellectual responsibility, less at propagating for specific social aims than at educating for social consciousness, less at moralizing than at focusing on the moral issues of democratic society. Wherever its place has been in the chain of cause and effect, it has been at the scene where things happened in the North.

Scandinavian Foreign Policy,

Past and Present

By BRITA SKOTTSBERG ÅHMAN

*Former Director of the Swedish
Institute of International Affairs, Stockholm*

FROM the outbreak of the First World War to the present it is possible to discern five periods in Scandinavian foreign policy, marked by natural dividing lines.

The first period is that of the First World War itself, during which Sweden, Norway, and Denmark were linked by a common neutrality policy, which was successfully carried through until the war ended with the collapse of Russia and Germany. The second period lasted from the end of the war, through the 1920's, and until 1933, when Hitler's ascension to power in Germany swiftly changed the whole European picture. The third period runs naturally from 1933, when international tension rose and put the League of Nations to tests it was unable to cope with (all three Scandinavian countries had been members of the League from its beginning), until the outbreak of the Second World War in 1939. The years of World War II, from 1939 until 1945, when occupied Norway and Denmark were liberated and isolated Sweden's communications were restored, constitute the fourth of the five periods. In the present period, which began with V-E Day, the Scandinavian countries, like all others, are contemplating a postwar world full of problems still waiting to be solved. The biggest of these problems is, of course, the latent conflict between East and West, in which the three neighboring countries in Northern Europe are groping for a course.

The title of this survey, "Scandinavian Foreign Policy," reflects the tendency to look at these three countries as a more or less homogeneous unit. This may be a natural approach when looking from afar at three small countries in a remote corner of the world. There is much talk of Scandinavian policy and Scandinavian problems, and, of course, there are such problems. Sometimes there has also been a Scandinavian policy at international council tables, as reflected by joint proposals offered or joint stands taken. But it would be a mistake to think that one can identify the three countries completely as one, lump them together, and be done with it. In addition to their common problems, they each have specific, individual problems of foreign policy, which in some cases have been with them for long periods of time.

Denmark alone of the Scandinavian countries has a common land frontier with Germany, and the area of Schleswig and Holstein has for centuries been the scene of a clash of nationalities. The Danish foreign policy toward Germany for a long time followed the line of pacification. After the First World War it seemed a natural thing for Denmark to co-operate with the democratic German Republic, and, in the thirties, when Hitler had come to power, fear of the aggressive German policy was an important reason for Denmark's sitting tight as far as Germany was concerned. Although the foreign policy of Norway and Sweden never could disregard Germany, the problem did not present itself quite as directly to these two countries.

Another point of specific Danish interest is the enormous Arctic subcontinent of Greenland, a possession of Denmark, where the United States acquired bases during World War II.

Norway also has a territorial problem all its own, which has been carried into the postwar phase. It is that of Spitzbergen, or Svalbard, as the Norwegians call it, the group of islands in the Arctic north of the Norwegian mainland.

Likewise the Åland Islands in the Baltic Sea between Sweden and Finland represent a problem in foreign policy for Sweden that does not particularly concern the other Scandinavian countries. Relations with Finland, on the whole, mean much more to Sweden than to the other two Scandinavian countries.

Recently the failure of the Scandinavian attempt to agree on a common attitude toward the North Atlantic defense alliance illustrated the warning against generalizing too much and speaking of Scandinavian foreign policy as though it were completely homogeneous. Summing up the failure of the Scandinavian defense conference the Norwegian prime minister said: "The reason we failed to reach agreement is the fact that the requirements of our national security are different."

Nevertheless for long periods there has been a common line of action by the Scandinavian countries, explained by the fact that they have had similar if not identical interests to protect and defend. Particularly in times of crisis there have been instances when the three countries have agreed formally to pursue the same policy. One such occasion, which brought the Scandinavian countries more closely together than they had been for a very long time, was the outbreak of the First World War in 1914.

Until that time, unity and co-operation between the three countries had not been very conspicuous. The differences between them had causes reaching far back into history. For several centuries Norway was a part of the Danish-Norwegian monarchy. She felt this as a suppression of her cultural and political self. When Norway was relieved of this dependence in 1814, she was linked instead with Sweden. This did not develop smoothly. The conflict over the control of the foreign policy of the two countries was long and bitter. In spite of the mutually independent administrations of Sweden and Norway, with the king as the titular head of both, they were as one in the field of foreign policy, with the policy being conducted by the Swedish minister of foreign affairs. Norwegian dissatisfaction with this subordinate position led to differences that caused the dissolution of the union in 1905. It is true that this dissolution was brought about peacefully, by mutual agreement. But it left the two countries in a state of suspicion toward each other and led them along different paths internationally. Furthermore, the Swedish attitude toward Denmark became cooler because the Danes had sympathized with Norway in her quest for independence.

THE FIRST WORLD WAR

The outbreak of the World War in 1914 changed the situation in Scandinavia. There were shadings of opinion in the three countries toward the belligerents, and if the question of choosing sides had arisen there would have been a danger of conflicting attitudes. Denmark's sympathies were entirely on the side of the Allies, and those of Norway were largely with Britain, but the Norwegians viewed Russia with a certain amount of mistrust. Sweden was the only one of the three countries in which there was a small, but rather vociferous, activist group that would have liked to see Sweden enter the war on the side of Germany. The reason was not so much love of Germany as fear of Russia.

But the common danger that the war of the great powers offered the Scandinavian countries made them relegate their internal differences to the background. It was no surprise that the path Scandinavia chose was that of neutrality. An overwhelming majority in all three countries had an ardent desire to keep the North out of the war. Neutrality was, perhaps, the only policy about which the three countries could have agreed. Furthermore, the policy of neutrality had become a tradition in Scandinavia after decades of isolation from entanglements in Europe. As an outward symbol of this joint policy the Scandinavian kings and their foreign ministers met at Malmö in Southern Sweden and issued a common declaration of neutrality.

This meeting at Malmö was the first of a long series of meetings of the kings and the ministers through the war years. The meetings were doubtless of considerable importance. The causes for irritation that had divided Scandinavia were buried in view of the importance of offering a united front toward the warring powers, the neutrality policy was co-ordinated, and social and economic questions were dealt with in consultation.

The interruption of international trade, which meant a lot to all the Scandinavian countries, made it necessary for them to develop their mutual trade, and a number of agreements were negotiated. The recurrent consultation between the three countries did not mean, however, that they were prepared to go any further in co-ordinating their policies by, for instance, forming a defense union or engaging in thoroughgoing military and political co-operation. The disruption of the union between Sweden and Norway was still a thing of the recent past, and the peoples of the North continued to think and to speak as Norwegians, Danes, and Swedes. Isolated voices were raised in favor of a military alliance or union, but they went unheard. Nevertheless, a foundation was laid for limited co-operation in meeting the problems of the peace that was to come.

The neutrality of Scandinavia was never seriously threatened from any quarter during the war. Sweden, however, was saddled with a special problem, which might have drawn her into the war. The problem was that of the Åland Islands. Ever since Sweden ceded Finland and the Åland Islands to Russia in 1809, Swedish foreign policy has never quite been able to disregard the danger inherent in Russian domination of the islands. Situated in the Gulf of Bothnia between Sweden and Finland, these islands would always be a suitable base for attacks on the Swedish mainland. In connection with the Peace of Paris in 1856 after the Crimean War, a convention was signed forbidding Russia to fortify the Åland Islands. Nevertheless, during the First World War Russia built some military installations on the islands, which were used as bases for Russian and British submarines in the Baltic. This more than anything else was seized upon by the small group in Sweden who urged that Sweden ought to enter the war on the side of Germany.

In November, 1917, immediately after the Bolshevik Revolution, the Russian government organ *Pravda* disclosed that the tsarist regime had demanded of the Allies that the clause about demilitarization of the Åland Islands be canceled. For public opinion in Sweden, this revelation confirmed suspicions that Russia intended to make the wartime fortifications permanent.

Another important disclosure about the Åland Islands was not made until twenty years later. Then it was revealed in an official Swedish publication of diplomatic documents that in December, 1917, Germany had informally asked the Swedish government whether it was willing to take over the Åland Islands on certain conditions. The German suggestion was that Swedish troops should occupy the islands, and Germany was to raise the question in her forthcoming peace negotiations with Russia. This offer the Swedish government rejected, stating that if Sweden were to obtain the Åland Islands with German support she would be abandoning her position of neutrality. The Swedish government limited itself to requesting that, in the peace negotiations with Russia, the Germans should urge the demolition of the fortifications of the Åland Islands. The Russians agreed, and the demolition was carried out two years later, in 1919.

FROM VERSAILLES TO HITLER

The only one of the Scandinavian countries that was represented at the peace conference was Denmark, which had a frontier problem to be solved in connection with the peace terms for defeated Germany. In 1864 Prussia and Austria had conquered the southernmost part of Denmark, the provinces of Schleswig and Holstein, which were subsequently incorporated into Prussia. The population in North Schleswig stuck stubbornly to its Danish character through the ensuing decades, while the leading circles in South Schleswig gradually veered more and more toward Germany. With the collapse of Germany after the war, the pro-Danish population saw a chance to return to the Danish crown, and they demanded a plebiscite. The Treaty of Versailles accepted this demand and stipulated that the frontier between Germany and Denmark was to be drawn according to the will of the population. In February, 1920, a plebiscite was held in two zones in Schleswig. In the northern zone 75 per cent voted for Denmark, while the southern zone, with the important town of Flensburg, went to Germany.

Although the Scandinavian states had managed to avoid being involved in actual warfare, they still could not escape the consequences of the war. Norway, for instance, lost almost half of her merchant fleet, and the reduction in international trade meant lack of fuel and food. And all the time the three nations feared that in the end they would be forced out of their neutrality. When the creation of an international organization for the maintenance of peace was proclaimed, as early as 1917, as one of the war aims of the Allies, the idea aroused vivid interest and sympathy in the Scandinavian countries. This resulted in opening a new field for Scandinavian co-operation. Government commissions in the three countries jointly drafted a plan for an "international juridical organization," the main object of which was to see that disputes were referred to an international court of arbitration or to special conciliation commissions. This plan indicated the Scandinavian attitude toward organized international co-operation, and it was framed in accordance with the interest these countries had in avoiding entanglements with the political conflicts of Europe. Therefore it did not so much as mention the question of sanctions against those who might break treaty obligations. What the Scandinavian countries wanted was not a political organization but a legal arrangement that would leave untouched the cornerstones of their traditional policy of neutrality.

It had been the hope of the Scandinavian states that after the war a general peace conference would be called, where belligerents and neutrals, victors and defeated, would meet for the settlement. There was bitter disappointment in Scandinavia when the neutral states were excluded from the peace conference and the actual shaping of the League of Nations. But when the invitations to join the League as charter members were issued, all three countries accepted. Denmark showed the least hesitation in accepting the invitation of the victors. There was little debate, and in the Danish parliament the affirmative decision was unanimous. In Norway there was much more criticism of the government's proposal to enter the League, but it was accepted in the Storting by

100 votes, with 20 in opposition. The strongest resistance came in Sweden, where the proposal gave rise to a hot debate in the press and in the Riksdag. But on the same day as the Danes and the Norwegians—the third of March, 1920—the Swedish Riksdag decided that Sweden was to join the League of Nations. In the lower chamber the vote was 152 to 67; in the upper chamber it was 86 to 47.

But in all three countries there was scant enthusiasm; criticism of the way the League had been organized was open. The League Covenant contained nothing about measures for conciliation and postponed the question of a permanent international court. Instead it created an outspokenly political organization and formulated provisions for military and economic sanctions. The dominant influence of the great powers in the League Council at the expense of the small states was strongly criticized. It was also pointed out that the obligations of the League members could not be identical. Above all, it was stressed that the provisions about sanctions must not cause the small states to be involved in warlike action. In spite of their disappointment the Scandinavian countries entered the League determined to co-operate loyally within its framework.

The first power whose loyalty was put to a test was Sweden, as the Åland question was the first international dispute of importance that was submitted to the League. After Finland had proclaimed herself an independent sovereign state in November, 1917, the Swedish-speaking inhabitants of the Åland Islands, in a petition to the king of Sweden, expressed their desire to be incorporated into the Swedish realm. The Ålanders held a plebiscite that showed 95 per cent for adherence to Sweden, and the Swedish government tried to persuade the Finnish government to recognize the right of the Ålanders to decide to whom they were to belong. Finland rejected the Swedish proposal, and tension grew strong between the two countries. Finally the British foreign secretary, in agreement with the Swedish government, approached the League Council and drew its attention to the dispute. *Rap-*

porteurs appointed by the Council visited Sweden, Finland, and the Åland Islands, and their report by and large approved the Finnish position. It said that Finland undoubtedly had sovereignty over the Åland Islands and that the principle of self-determination did not apply in this case. The *rapporteurs* also gave a number of reasons, which they themselves designated as political. By repelling communism Finland had rendered great service to other countries, and from a European point of view it was important that Finland should be retained within the group of Scandinavian states as a bulwark of peace in Northern Europe. If Finland were deprived of the Åland Islands, there was a danger that she might go further away from Scandinavia and be driven into alliances directed against Sweden.

In June, 1921, the Council took up the question for final action and awarded Finland the sovereignty over the islands. At the same time the government of Finland pledged itself to create legislative guarantees for the Swedish elements in the population. In the same year an agreement about the international and military position of the Åland Islands was signed by ten powers: Sweden, Finland, Denmark, Estonia, Latvia, Poland, Germany, France, Britain, and Italy. The understanding was that as soon as a Russian government had been recognized, Russia also would be invited to sign the agreement. This international convention stipulated the neutralization and demilitarization of the islands.

Disappointment with the decision of the League was keen in Sweden. But the government accepted the verdict, and it was not long before the Swedish public also accepted it. There was peace concerning the Åland Islands until the clouds of war again began to gather over Europe.

There were further complications, however, in the relations between Sweden and Finland, complications that had no counterpart as far as Norway and Denmark were concerned. The position of the Swedish-speaking minority in Finland constantly irritated public opinion in Sweden. But above all, the question of Finland's relations with the Soviet Union and the risks that Russian hostilities against Finland would entail for Sweden determined the Swedish position toward the East. Finnish foreign policy was dictated by need for support in its relations with Russia, of which Finland stood in traditional fear. One course favored by Finnish policy makers was a close association with the Scandinavian countries. In October, 1923, the Swedish foreign minister recommended a Swedish-Finnish defense agreement. His idea was that Sweden should pledge herself to come to the assistance of Finland, if Finland were subjected to an unprovoked attack by Russia. The Swedish government did not back up the foreign minister, who also made it clear that he had not spoken on behalf of the government. The result was that the foreign minister resigned, and the idea of a defense union with Finland was dropped.

During this period discussion about closer political and military co-operation between Sweden, Norway, and Denmark also receded into the background. With the end of the war and the revival of international trade relations, the co-operation that had developed during the war years became less important. The meetings of Scandinavian ministers, which had almost become a fixed institution, were not continued. There was not a single such meeting from 1920 until 1932. In 1929 the leader of the Conservative party in Denmark, Christmas Möller, spoke in the Danish parliament in favor of inter-Scandinavian negotiations on defense, but this proposal aroused little interest. The question of closer political co-operation in Scandinavia seemed all but forgotten. In Norway, particularly, the idea of political Scandinavianism was severely criticized. In other fields, however, there was valuable co-operation.

During this period there was little Scandinavian foreign policy except within the framework of the League of Nations, and in the course of their work in the League the Scandinavian countries often formed a common front and fought for the same ideas. What opposition there had been to joining the League abated gradually, and a distinctly positive attitude took its place. This did not mean, however, that the Scandinavian powers had shelved their ideas about the forms in which international co-operation ought to be conducted. They continued their attempts to change the League, to transform it from a political organization into an instrument for the peaceful solution of all disputes.

One principle for which the Scandinavian states worked was that of the universality of the League. They were determined opponents of differentiation between victors, neutrals, and defeated, which had been introduced when the League was created; and the longer this difference was maintained, the more they opposed it. Above all, they were anxious from the very outset to have Germany admitted. And it was the same with Russia. A vast majority in Scandinavia feared and detested Bolshevism, but enlightened opinion there favored the entry of the Soviet Union into the League.

There was great disappointment in Scandinavia when the United States did not join the League, and yet perhaps there was more understanding for the American attitude in Scandinavia than in many other quarters. In the Scandinavian countries there was a tinge of the same isolationism that kept the United States away from the League, a certain feeling of mistrust toward European politics, an urge not to get mixed up in it all.

A matter of constant concern to the Scandinavian countries in the League was the rivalry between the great powers and the smaller states. The Council of the League, by its very organization, was principally an instrument of the great powers, while the Assembly was the forum of the smaller states. One of the most important points in the League policy of the Scandinavian countries, therefore, was quite naturally to strengthen the position of the Assembly and to assert its supremacy. They used every opportunity to assert the right of the Assembly to check on the activities of the Council, and they often criticized the Council, that is, the great powers. Some people liked to label the Scandinavian states in the League a group of "Latter-Day Saints," and there certainly was a strong conviction in Scandinavia that the mission of the smaller states was to plead the cause of justice and to function as the conscience of the great powers.

During its first years the League was busy trying to build up the new organization in a way that would safeguard world peace. The three great problems were these: how to settle disputes between states, how to carry out the general disarmament foreseen in the League Covenant, and how to create guarantees for achieving international security. In the early years of the League these questions were largely dealt with separately, and the Scandinavian countries had their own course here and stuck to it stubbornly. From the very start they were among the most eager advocates of arbitration and disarmament, but they were strongly opposed to the idea of creating security by a system of guarantees.

In view of the juridical perspective in which the Scandinavian states regarded international relations it is no wonder that they attached extraordinary importance to the creation of procedures for arbitration. For them it was a triumph of justice when the Permanent Court of International Justice was created in 1920. The Scandinavian states, like a number of other small states, immediately decided to recognize unconditionally the competence of the court in certain legal disputes, whereas it took the great powers in the League Council several years to accept the compulsory jurisdiction of the court.

There can be no doubt that the Scandinavian states were the principal motivators in getting the competence of the court recognized. But this did not satisfy them. They not only worked on judicial procedure before the court but also spent much energy on the attempt to create efficient machinery for the peaceful settlement of political disputes, which did not lend themselves to a judicial court procedure. The technique of conciliation and arbitration was the field in which the Scandinavian states, with Sweden taking the lead, played a really important part and made their most active contributions. What the Scandinavian states wanted to avoid was the involvement of the League Council, the political character of which seemed to them to make it inappropriate as a conciliation organ. In 1924 Sweden, Norway, Denmark, and Finland concluded bilateral agreements with one another establishing permanent conciliation commissions for the solution of all disputes that did not come under the Permanent Court.

In the big question of general disarmament the Scandinavian countries also had their own clear-cut line of action. From the start these three small states were among the most ardent advocates of swift disarmament. As they saw it, the chief task of the League was to prevent war, and general disarmament seemed to them the safest way of performing this task.

The Scandinavian states did not feel themselves threatened by anybody. The only thing they feared was that a new war among the great powers might endanger their neutrality. General disarmament would contribute greatly to the security of Scandinavia, because it would increase mutual confidence among the great powers and therefore reduce the risks of a new war among them. Combined with an efficient system for the peaceful solution of all disputes, disarmament would offer guarantees for the security that was the watchword of the League.

But some of the great powers, especially France, were firmly opposed to Scandinavian attempts to speed up general disarmament. To them the problem of security looked different. Disarmament would have to wait until the atmosphere in the world was more peaceful. What they sought was a different kind of security, a security through guarantees. The Scandinavian states rejected the idea of guarantees. When they had first joined the League of Nations the Scandinavian governments had indicated that they did not admit any obligation to employ military sanctions. They also had pushed through a provision empowering the Council to postpone the application of economic sanctions. They did not want to see the system of guarantees further elaborated.

The Geneva Protocol of 1924 was an attempt by the League to join together the three different aims that had been in competition ever since the League was created: arbitration, security, and disarmament.

According to the Protocol all judicial disputes were to be referred compulsorily to the Permanent Court, as the Scandinavian states had demanded ever since the League started. But the Protocol went further than that. It went further than the Scandinavian states had gone before and stipulated compulsory arbitration even of political disputes, with a few exceptions. The security problem was to be solved by an addition to the sanctions clauses of the Covenant. Finally, under the Protocol a conference to reduce armaments was to convene in 1925.

This was the only major attempt by the League to solve these problems as one whole. The Scandinavian countries gave it their very serious attention. They greeted with great satisfaction the prospect of seeing the principle of compulsory arbitration and the compulsory jurisdiction of the International Court realized at last; they rejoiced that disarmament was to be taken up in earnest; but their opposition to the sanctions clauses remained. It is doubtful that the Scandinavian countries would even have ratified the sanctions provision unless it had been definitely understood that no obligation rested upon them to yield military assistance without their own consent. But they never had to make a decision concerning the Geneva Protocol. When Britain declared that she could not accept it, its fate was sealed. Although several states had already signed it, it was taken off the agenda of the League.

The failure of the Geneva Protocol was a serious defeat for the League, but nonetheless international tension continued to decrease for a time. The Locarno treaties of 1925, which guaranteed the frontier between Germany and Belgium and France and stipulated procedures of conciliation and arbitration between Germany and its neighbors, and the subsequent entry of Germany into the League in 1926 were greeted in Scandinavia as gratifying signs of health.

At the same time Scandinavia became a region in which arrangements were actually made for the peaceful settlement of any dispute that might arise. The three Scandinavian countries in 1925–1926 concluded conventions with each other and with Finland to this effect. Under these conventions all political disputes that had not been solved by conciliation were to be referred to a specially created arbitral tribunal. Sweden and Denmark ratified the Scandinavian arbitration treaties immediately and without debate. In Norway the matter took a full year. The reason for the Norwegian criticism and hesitation was the feeling aroused over the Greenland dispute between Norway and Denmark. In the end, however, the essential feature of the Greenland dispute was perhaps the illustration it offered of the fact that the Scandinavian countries were prepared to put into practice the ideas they fought for in the League of Nations.

Greenland was originally a Norwegian crown possession, but during the long period in which Norway was joined to Denmark it was administered from Copenhagen. When Denmark ceded Norway in 1814 and Norway was joined with Sweden, Denmark kept Greenland, and Norway expressly renounced all claims to it. The settled parts of the west coast of Greenland were administered as a Danish colony. Access to this colony without special permission was prohibited, not only to foreigners but also to Danes. Gradually Danish colonization was extended to the rugged east coast also, and, in 1916, when Denmark sold the Virgin Islands to the United States, she received American assurance that the United States had no objections to the extension of the Danish monopoly to the whole of Greenland. Similar assurances were obtained from a number of other countries. The Norwegian foreign minister also declared that the Danish plans would meet no difficulties from the Norwegian government. In May, 1921, the Danish government announced that the whole of Greenland would henceforth be administered as a Danish colony. In spite of its earlier assurances, the Norwegian government protested, declaring it had never recognized, nor did it intend ever to recognize, this extension of the Danish sovereignty, since it would mean that the whole of Greenland would be closed to Norwegian sealers, hunters, and fishermen who plied their trade there. After long negotiations the two countries concluded the East Greenland Treaty in 1924. This treaty, for a period of twenty years, allowed free access to Norwegian ships, persons, and companies to most parts of the East Greenland territories for the purpose of landing, hunting, fishing, and taking possession of lands as users, but not as owners. By explicit agreement the question of sovereignty was not mentioned in the treaty.

The Norwegians continued, however, to consider East Greenland as no man's land, and in 1930 and 1931 Norwegian expeditions occupied areas on the east coast, and nationalist opinion in Norway persuaded the government to back the occupation. Denmark decided to refer the matter to the International Court at The Hague. To this Norway had no objections. The verdict of the Court came in April, 1933, and it recognized Danish sovereignty over the whole of Greenland. Norway loyally accepted the verdict. The East Greenland Treaty remained in force.

THE TIME OF RISING TENSION

On January 30, 1933, Hitler had become the master of Germany. This is not the place to go into detail about how the ascension to power of the bellicose Nazi party affected the international situation. Naturally it did not leave the Scandinavian countries indifferent. The new course in Germany was regarded not only with misgivings but also with strong antipathy in all the Scandinavian countries. From this time onward international tension rose without interruption, and the Scandinavian states were faced with the failure of fifteen years of effort.

After many delays the international disarmament conference finally met in 1932 and was greeted with joy by the Scandinavian states, but the negotiations broke down. In 1933 Germany left not only the disarmament conference but also the League of

Nations, and two years later, denouncing the military clauses of the Versailles Treaty, Germany officially started her rearmament. The Council of the League of Nations took up a resolution condemning the German action. At that time Denmark had a seat in the Council, and the resolution placed her in a delicate position. The Danish attitude toward the Nazis was no different from that of the other Scandinavian countries, but Denmark was the only one of the three that had a common frontier with Germany, and her concern about the position of the Danish minority in South Schleswig on the German side of the frontier was a compelling reason for Denmark not to do anything that the Germans could consider a challenge. For this reason, the policy of Denmark during these years was perhaps somewhat more cautious than that of the other two. When the resolution was passed by the League Council, the Danish representative abstained, after consultations between the three Scandinavian foreign ministers.

The League got weaker and weaker, with the conflict between Italy and Ethiopia a definite defeat for it. After Mussolini invaded Ethiopia in October, 1935, without a declaration of war, the League appointed a special committee to prepare sanctions procedures. The Scandinavian countries immediately accepted the economic sanctions recommended by the committee, but it soon became apparent that the sanctions in no way stopped Mussolini, who conquered Ethiopia and drove its emperor into exile. The League was faced with a *fait accompli*, and the Assembly in June, 1936, rejected an Ethiopian proposal that annexations by armed force should not be recognized. Instead the Assembly came out for the abolition of the sanctions against Italy.

Shortly after the League had recognized its failure and abolished the sanctions it had introduced, the three Scandinavian foreign ministers, together with those of Finland, Holland, Switzerland, and Spain—Republican Spain—issued a statement declaring that as long as the Covenant was applied only incompletely and inconsistently, with the disarmament clause a dead letter, they were obliged to bear that fact in mind in connection with the application of the sanctions clause.

The Scandinavian countries had always been opposed to compulsory military sanctions, though they had recognized the obligation to join economic sanctions. Now a leaf was turned, and during the three years that remained until the outbreak of the Second World War the Scandinavian states returned more and more to the line of absolute neutrality. The passivity of the League when Hitler marched into the Rhineland, the increasing aggressiveness of his policies, the annexation of Austria and Czechoslovakia—all these things convinced the Scandinavian states that they could no longer expect security through the League. After Germany, Italy, and Japan had left the League and joined in the Anticomintern pact, there remained in the League only three great powers, representing one of the opposing blocs. The time had come for the Scandinavians to look after their own house.

In April, 1938, the three Scandinavian foreign ministers and their colleague from Finland gathered in Oslo and declared that the Northern countries, now as before, were resolved to keep away from the power groups that were being created in Europe and to do everything they could in order not to be involved in a war between these groups. In the three Scandinavian countries statements were also made that indicated an identical attitude toward compulsory sanctions. During a meeting in Copenhagen in the summer of 1938 between the so-called "Oslo states"—the Scandinavian states, Belgium, Holland, and Luxemburg—a clear statement to this effect was made.

Convinced that their countries should continue to co-operate in the work of the League, the foreign ministers have established that their governments are determined to stick to the line . . . that the sanctions system, in the present circumstances and thanks to the practice that has been followed in the past, has taken on a noncompulsory nature. Further they are of opinion that this noncompulsory nature of the sanctions applies not only to a special group of states, but that it exists for all League members. They are convinced that it is in the interest of the League itself that this right to judge freely is being established.

The Swedish foreign minister shortly afterwards stressed that the League would have to recognize the Scandinavian view, because otherwise the fears that the League and the Covenant were being reserved as an instrument for one combination of great powers against another would ruin the authority of the League in states that were not willing to let themselves be used as tools for such a policy. The illusions about the value of collective security had been completely shattered in Scandinavia, and this statement was a farewell to the ideas of the twenties.

Concern for their own security, in these last years before the war, became the leading idea in Scandinavian foreign policy. During the twenties Scandinavian co-operation had been concerned principally with the League and the construction of a system for international security, but now it took on a different character. With the weakening of internationalism the Scandinavian problem was pointed up and brought to the fore. Just as at the outbreak of the First World War, each country turned to its neighbors who also wished to stay out of the war that seemed more and more inevitable.

Economic co-operation had begun in 1930, through the Oslo Convention, to which Finland later adhered, and in 1934 the Scandinavian governments appointed special delegations to further economic co-operation in the North. In connection with trade negotiations the meetings of Scandinavian ministers were revived. They soon became a recurrent institution, and their program was widened to include political questions. In 1938 Sweden, Norway, Denmark, and Finland separately issued sets of neutrality rules, which had been drafted jointly. Official declarations began to stress more and more the value and importance of Northern co-operation, but mostly this was done in rather vague phrases. Detailed proposals about an organized political or military co-operation were only rarely put forward by authoritative politicians, but they were the subject of lively discussion in the press. Just as in the early twenties, the idea of a defense alliance was embraced most positively in Finland, where support from Sweden was seen as a chance of averting the constant threat from Russia. In Denmark certain proposals for a defense alliance were put forward, but they were rejected by leading politicians. Nazi Germany was a potential danger for all the Scandinavian countries, but Denmark was closest geographically, and there was a certain change in the Danish attitude. In October, 1933, the Danish prime minister, Stauning, stated that the Danish southern frontier was the frontier of Scandinavia, and that an attack on this frontier was an attack on the whole of Scandinavia. In March, 1937, he made a speech in which he reversed himself. It attracted a great deal of attention at that time. Stauning declared that the countries of the North had interests that were too diversified for an alliance between them to be possible. "A Northern defense alliance, in my opinion, is utopian. To concern oneself seriously with such a thing will create a new danger zone, call forth a suspicion which hardly exists now and which in any case is unjustified." The principal aim of Danish foreign policy was to undertake nothing that might cause displeasure in Germany and increase the danger of a German attack. Denmark was therefore the only one of the Scandinavian states that, in 1939, accepted Hitler's offer of a nonaggression pact.

Norway was weakest in its interest in closer political or military co-operation in the North. The memories of the union with Sweden and the differences with Denmark over Greenland had an inhibiting effect, and Norway felt safe behind the other Scandinavian states, since there was no threat from the West.

In any Scandinavian co-operation, Sweden would have to play the central part. This was mainly because Sweden had started reorganizing her defenses under the pressure of increasing international tension and was the only one of the Scandinavian states having a military establishment of any real importance. Nowhere was the debate about a Scandinavian alliance as lively as in Sweden. However, the situation in Scandinavia was more complicated now than during the twenties. Denmark feared a German attack, Finland a Russian one. Russia had always been distrustful of any attempts at closer Scandinavian co-operation, and now both the German and the Russian press strongly criticized all plans for co-ordination in Scandinavia.

During this last period before the outbreak of the Second World War, Sweden was again faced with the problem of the strategic value of the Åland Islands. When the League of Nations settled the question in 1921, the decision was accepted by the Swedish public and there had been no discussion of the problem. Now the situation was changed by the bankruptcy of collective security, the risk of a war between the great powers, the increasing orientation of Finland toward Scandinavia, and the strengthening of Swedish defenses, which made possible military commitments. The Swedish and Finnish governments early in 1939 submitted a plan for a revision of the Åland convention so as to permit defensive military installations in certain parts of the islands. The government turned to the countries that had signed the convention, asking them to accept the easing of the demilitarization provisions. In the notes making this request it was added that the approval of the League of Nations was to be sought afterwards. At the same time the Soviet Union, though not a signatory, was asked in its capacity of Council member to help obtain approval for the Swedish-Finnish proposal.

All the signatories in due time replied affirmatively, and early in May the Swedish government asked the parliament to approve the "agreement for protection of the neutrality of the Åland Islands." The proposal was never taken up by the Swedish parliament, however, because of Russian opposition to a revision of the convention. The League Council never took any decision, and Foreign Commissar Molotov declared that the Soviet Union was firmly opposed to approval of the Swedish-Finnish project and regarded remilitarization of the Åland Islands as a direct threat.

In contrast to the Swedish government, the Finns nevertheless went through with their action and obtained the approval of their parliament. During the summer of 1939, when the danger of war drew nearer, Swedish enthusiasm for the Åland plan cooled a great deal, and when war broke out Sweden dropped the plan altogether.

THE SECOND WORLD WAR

When Germany started the Second World War by sending its troops across the frontiers of Poland on September 1, 1939, the Scandinavian governments all declared that they intended to maintain strict neutrality. There can be no doubt that the vast majority of the people of Scandinavia viewed the German aggression with genuine abhorrence and that their sympathies were entirely on the Allied side. But the peace tradition and the faith in neutrality were deeply rooted. There was complete agreement in the three countries not to let themselves be drawn into the war voluntarily.

The first critical test for Swedish and Norwegian neutrality came with the Finnish-Russian winter war of 1939–1940. The Russian attack on Finland on the last day of November aroused a storm in Scandinavia—strongest perhaps in Sweden, which traditionally had more ties with Finland than the others. Voices were heard in Sweden demanding active intervention on the Finnish side. Germany, tied to Russia through the Ribbentrop pact, let it be clearly understood that active official Swedish intervention in Finland would be regarded as a hostile attitude toward Germany. An official Swedish intervention in Finland would, with certainty, involve the whole of Scandinavia in the war between the great powers. This view was shared by Norway and Denmark.

Instead, Sweden practiced a policy that might be called "nonbelligerent interventionism"; she sent considerable quantities of arms to Finland and permitted the recruiting of volunteers, which added about 9,000 fully equipped men to the fighting forces of Finland. Norway and Denmark also sent aid, though to a lesser extent.

Both Britain and France were eager to support Finland, and not for moral and idealistic reasons alone. One reason was that in this way the ability of the Soviet Union to yield material aid to Germany would be reduced. Both Britain and France, therefore, in December, 1939, asked the Swedish and Norwegian governments whether they would agree to let war material pass through to Finland. The Soviet Union protested in Stockholm and Oslo, but the Scandinavian governments rejected the protests as an attempt to interfere with their freedom of action. They maintained that such transit rights did not conflict with the principle of neutrality. In January, 1940, both governments agreed to the British and French request, and the transit of arms was started.

But it soon became clear that in the long run Finland would not be able to withstand the overwhelming might of the Russians. The Allies then developed plans to send troops to Finland, and these would have to go via Norway and Sweden. It was not until the second of March, however, that the Swedish and Norwegian governments were notified that Britain and France were prepared to send troops, if Finland so requested, and were asked what their attitude toward such a project would be. The next day the Swedish government declared it could not permit troops to pass, and the Norwegian government gave the same answer. Sending French and British troops to Finland would mean war between the Western Allies and Russia, which at that time had not entered the big war, and the Scandinavian countries would thereby become a battlefield for the war of the great powers.

Actually, Finland never requested troops, and in any case the Allied offer came too late. As early as January, Finland, with Sweden acting as intermediary, had started sounding out conditions of peace, and on March 12, 1940, the peace between Finland and the Soviet Union was signed in Moscow. All over Scandinavia the peace terms were considered very hard on Finland.

When Denmark and Norway were invaded by the Germans less than a month later, while Sweden was left in peace, the Scandinavian united front was broken. Whatever the motives of the Germans in sparing Sweden, it is certain that they counted on Sweden's resisting as Norway did. A conquest of Sweden would probably have delayed the German timetable considerably. There were also certain advantages to Germany of Sweden's remaining outside the war but serving as a source of important supplies. Another reason, and a more important one, was the attitude of Russia. The Russian government told the Germans that it would regard a German attack on Sweden with disfavor. And at this early stage, with the battle with the Western powers still to begin, the Germans could not afford to disregard such a Russian view.

The occupation of Denmark was a matter of hours. The Danish frontier units put up a desperate resistance, but being practically unarmed Denmark could do nothing to defend her territory against the invaders. The king and the government therefore surrendered, under protest, to the ultimatum of the Germans. The lawful government, parliament, judiciary, and administration continued to function, and on the surface the change was less radical, to begin with, than might have been expected. Denmark considered herself as an occupied, but still neutral, country. No exile government was organized, but the Danish Council in London served as an organ of resistance. Denmark was, of course, unable to conduct an independent foreign policy apart from the bidding of Germany, and one consequence of this was that Denmark was made to sign the Anticomintern pact. The Danish minister in Washington, Henrik Kauffmann, however, proclaimed himself the representative of the king of Denmark and on Denmark's behalf concluded an agreement with the United States in April, 1941, which gave the United States bases on Greenland.

During the first three years of occupation Denmark was treated quite differently from other occupied countries. She was Germany's showpiece of the New Order in Europe. Even if the Germans did not ostensibly interfere with Danish internal affairs to begin with, their presence in the background could, of course, not be ignored. But with the Danish people feeling definitely that they belonged in the Allied camp, passive resistance grew, and with it German pressure. Late in August, 1943, the Germans put an end to their "model protectorate." They proclaimed a state of emergency and introduced martial law. The cabinet resigned, the parliament ceased to function, and the king became a prisoner in his palace. From that moment onward Denmark was in a state of war with Germany; it was conquered enemy territory; the resistance movement grew; and there were many victims of German terrorism. The Allies recognized Denmark as an associated power, and her diplomatic representatives abroad were recognized as representing free Denmark. When liberation came on May 5, 1945, the underground resistance movement could take over, and a new Danish cabinet was immediately formed.

In Norway the situation was different from the outset. After the Norwegian government had rejected the German demand for submission and put up resistance, the British and French landed troops along the coast of Norway. They could not, however, achieve much. On June 7 resistance on land was ended, and the Germans were masters of the whole country. The king and the government established themselves in London and led Norwegian resistance from there.

With its exile government in London and the Germans administering Norway through a German commissar and the Quisling puppet government, Norway was recognized as an Allied power from the beginning, and foreign countries had their envoys accredited to the king and the government in London. Thus, Norway, all through the occupation, had a free government out of reach of the Germans, which was able to return to Norway when liberation came in 1945.

While Denmark, by the nature of things, was unable to conduct a foreign policy during the years of occupation, Norway was not placed in the same position. With all interests subordinated to the common effort to win the war, there was, however, little room for activities aiming beyond actual liberation.

Trygve Lie, as foreign minister of the Norwegian government in London, on occasion dropped hints that Norway after the war envisaged for herself a role as a member of the Atlantic community in preference to a place as the western half, or third, of Scandinavia. At the same time, his government was undoubtedly alive to the problems arising from the potential postwar differences between the Western powers and the Soviet Union, and at one time it was a popular phrase in official Norwegian circles to speak of Norway as a bridge between East and West.

In one concrete case, the potential differences between the Soviet Union and the West were brought up officially during the war. That was in the case of Spitzbergen, the island group north of the Norwegian mainland. The Russians have long had an interest in these islands. As early as 1871, when the first serious attempt was made to bring them under Norwegian sovereignty, the Russians filed a protest. Norwegian sovereignty over Spitzbergen was definitely established through an international treaty in 1920, immediately after the First World War, but the Soviet government did not recognize this treaty until four years later and did not subscribe to it without reservations until 1935. By the terms of this treaty Norway was bound not to erect, or permit the erection of, naval bases or fortifications in the areas covered by the treaty, nor ever to use them for purposes of war. During the Second World War, Spitzbergen nevertheless became militarily important, and in the fall of 1944 the Soviet government approached the Norwegian government in London about a revision of the Spitzbergen treaty. What the Russians wanted was an arrangement for joint Norwegian-Russian defenses. In April, 1945, shortly before it was able to return to its homeland, the Norwegian government told the Moscow government that it was prepared to sign a preliminary joint declaration, expressing its willingness to negotiate with Moscow about the military utilization of the islands. Such a declaration was, however, never signed, and it was not until 1947 that what had occurred was made public. By then, the foreign minister of the Soviet Union had again broached the matter to the Norwegian foreign minister on two occasions— at the Peace Conference in Paris and during the United Nations meeting at Lake Success in the fall of 1946. The Norwegian point of view was that a change of the demilitarized status of Spitz- bergen required the approval of all the signatories of the 1920 treaty. The other powers involved in this treaty were the United States, Britain, France, Holland, Denmark, and Sweden. Of these, the United States and Britain were kept informed from an early stage; the others were told about the Russian desire for revision of the treaty only after renewed Soviet approaches in 1946. From early in 1947 until now nothing more has been done about the matter. Apparently the Norwegian view that the approval of all treaty signatories was needed has been the reason for this. The Norwegian attitude on the arrangement to be discussed with Mos- cow has been that it should be not only a joint arrangement between the two in the interest of increasing the security of Nor- way and the Soviet Union but also a regional link in a universal security arrangement.

During the war years Sweden was on her own in Scandinavia. On the day Denmark and Norway were invaded, the German government demanded an assurance from Sweden that she would remain strictly neutral, particularly in the matter of refraining from military mobilization or deployment. The Swedish govern- ment replied that it would adhere to the policy of neutrality. Far from renouncing her right to use her military resources as she found best, Sweden undertook mobilization.

The same assurance of neutrality was given to the West when Britain wanted to know whether Sweden intended to declare war on Germany or send troops over the frontier and when France said she was willing to help Norway and aid Sweden in warding off threats to her independence. The Swedish attitude toward Norway was the same. The Norwegians were told that, since

Sweden had undertaken not to take any measures to prevent the occupation, she could not aid Norway with arms, as she had done for Finland during the winter war, nor could Sweden permit exports of arms and munitions to the fighting Norwegian forces. The Germans applied strong pressure to make Sweden allow the transit of war materials to the German forces in Norway. But this demand, while the fighting on land was still going on, was rejected by Sweden. The difference between the situation in Norway and that in Finland was explained to be this: Sweden did not regard the war in Norway as a local war, like the Russian attack on Finland in 1939, but as a part of the great power war between Germany and the Allies, and therefore she had to abstain from all measures that could be considered siding with one or the other of the belligerent camps.

Toward the end of hostilities in Norway the Norwegians considered asking for an armistice that would allow them to retain their control of the northernmost part of the country. There were negotiations with Sweden about neutralization of the Narvik area, which under this armistice plan was to be occupied by Swedish troops. This was an opportunity for Sweden, with her sympathies completely on the side of the Norwegians, to do something without becoming involved in the war. The Germans were in difficulties in the Narvik area when diplomatic talks about this scheme started and did not seem uninterested in the beginning. But when the whole thing had been worked out, they did not answer. By then it had become clear that the Allies would be forced to leave not only Narvik but the whole of Norway, and thus nothing came of the neutralization idea.

With Germany the master of Denmark and Norway, Sweden was placed in a very difficult position—isolated from the West and in many respects at the mercy of the Germans. This difficult position was further stressed when Holland, Belgium, and France succumbed to the German armies. The German government soon sharply repeated its demands that Sweden should allow the transit to Norway not only of civilian goods but also of war materials and troops. This time Sweden did not feel she could withstand the pressure. An agreement was made giving the Germans the right to send all kinds of goods, including war materials, to and from its forces in Norway. They were also allowed to transport through Sweden soldiers on furlough from Norway and to send the same number of soldiers from Germany back to Norway. These soldiers in transit were not allowed to carry arms. The official Swedish explanation was that after hostilities had ceased in Norway it was not a breach of neutrality to allow this transit arrangement, since it did not lead to any reinforcement of the German occupation forces in Norway.

There was much bitterness in Norway over this Swedish concession, and the Norwegian government in London protested, rejecting the view of Sweden that hostilities between Germany and Norway had ceased. Britain also presented a protest note, declaring that His Majesty's government took a grave view of the matter, since it was a direct service to the enemy and therefore a serious breach of neutrality. In rejecting the protests, Sweden again stressed that the Swedish action could not damage British or Norwegian interests in Norway, since it did not increase the German forces in Norway. The Swedish public was dismayed at the concession, which was made under duress. At one point a hint of this even crept into a Swedish diplomatic document. That was when, in replying to a Norwegian protest, Sweden said, "All neutrality policy has its limitations in the means which are at the disposal of the neutral state." But as neither Norway nor Britain wanted to see Sweden involved in the war at this point, the protests were never followed by actions. Circumstances forced Sweden to favor the Allies in a way that was also unneutral. The German blockade cut Sweden off from half of her ocean-going merchant marine, and Sweden leased this tonnage to the Allies.

When Germany attacked Russia on June 22, 1941, Sweden was faced with further German demands. The most important of these was that Sweden was to allow the transit of one fully armed German division from Norway to Finland. Finland, which had entered the war under German pressure, led by a desire to regain what she lost in the winter war, associated herself with this demand. To agree to it would mean a bigger step away from the course of strict neutrality than any Sweden had so far taken, and the German demand caused a split within the Swedish government that almost broke up the National Coalition in office. The final answer, however, was "yes," with particular stress on the fact that this was to be a one-time concession, not to be repeated. It was explained that it did not mean that Sweden had made her choice between Germany and the Allies; it only meant that in this particular instance Sweden had taken Finland's side. "We also have Sweden's own interest in mind," it was added. "Our main purpose is to preserve our independence and keep out of the war between the great powers."

As a proof of the declaration that this concession was for one time only, demands for further transports of the same kind and for furlough traffic to and from Finland on the Norwegian pattern were refused. The British government, while protesting against the concession, also confirmed that relations with Sweden "remained normal."

A veritable stream of demands followed from the Germans, who never were content for long with what they got. Many of these demands were met with a firm "no" in Stockholm. But it was one of the difficulties of Swedish diplomacy in those days that whenever a concession had to be made, it had to be officially announced, but whenever the government said "no," it kept silent about it in order not to make it a point of prestige for the Germans to put on further pressure. In the spring of 1943, marked by the German collapse at Stalingrad and the Allied advances in North Africa, German pressure on Sweden was reduced. Toward the end of July, 1943, Sweden notified the German government that military transit to and from Norway would have to stop in the course of the following month. For months before that protests against the transit from within Sweden itself had become increasingly insistent. When the government canceled the concession, this also removed the greatest single strain on Swedish relations with Norway.

Generally speaking it may be said—as was remarked at the time by the *Times* of London—that these concessions and counterconcessions and cancellations of concessions were regarded by Sweden not as inconsistencies but as a sort of defense in depth of neutrality when it became clear that there was no Maginot line at which this main objective—neutrality—could be defended.

Consequently in the Swedish view there was no lack of logic in the fact that in the later stages of the war many other concessions were made to the Allied side, where Sweden had her sympathies anyway. The most important of these were in the economic field and culminated in the stopping of all exports of ball bearings and iron ore to Germany. In its relations with Denmark and Norway, Sweden was also able to add to the aid she had given to thousands of refugees. Thus the Norwegian authorities were allowed to train and equip troops in Sweden for so-called police duties in connection with the liberation of Norway, and smaller units of Danish police troops were similarly trained and equipped.

THE POSTWAR PERIOD

At the end of the Second World War the Scandinavian countries faced the postwar problems with different backgrounds of recent experience and with different international positions. Norway and Denmark had both been recognized as Allied powers during the war, but Sweden remained outside this wartime community of nations. In Denmark and Norway resistance movements had fought bitterly against the German invaders. Sweden, isolated within the German sphere of power, had managed to maintain her territorial integrity, but only by deviations from the strict neutrality she had proclaimed. Sweden was intact, whereas both Denmark and Norway had suffered heavy material losses during the German terrorism. In both countries an enormous task of reconstruction and rehabilitation had to be fulfilled in order to secure a decent standard of living for the people.

In addition, Denmark had her own problems, not shared by the other two countries. When the hostilities were over there remained in Denmark more than 200,000 German refugees from the Eastern German provinces; they had been sent there by the Nazis, in the concluding months of the war, to escape the Russian advance. All these undesirable guests, originally placed in about a thousand camps all over Denmark and later in a few large camps, were a heavy burden for a small country to provide for. The Danish government entered into negotiations with the Western Allies, and by and by these refugees were transported to the Western zones of Germany. By February, 1949, the last of them left Danish territory.

The end of the war brought Denmark two other problems that put her in even more direct contact with the great powers than had the question of the German refugees. One was the South Schleswig problem. The plebiscite in 1920, although carried out according to the principle of national self-determination, failed to put an end to the Danish-German frontier problem. As a result of the new delineation, Denmark was saddled with a German minority in North Schleswig, which was granted by the Danes the right to a national life within the framework of the Danish state. Nevertheless, this German minority worked for a frontier revision all the time until the end of the Second World War, and the German penetration into this area made itself strongly felt during the Hitler regime. On the other hand, there was a Danish minority in South Schleswig, which was subjected to severe pressure by the German authorities. This minority, however, stuck to its Danishness, and during the war a somewhat astonishing development took place. Although this part of Schleswig, in the period between the two wars, had become more and more Germanized, toward the end of the last war a large part of the German-speaking population joined the pro-Danish movement, which demanded that the region should be taken away from Germany and incorporated into Denmark. After the surrender of Germany in 1945, South Schleswig, as a part of the German province of Schleswig-Holstein, was occupied by the British forces, and it became one of the tasks of the occupying authorities to deal with the pro-Danish movement.

As far as Danish foreign policy was concerned, there were two aspects to the problem of South Schleswig. One was the safeguarding of the interests of the Danish population there; quite another was the question of the incorporation of the region into Denmark. There could hardly be any doubt that one of the main reasons why large numbers of people suddenly joined the Danish movement in South Schleswig was to save themselves from the German collapse. There was, therefore, a great deal of doubt in Denmark about how durable and reliable this change of opinion among the German elements in the area would be.

The frontier question caused sharp differences in Danish politics. The first announcement about the position of the Danish government was made immediately after the liberation of Denmark, when Prime Minister V. Buhl, on behalf of the coalition government, declared: "The frontier of Denmark remains fixed." The main argument for this stand was that Denmark must be careful not to acquire a large German minority by a frontier revision and thereby lose her character as a homogeneous national state. But the declaration of the prime minister did not end the matter. Strong opposition was organized against the official view, and certain parties loudly demanded the right of South Schleswig to decide where it wanted to belong by a plebiscite. There was a series of exchanges between Denmark and Great Britain about the Schleswig question. In a note in the beginning of September, 1946, the British government said it understood Denmark to desire the immediate incorporation of the Danish population in South Schleswig with Denmark, and it wanted to know whether Denmark desired this in the form of an exchange of populations or a frontier revision with or without a preceding plebiscite. After a lot of domestic debate, some of it rather acrimonious, Denmark replied in October, 1946, that she did not want to make any proposals about an alteration in the status of national allegiance of South Schleswig, and therefore could not accept any of the British alternatives. It was up to the population of the area if it wanted to demand an opportunity to exercise its right of national self-determination.

The matter was introduced into a larger context when Denmark was invited, along with other countries, to state her views on the German problem in connection with preparations for the meeting in Moscow of the Council of Foreign Ministers in 1947. The Danish memorandum stressed the interest of Denmark as a neighbor country of Germany in the complete disarmament of Germany and in seeing that German militarism was lastingly exterminated. Great importance was attributed to safeguarding the rights of non-German groups of population within Germany, and attention was drawn to Danish national interests in South Schleswig. The memorandum repeated that the Danish government did not intend to propose any frontier revision and stated that the people of South Schleswig must decide for themselves if they wanted to raise the question of exercising their natural right of self-determination.

Denmark also called attention to the serious problems arising out of the settlement in South Schleswig of 400,000 German refugees, a number almost as great as that of the indigenous population. The presence of the refugees enormously increased the German-minded part of the population, thereby altering its composition to the detriment of the Danish element. The Danish government also expressed concern over these refugees as constituting a threat to the future security of the Danish frontier.

At a meeting of the Scandinavian foreign ministers in September, 1949, Denmark brought up the question of support from her neighbors for her efforts to lessen the pressure of the refugees in South Schleswig. It was agreed that a satisfactory solution of this problem was a joint Scandinavian interest. In the beginning of

November the Norwegian, Swedish, and Icelandic envoys made *démarches* to this effect in London, Paris, and Washington. The high commissioners of the occupation powers were also informed, with the request that the views of Denmark's neighbors be made known to the West German government. By the end of 1949 only a few thousand of the refugees had been moved from South Schleswig to other parts of the West German republic.

Thus frontier revision and the demand for a plebiscite have been written off as far as official Denmark is concerned. The main problem for Denmark is to achieve the best possible protection for the Danish minority in South Schleswig within the framework of a German state. The British have recognized an organization named Sydslesvigsk Forening as representing the Danish activities in the area and have accorded it strictly limited political authority, treating it mainly as a cultural organization. A series of British-Danish talks have been held on the question of a special status for the members of the Danish-minded minority that would secure them, in addition to their normal civic rights, the freedom to enjoy their ancient Danish culture. Within South Schleswig itself, however, voices are still heard in favor of moving the frontier. Thus South Schleswig remains a political problem, but its solution depends on factors outside the area itself, principally on what definite decisions are taken about the organization of Germany as a whole.

In Greenland Denmark had another international problem that came up once the war was over. During the war Quisling, with the Germans prompting in the wings, laid claim to Greenland on Norway's behalf. When the Norwegian government in exile returned to actual control of the country after the war, Danish-Norwegian relations in connection with Greenland were settled by a supplementary clause to the East Greenland Treaty that stipulated that, in spite of Danish sovereignty over Greenland, Danish decisions about Greenland were to be preceded by consultations with Norway. But now there was also another interested party, the United States.

William H. Seward, secretary of state under Lincoln and Andrew Johnson, had wanted the United States to buy Greenland in order to acquire a strategic base against Russia. His plan was considered a foolish whim at that time, but during the Second World War American attention was again fixed on Greenland. When the Germans increased their activities in this neighborhood, the United States in 1941 concluded a treaty with the Danish minister in Washington, Kauffmann, as has already been mentioned. That treaty gave the United States bases on Greenland. It said that the arrangement should be discontinued when the parties agreed that the present danger to the American continent had ceased. The danger referred to was, of course, the policy of conquest of Nazi Germany, which is now a thing of the past. After the end of hostilities the United States tried to establish a new agreement with Denmark to take the place of the Kauffmann treaty since the Greenland bases had become an important link in postwar American polar strategy. The Danish foreign minister told the American secretary of state that Denmark wanted the United States to evacuate Greenland entirely. Negotiations between the two countries have been going on intermittently. They entered a new phase after Denmark joined the Atlantic pact (see below, p. 304). In the hemisphere pact of Rio de Janeiro in 1947, Greenland was placed inside the security region of the Western hemisphere. If one remembers that American interest in this part of the Arctic has a counterpart in Russian interest in Spitzbergen, it becomes clear that the Greenland problem is only one of numerous questions that arise out of the tension between East and West. Denmark thus has a problem that, more immediately than any other, points up its position between the two great rivals.

During the concluding months of the war, when a conference to form a new world organization was called in San Francisco, both Norway and Denmark were invited to participate, as members of the wartime grand alliance. Both became charter members when the United Nations Organization was formed in June, 1945.

Sweden was one of the first three noncharter members admitted to the United Nations in October, 1946. The parliaments of the three countries unanimously voted for adherence to the UN, and it was very striking how much less debate there was than when the question was whether to join the League of Nations. With the UN an outgrowth of the wartime alliance, it was natural that Norway and Denmark should consider it a matter of course to carry over into the peace the wartime co-operation of which they had been a part. But there was no opposition in Sweden either this time, whereas adherence to the League of Nations had been very strongly criticized. There was, however, less enthusiasm. It was realized that Sweden could not stay outside this new community of nations, but no miracles were expected of the United Nations. The disappointments of the League were not forgotten.

Inside the United Nations the Scandinavian states started pursuing a common course, just as they had done during the days of the League, and this course offers important parallels to that of the prewar years. The principle of the universality of the UN is a matter of concern to the Scandinavian countries, and the Swedish delegations to the UN have tried to urge this point whenever the question of admittance of new members has come up in the Assembly. The Security Council has received a large number of applications for membership, but most of these have been rejected, some because of the veto of the Soviet Union, others because they failed to get the stipulated majority. It has been evident that political reasons blocked the entrance of these rejected countries. This fact has been strongly criticized in the Assembly, and in the general debate in 1947 the Swedish foreign minister, Undén, stressed universality as one of the basic principles of the UN. To admit all the states that had applied for membership would be in accordance with the spirit of the Charter. When the membership question was debated in the political committee of the Assembly, the Swedish delegation submitted a draft resolution, according to which the Assembly was to ask the Security Council to reconsider the applications "in the light of the principle of universality." The

Swedish draft resolution was, however, defeated, although it had the support of all the Scandinavian delegates. The latter then voted for a resolution that declared certain specified states qualified for membership.

The rivalry between the great powers and the smaller states has made itself felt in the United Nations as it did in the League. The Scandinavian delegations have been anxious to participate in all measures that would serve to strengthen the position of the Assembly and assert its supremacy over the Council, which by its very nature is an instrument of the great powers. They therefore voted for the American proposal in 1947 to create an interim committee for peace and security, the so-called "little assembly," which was to function during the time between the sessions of the General Assembly. One of the motives behind the forming of this new organ was the necessity for increasing the efficiency of the United Nations, which was seriously threatened by the split in the Security Council, where the steady use of the veto by the Soviet Union hampered the solution of important questions and endangered the functioning of the whole organization.

The veto question has been one of the great problems of the United Nations, and on several occasions proposals have been made either to abolish the veto or to introduce certain restrictions. The Scandinavian delegations have declared themselves to be against any attempt to alter the Charter in this respect. Their view has been that it is too early to convene a general conference for the purpose of reviewing the Charter. They have seen the use of the veto as a symptom of the existing political situation and not as the cause of it. Instead they have favored all attempts to investigate the whole question and to recommend that the Security Council try to solve the difficulties through agreements within itself. The Scandinavian delegations supported the resolution that commissioned the "little assembly" to investigate the entire problem of the veto power and to report to the General Assembly.

In the Palestine question Sweden has played a rather active role. Sandström, the Swedish representative on the Palestine committee, which worked out the scheme for the partition of the Holy Land, became the president of that committee. He was also president of the special committee that, during the Assembly in 1947, drafted the resolution concerning partition that was accepted by the Assembly. A Swede, the late Count Folke Bernadotte, was the first UN mediator for Palestine and as such was killed by an assassin's bullet. Denmark became a member of the new Palestine commission, which was set up by the 1947 Assembly to carry out the partition scheme.

Sweden has not yet had a seat in any of the main organs of the United Nations, whereas Denmark is a member of the Economic and Social Council and Norway, after two years in this council, succeeded to a seat in the Security Council on January 1, 1949.

The election, early in 1946, of a Scandinavian, Trygve Lie of Norway, as Secretary-General of the new world organization was not without its significance. It indicated a tendency at that time among the member nations, and more especially in both great power camps, to attribute to this part of the world a somewhat intermediate and disinterested position, less closely identified than that of many other nations with either side in the East-West tensions that were already becoming apparent.

On the whole the Scandinavian countries have played a much less active role in the UN than they did in the League. One of the main reasons for this has obviously been the tension among the great powers, which the Scandinavians have tried to side-step. Membership in the United Nations meant a farewell to the old Scandinavian conception of neutrality. The Charter imposes on member states the duty of taking part in sanctions—both economic and military—against an aggressor state at the bidding of the Security Council. But as the Security Council is constructed by the Charter, it cannot start any coercive action against one of the great powers because of the veto of the permanent members of the Council. Therefore, if a conflict between the great powers should occur, the whole problem of neutrality would—or, at least, could—come up again. This was immediately pointed out in official pronouncements in Denmark. The Swedish official commentary on the UN Charter states the position clearly. If the composition of the Security Council should be changed, it says, particularly if this should happen through the withdrawal of one of the great powers, the authority of the Council would be automatically canceled. In other words, if, for instance, Russia were to leave the UN, Sweden would not feel bound automatically by decisions of the rump Security Council that would remain.

Even though the position was stated differently, the general attitude was the same in all three countries. It recalled the traditional Scandinavian concern about neutrality. The next conclusion was that it would be in the interest of the Scandinavian countries not to join any bloc or alliance that might put this neutrality in danger. The task was set to maintain good relations toward both the West and the East. The postwar disappointments, the inability of the Security Council to achieve anything because of the differences between the great powers, had their reflection in the attempts of the Scandinavian countries to steer some kind of middle course in questions in dispute between the two great rivals, the United States and the Soviet Union. At least in part, the Scandinavian countries started the postwar era by returning to their old course of neutrality. Just as they did during the period when Germany was the great menace, these three small countries in the close vicinity of Russia have tried, by a cautious policy, not to challenge one whom they fear.

But by degrees the Scandinavian states have been driven out of their isolationism, at least in part. At first this applied only to the economic field. After the American secretary of state made the suggestion, in a speech at Harvard in June, 1947, that gradually led to the development of the Marshall Plan, the Scandinavian countries took part in all the conferences that finally resulted in the creation of the Organization for European Economic Cooperation. This is a matter that will not be dwelt upon here since it is the subject of another chapter of this book (see Chapter II).

It should be pointed out, however, that from the beginning

the Scandinavian countries, and particularly Sweden, strongly stressed the fact that the Marshall Plan was strictly an economic matter and did not entail any political obligations of closer co-operation. There was a parallel here with the postwar credit agreement between Sweden and Russia, which is often represented in the United States as having been political in nature. Nothing of this kind is recognized in Sweden, where this agreement has been described as motivated by a desire to safeguard against a postwar slump in the United States and to compensate for the disappearance of Germany as a market and a source of supply.

The problem of political co-operation versus neutrality was pointed up when British Foreign Secretary Bevin said, in the House of Commons on January 22, 1948, that the time was ripe for a consolidation of Western Europe. He recommended regional agreements between Britain, France, and the Benelux countries as the backbone of a united Western Europe. He further said that this unity was not to be limited to Britain's closest neighbors but that contact ought to be established also with other countries. Although he named none of these except Italy and did not even hint at Scandinavia's part in a Western bloc, his speech touched off a fresh foreign policy debate in all the Scandinavian countries.

In the course of the spring of 1948 a number of declarations were made by leading government spokesmen in the three countries. To begin with, there was no real certainty about what Bevin had meant, and some of the Scandinavian declarations were correspondingly vague. Later three things happened in the outside world to give this debate more precision. One was the fact that Bevin's speech and what followed actually led to a Western European military union. The second was the Communist coup in Czechoslovakia, which increased the feeling of a critical situation in Europe and the necessity for certain decisions, one way or the other, about the problem of neutrality versus co-operation. The third, of course, was the American attitude of increased interest in association with the Western Union, first officially expressed in the Vandenberg resolution of the United States Senate and later through the negotiations for a North Atlantic alliance.

First to comment on Bevin's speech was Swedish Foreign Minister Undén. In the Swedish parliament he said:

The Government is convinced that an overwhelming majority of the Swedish people does not wish to join any great power bloc, either by express treaty or alliance or by silent acquiescence in joint military measures in case of conflict. If the United Nations functions according to its program, Sweden's attitude in such situations will be determined with regard to the obligations which the UN membership imposes on us. If the new security organization is being undermined through the creation of political blocs, or if it is otherwise paralyzed in its capacity for action, our country must have its freedom to choose the road of neutrality. Whether a policy of neutrality in this hypothetical situation is possible to carry out or not does not depend on ourselves alone, and the chances can therefore not be appraised in advance. But we do not wish, through advance commitments, to renounce the right and the chance to stay outside another war.

Prime Minister Hedtoft, of Denmark, also made a declaration in favor of the right to neutrality:

We do not want to place our country in any bloc at all. We are sticking to stating our views freely towards East and West. In my view it cannot be a Danish or Scandinavian interest to widen the obvious differences between East and West.

The first Norwegian statements were rather general and cautious. Foreign Minister Lange in February, 1948, declared:

A stable, democratic and independent Western Europe with free co-operation between sovereign states has a great task to fulfill in smoothing out the differences between East and West.

But at the same time he repeated the earlier declarations of the Scandinavian countries that, by participating in the Marshall Plan, they did not take a stand on the creation of a political bloc, and he expressed his satisfaction that Marshall had stressed that the economic program contained no political conditions. Some days later, however, he did add that Undén, the Swedish foreign minister, had not spoken on behalf of the whole of Scandinavia.

Lange went much further in a speech on April 19, after the Czech coup and the Russian proposal of a military alliance to Finland, which naturally affected the political atmosphere in Scandinavia. In this speech, the Norwegian foreign minister demonstrated that the attitude of Norway was moving toward the West. He said in part:

Towards the Bevin plan we have taken the position that we do not want to bar ourselves from the possibility of discussing a closer co-operation westwards in the cultural and political fields also. We do not consider Mr. Bevin's suggestion of a consolidation of Western Europe as an aggressive step, but feel that such a consolidation may become a step towards a stabilization of conditions, a contribution to the creation of a new equilibrium and the foundation of an independent contribution which might counteract the tension between the two leading great powers. We have considered that a closer Western European co-operation has possibilities of creating a real basis for an independent democratic peace policy by the Western European countries, and it has been clear to us the whole time that such closer co-operation between the countries in our part of the world is by no means in conflict with the United Nations Charter. As tension between the great powers increases it becomes necessary for us to make it clear to ourselves where we belong. There cannot be the slightest doubt that we are part of Western Europe, both geographically, culturally and economically, and that we are and want to be a Western European democracy.

Lange went on to stress that this must not prevent Norway from establishing good relations and expanding economic exchange with Russia and other countries in Eastern Europe. But because of rumors that Russia planned to offer Norway a pact similar to the one Finland had concluded, Lange announced that, if such a Russian offer came, Norway had no intention of entering any separate military agreement.

He continued:

We have also discussed the question of expanded co-operation in Western Europe. The question of such co-operation apart from the purely economic, which we have already declared our willingness to take part in, has not been raised from any quarter in connection with the Marshall Plan. It is completely clear that neither the British Government nor any other parties to the Brussels pact have plans to ask us to join this pact unless we ourselves expressly desire to join it. Personally I attach very great importance to our finding, as far as possible, our way to a policy which the three Scandinavian countries can agree upon. There must be very compelling reasons before we choose a course which may take us away from Sweden and Denmark or one of them. On the other hand we must realize that the problems of military policy and security which face the three Scandinavian countries are not identical, and that this fact may create certain difficulties in the work to find a common solution.

This final passage in Lange's speech had a direct bearing on inter-Scandinavian negotiations that were taken up later in 1948 to see what could be done about military co-operation between the three countries. It was widely reported that an earlier plan to negotiate failed because Sweden and Norway could not agree on the basis for the talks. Norway wanted to adapt them to a greater co-operation with Western Europe. Sweden wanted advance assurances that Scandinavian military co-operation was not to prejudice Sweden's wish to stay outside blocs of the great powers. In September, 1948, agreement was finally reached to start a joint inquiry into the possibilities of Scandinavian military co-operation. It was then agreed that this inquiry was not to begin with any assumptions regarding Scandinavian neutrality or co-operation with the Western powers. It was to be more technical in nature, with the political angle temporarily disregarded.

Before this inquiry was concluded, in January, 1949, the political issue was brought to a head, however, and the situation that the Norwegian foreign minister had described with such reluctance arose—a situation in which the question was whether the Scandinavian countries were to follow a joint policy or go their separate ways.

In the course of conversations about a North Atlantic defense alliance held in London, Paris, and Washington in the summer and fall of 1948 the question of Scandinavia was brought up, since the United States was particularly interested in having the Scandinavian countries join as the northern wing of a Western European defense system. Around the New Year, Norway and Denmark were informally approached by the United States and told about the progress made in the North Atlantic pact negotiations. At the same time they were given to understand that, if they so desired, the seven negotiating powers were willing to invite them to participate in the talks. The immediate result of this intimation was that, at the request of the Norwegian government, a meeting of the prime ministers, foreign ministers, and defense ministers of the three Scandinavian countries was called in Karlstad, in Southwestern Sweden.

At this meeting, on January 5 and 6, 1949, Sweden offered the other two Scandinavian countries a ten-year military alliance, constructed as a regional agreement according to Article 52 of the United Nations Charter. From the Swedish point of view this was a considerable departure from her traditional policy of neutrality. But Sweden proposed a clause in the treaty according to which the members of the alliance were to pledge themselves not to enter any military alliance with other countries. In this way, as was later explained in a declaration to the Swedish parliament, the Swedish government proposed to extend to the whole Scandinavian area the principle of staying out of entanglements with the great powers. The aim of the alliance was to be to keep the three countries out of war unless one of them was attacked or military sanctions were ordered by the United Nations Security Council. To make possible the rearmament necessary under the plan for joint action in case of attack, the possibility of receiving supplies of arms from the United States on reasonable conditions was to be investigated.

After consulting their respective parliaments, the ministers met again in Copenhagen on January 22, accompanied by a number of members of the parliamentary foreign affairs committees. At this meeting it became clear that the stumbling block to the Swedish proposal was the clause preventing any member of the alliance from entering other military arrangements. Norway considered the protection offered under an exclusive Scandinavian alliance insufficient and proposed: (1) that the three Scandinavian powers should seek a unilateral United States guarantee and (2) that, if such a guarantee was obtained, they should enter into immediate military conversations about preparatory measures to render it effective. Sweden thought that this proposal went so far beyond the whole concept of a Scandinavian alliance apart from the North Atlantic pact as to be unacceptable. After a third Scandinavian meeting in Oslo the failure of the Swedish plan was formally acknowledged on January 30.

Meanwhile two things had happened to emphasize how this whole discussion caught Scandinavia in the cross draft of Western and Soviet interests. On January 14, between the meetings in Karlstad and Copenhagen, a spokesman of the United States State Department announced publicly that American military supplies available for export would have to go, in the first place, to countries associated with the United States in collective security arrangements. Similar statements were made some days later to the governments in Copenhagen, Oslo, and Stockholm by the American ambassadors. Finally, just before the Oslo meeting the Soviet Union addressed a diplomatic note to the Norwegian government inquiring about Norway's intentions with regard to the North Atlantic pact, which Moscow denounced as directed against the Soviet Union. Recalling that Norway had a common frontier with the Soviet Union, the Moscow note specifically inquired whether Norway intended to make bases on its territory available to foreign powers.

In Scandinavia the American announcements concerning arms supplies were widely considered to be in the nature of diplomatic pressure, although this was denied by United States spokesmen. Nor could there be any doubt that the Soviet inquiry, which was immediately made public by the official Soviet news agency, had the object of influencing Norway's attitude. After a few days Norway replied to the Soviet note stating that considerations of her own security prompted her to investigate, in view of the failure of the Scandinavian defense alliance plan, in what form and on what conditions Norway could take part in a regional security system embracing the countries bordering the Atlantic Ocean. The Norwegian note asserted that Norway would never contribute to a policy with aggressive aims and added: "The Norwegian government will never join in any agreement with other states that contains obligations for Norway to open bases for the military forces of foreign powers as long as Norway is not attacked or subjected to threats of attack."

Two days later the Norwegian government decided to send Foreign Minister Halvard Lange to Washington to inquire personally into the conditions on which Norway might enter into the North Atlantic pact conversations. Just before Lange left a second Soviet note was delivered in Oslo. It rejected as unconvincing the Norwegian assurance concerning bases, renewed the denunciation of the North Atlantic pact, and concluded by offering Norway a nonaggression treaty with the Soviet Union.

The Soviet offer created an immediate stir all over Scandinavia. Public comment not only in Norway but also in Sweden and Denmark dwelt on the parallel with Hitler's offer of nonaggression pacts to the Scandinavian countries before World War II. It was immediately clear that Norway would reject the Soviet offer, but it was some time before the reply was made officially. After a week of conversations in Washington with Secretary of State Acheson and other American representatives, Lange went to London for similar talks with British Foreign Secretary Bevin before returning to Oslo to make his report. At a closed meeting of the Storting on March 3 it was decided by 118 votes to 11 (the negative votes were cast by Communists) to notify the United States that Norway was willing to accept an invitation to participate in the preliminary discussions about the Atlantic pact. Upon delivering this notification, the Norwegian ambassador in Washington was immediately invited to take part in the discussions. He took his place in the group of Western European ambassadors on the following day.

In rejecting the Soviet offer of a nonaggression pact the Norwegian government pointed out that such a pact was unnecessary in view of the adherence of both countries to the United Nations Charter, which obligates member states to desist from the threat or the use of armed force against the territorial integrity or political independence of any state.

With Norway's decision to join the pact talks in Washington and the virtual certainty that she would eventually adhere to the pact, a new situation arose for the other Scandinavian countries. Denmark, whose position so far had been an intermediate one aimed at reconciling, if possible, the divergencies between the Swedish and Norwegian attitudes, for one brief moment seems to have toyed with the idea of a Swedish-Danish alliance. But it immediately turned out that there was no support for such a solution. While Sweden returned to her neutrality policy, Denmark sent her foreign minister, Gustav Rasmussen, on an exploratory visit, patterned after Lange's, to Washington. In his conversations with Secretary Acheson and others it was made clear that Denmark also could become a charter member of the North Atlantic pact—if she acted promptly, since by that time, the second week of March, the date for the signing of the pact had already been set, tentatively, for April 4. Upon Rasmussen's return the Danish parliament considered a government proposal that Denmark join the pact. On March 24 the Folketing, the lower chamber, accepted the proposal by a vote of 119 to 23 (the negative votes were cast by Liberal and Communist party adherents). In the Landsting, or upper chamber, the affirmative vote the following day was 64 to 8. On March 29 the Norwegian Storting voted, 130 to 13, in favor of Norway's adherence to the pact. Both Denmark and Norway thereupon became original signatories when the pact was signed in Washington April 4. On January 27, 1950, the two countries were among the signatories, in Washington, of bilateral agreements making them, like other pact members, eligible for aid in the form of American arms deliveries.

One specific subject discussed between Denmark and the United States in connection with the Danish foreign minister's visit in Washington was the Greenland bases held by the United States since World War II. During the pact debate in the Danish parliament it was announced that if Denmark joined, the defense of Greenland would no longer remain a question between the United States and Denmark, but a problem to be discussed within the defense council that was to be formed under the pact. In this council Denmark would be one of the states represented. After declaring that there could be no question of erecting foreign bases in Denmark, Rasmussen announced that Secretary of State Acheson had stressed the purely defensive character of the Greenland bases. Since the establishment of the Atlantic defense alliance and the formation of a number of regional groupings within its framework, discussion about the future of the Greenland bases has begun within one of these groups, the one in which, besides the United States and Denmark, all the other pact members with a coastline bordering the North Atlantic have seats.

The public debate in the Scandinavian countries preceding the decisions now outlined showed one point that must not be overlooked: the differences in attitude toward the question of forging political and military links with the West cannot be traced to ideological differences between the three countries. In Sweden, which has managed to keep out of two world wars, the argument that a country should not sacrifice in advance the chance that a third conflict might by-pass Scandinavia, as an area of secondary importance, has great appeal. Norway, with her experience of German occupation, is more keenly aware of the importance of her coastline as a base for naval warfare and has tended to discount arguments that Scandinavia's strategic importance is secondary. Different views about the military efficiency of a self-contained alliance, as proposed by Sweden, have obtained. The joint Scandinavian inquiry into the possibilities of military co-operation has been concluded, but nothing has been made public about its findings. The fact that Sweden's national defenses are considerably stronger than those of her Scandinavian neighbors may have contributed to a more optimistic evaluation both of the efficiency of an isolated military alliance and of the possibility of her staying apart even after Norway and Denmark joined the North Atlantic pact. Both Norwegian and Danish spokesmen have made it clear that one strong motive for their countries' joining has been the realization that nowhere but in the United States, Canada, and Britain could they hope to find the military equipment needed to bolster their defenses.

The arguments against directly linking Scandinavia's defenses with those of an Atlantic alliance have not been concerned only with reluctance to give up in advance the chance to stay out of another war. In fact, even among the advocates of an "isolated" alliance there have been those who admitted that the hope of neutrality in another conflict is unrealistic. What has made them take their position, some have indicated, has been their concern, not about what would happen if war broke out but about what would be the consequence for Scandinavia of an Atlantic link if war did *not* come, if there was a period of prolonged tension, conceivably extending through many years. In this case, it has been argued, adherence to a North Atlantic pact would in effect mean pulling the cold war right into Scandinavia, making the Scandinavian countries one of its focal points. Fears have been expressed in Sweden, particularly, that such a step would prompt the Soviet Union to extend its military grip over Finland by invoking the mutual assistance treaty, in effect occupying the country, and thus advancing its positions westward to Scandinavia's very doorstep.

x

Co-operation between the Scandinavian Countries

By GUNNAR LEISTIKOW

New York Correspondent of Ørdags-avisen,
Copenhagen, and Verdens Gang, *Oslo*

WHAT is known in Scandinavia as *nordisk samar-bejde*, approximately "Scandinavian co-operation" in English, is one of the outstanding examples of mutual collaboration between peaceful and friendly nations.[1] In a way it is similar to the co-operation of the members of the British Commonwealth of Nations. It works smoothly without any over-all machinery. It is very down to earth and factual in its approach to problems. And it is based on mutual understanding of each other's languages without any need for translations and interpreters, and on a common ground of nearly identical cultural traditions.

There has even been achieved a common legislation for many of the most important fields of commerce and daily life, to the extent that there is today a greater similarity of law between the Scandinavian states than, say, between New York state and Florida. Other aspects of Scandinavian co-operation are co-ordination of foreign policies, cultural ties, and inter-Scandinavian forums ranging from meetings of cabinet ministers, bishops, and parliament members to conventions of societies for the prevention of cruelty to animals.

SCANDINAVIAN BROTHERHOOD

The basis for all these activities is a strong feeling of kinship between the Scandinavian nations. This emotion is decidedly less

---

[1] This chapter is an extended and re-edited version of an article that was first printed in the June, 1948, *Forum*, "How Scandinavia Co-operates." It is reprinted with the permission of the editors of *Forum*.

intense than the feeling of nationalism and allegiance to the individual country, but it is more pronounced than the feeling of solidarity between the Anglo-Saxon nations.

This emotion is not of any recent origin. It is as old as the Scandinavian peoples. When the three Northern kingdoms developed about a thousand years ago, linguistic differences were so slight that the old Norsemen conceived of their vernaculars as one single language, the "Danish tongue," as it was then called.

This community of speech seems to be the root of the idea of kinship and solidarity. The law code of the old Icelandic vikings accorded to "heirs of Danish tongue" and "men from the three kings' realms where our language is spoken" a privileged position compared to that of other foreigners. In a similar way the law code of the Swedish province of Västergötland about 1200 stipulated a higher *wergild* for the manslaughter of a Dane or Norwegian than for the killing of an Englishman or German.

The feeling of Scandinavian brotherhood even became a matter of practical politics during the later Middle Ages when peasants from the Norwegian-Swedish border regions met and pledged themselves in solemn "peasant peace treaties" to maintain peace and brotherly relations, no matter how much their soldierly kings warred against one another.

Even today affinity of language is one of the basic elements of Scandinavianism, although mutual understanding is no longer quite so easy as in bygone times. Danes, Norwegians, and Swedes can become accustomed to the sound of each other's languages within a few weeks. Modern Icelandic, however, is no longer understood outside Iceland and the Faeroe Islands, and Finnish, a language of Asiatic origin, is entirely unintelligible to any Germanic Scandinavian. But although Iceland shed her last legal ties with Denmark when she became a republic in 1944, she still upholds cultural connections with her Scandinavian sister countries by teaching Danish in Icelandic schools. In Finland, Swedish is recognized as the second official language and since 1947 has been taught in all schools, although it is the native language of only 11 per cent of the inhabitants. So, wherever conationals of the five nations gather, understanding is assured without interpreters, simply through alternating use of Danish, Norwegian, and Swedish.

Feelings of brotherhood between the Scandinavian nations were running particularly high in the middle of the nineteenth century. When the surge of pan-German nationalism imperiled the frontiers of the southernmost Scandinavian monarchy, Denmark, volunteers from Norway and Sweden swelled the ranks of the Danish army during the German-Danish war of 1864, but stein, and Lauenburg. Attempts were also made to link the throne this could not prevent the loss of the duchies of Schleswig, Holof Denmark with that of the already united kingdoms of Sweden and Norway by electing King Oscar I of Sweden-Norway hereditary prince of Denmark. But nothing came of this scheme.

Such personal unions were a well-known instrument of government in Scandinavia. From early times the Scandinavian thrones were repeatedly linked together. Denmark and Norway were united for over four hundred years, from 1375 to 1814; and when Norway was ceded to Sweden, she was not absorbed by the Swedish state but remained an autonomous entity under a common Swedish-Norwegian king until 1905. Another union was instituted as late as 1918, when Denmark recognized the independence of Iceland under the condition of joint royal power. But this combination came to an end in 1944, when Iceland in a plebiscite chose a republican form of government in preference to a foreign monarchy.

However, attempts to unite all three kingdoms were generally unsuccessful. A union comprising Denmark, Norway, and Sweden existed during the later Middle Ages, from 1397 to 1527. During the following centuries, when Denmark and Sweden fought each other for the mastery of the Baltic Sea, a royal union was repeatedly but unsuccessfully recommended as a means of ironing out conflicting interests.

Today such unions are no longer practical politics. Experience has shown that joint royal power is usually considered very unsatisfactory in the countries where the union king does not reside. Thus both Norwegians and Icelanders felt that their unions were to their disadvantage, and they freed themselves at the first opportunity. In our time the royal power in the Scandinavian states is so limited that only a very few problems could be solved by merging the heads of state into one. The issue is also complicated by the fact that two of the five countries, Finland and Iceland, are today republics headed by elected presidents.

COMMON LEGISLATION

Practical Scandinavianism had, therefore, to seek different ways. One successful approach was found in the 1870's by means of a Scandinavian monetary convention along lines similar to one in the Latin countries. From then on until the convulsions of World War I, Danish, Norwegian, and Swedish coins and notes, all denominated in kroner and öre, were legal tender in all three countries.

This reform favored closer commercial ties. The ensuing extension of commerce in turn created the need for better co-ordination of the laws covering bank drafts. This was achieved in 1880 through the unprecedented procedure of enacting an identical bill in all three countries, after a joint committee of members of each of the three parliaments had agreed on exactly corresponding texts.

This inter-Scandinavian Bank Drafts Act of 1880 was a tremendous, history-making success. From then on almost every important new codification was created in the same way, whenever conformity of law was considered advantageous. When Finland and Iceland obtained independence in 1918, they too started participating in the co-ordination of civil law. The most important of such common codifications are the Navigation Act of 1892, the Law regarding Purchase and Selling of 1905–1907, the Marriage Law of 1921–1925, and many laws regulating the use of trade-marks, insurance, trade registers, bank checks, commercial agents, selling on the installment plan, promissory notes, property in various aspects, and air traffic. A bill concerning corporation law is in preparation.

Within the scope of family law, co-ordination has been achieved between all five countries concerning marriage and divorce and the legal effects of marriage and adoption. Some of the countries have agreed on common regulation of problems of minority and tutelage and of certain aspects of legacy.

Less necessity has been felt for conformity in criminal law, because the aim of common legislation was highly practical; that is, the legislators were mainly concerned with removing obstacles obstructing trade and communications. However, problems of criminal law have often been discussed on an inter-Scandinavian level, and certain basic principles have been worked out in common, for instance, concerning juvenile delinquency, alcoholism, and criminal abortions. Denmark and Sweden have adopted nearly identical laws about citizenship. During World War I, Denmark, Norway, and Sweden agreed upon identical regulations for maintaining their neutrality in dealing with the belligerent powers. This kind of co-operation within international law was renewed in 1939, immediately after the outbreak of World War II.

These efforts to obtain greater harmony in legislation are greatly facilitated by the fact that principles of law and concepts of justice are largely identical in the Scandinavian countries. The common law of these countries is practically the same; the inter-relations centuries ago created great legal conformity within two wide areas. As an integral part of Sweden until 1809, Finland participated in the major reorganizations of Swedish law in the eighteenth century, such as the codification of civil law in 1734. Finland's autonomy under later Russian rule enabled her to keep these acts on the books. Norway, on her part, achieved codification in 1687. The so-called "Norwegian Law of Christian the Fifth" was to a great extent an adaptation of the corresponding "Danish Law of Christian the Fifth." Iceland was at that time a Norwegian dependency, and the Norwegian code was therefore in force in that country also. Thus Scandinavian legislation was basically organized in two wide spheres, one Swedish-Finnish and the other Danish-Norwegian-Icelandic, as early as in the seventeenth and eighteenth centuries.

The co-ordination of Scandinavian civil law is not only extremely comprehensive, but at the same time flexible and adaptable to local conditions. There is no obligation for any parliament to adopt every detail of a bill drafted in joint committee. Each state is free to make its own changes in an agreed-upon text, and this is done every once in a while, mostly with regard to some minor item rather than a basic principle. One of the countries may refrain from enacting a bill that the others put on their books. The co-ordinated texts being in no sense treaties, each state is at liberty to amend or abolish such laws at will. Since the goal is increasing co-ordination of law, the parliaments are generally reluctant to use their sovereign rights to make such changes without first negotiating with the other countries. Forums for such negotiations are the periodical joint sessions of the Scandinavian ministers of justice, the Scandinavian Inter-parliamentary Union, or the Scandinavian Jurists' Conventions.

Another area of inter-Scandinavian co-ordination is that of social security. Co-operation between the social security agencies of Denmark, Norway, and Sweden began in 1907, when on the initiative of the Swedish social security director, John May, representatives of the three countries met in Copenhagen to discuss problems of workmen's compensation. Since then similar meetings have taken place periodically. After 1919 Finland also participated, and in 1948 Iceland was represented for the first time. Since World War I the ministers of labor and social affairs and their experts have met regularly every two or three years in order to discuss problems of social security.

Co-operation in this field did not aim primarily at co-ordination of social legislation. The main purpose was to carry out the principle of reciprocity within the main branches of social insurance, workmen's compensation, health and unemployment insurance, and lately even employment service. That is, it was considered of paramount importance that nationals of one Scandinavian country who were residents of another should be able to receive the same benefits in their country of residence as that country's own citizens, and that such benefits should be paid in full even if the national concerned had paid part of his contributions in his own country. On a secondary level, co-operation concerned administrative problems, exchange of information and experiences, and so forth. Reciprocity has been achieved by stages and within varying limits, including to date industrial accident insurance and health and unemployment insurance. Old-age pensions and disability insurance have not yet been co-ordinated.

The reciprocity principle was applied earliest and to the fullest extent for industrial accident insurance. A reciprocity convention between Denmark, Norway, and Sweden was signed in 1919. In 1923 reciprocity was extended to Finland and in 1927 to Iceland. In 1937 all five countries concluded a new convention that extended the principles also to cases in which the incapacitated worker was not a resident of the country where he was injured.

A health insurance convention between Denmark and Norway was signed in 1926. It enabled members of an approved health insurance society in one country to be transferred to a similar society in the other regardless of age or health. It was not possible to achieve a similar arrangement with Sweden until Swedish legislation concerning health insurance societies was amended. This was done in 1939, but the outbreak of World War II and the ensuing German occupation of Denmark and Norway made it necessary to postpone a convention until after the war. Nevertheless, during the war the Swedish societies voluntarily accepted many Norwegian and Danish refugees as transferred members. After the war Danish-Swedish and Norwegian-Swedish conventions were concluded in 1947 and 1948, respectively, along the lines of the Danish-Norwegian agreement.

Finland never did participate in these negotiations because its voluntary health insurance has not been developed to the same extent as the health insurance schemes of the other Scandinavian countries. Iceland signed a convention with Denmark in 1939 after the pattern of the Danish-Norwegian arrangement of 1926. This Danish-Icelandic convention was revised in 1948 in accordance with the new Icelandic national insurance law; the revision is expected to become the basis for similar agreements between Iceland, Norway, and Sweden.

There is less reciprocity as far as unemployment insurance is concerned because of greater differences in legislation. For instance, in Denmark and Norway resident foreigners are eligible for membership in unemployment insurance societies on the same conditions as citizens. But in Sweden this is only the case if they belong to a country which, like Denmark since 1936, has a reciprocity arrangement with Sweden. Again, Norway has had compulsory unemployment insurance since 1939, while Denmark and Sweden still keep this insurance on a voluntary basis.

However, reciprocity in the eligibility of foreigners for insurance society membership is not an issue of such practical importance as the transference of members from the societies of one country to those of the other. Particularly since World War II has this become an important question for Denmark and Sweden, because migration has been considerable between the two countries. In May, 1946, therefore, representatives of Danish and Swedish unemployment insurance societies met and worked out a standard agreement concerning the transference of members without loss of status. This standard agreement was adopted by sixty-one Danish societies representing 560,000 members and thirty-four Swedish societies with 890,000 members. Only six Danish and two Swedish unemployment insurance societies have refrained from signing up. As a result of this, most workers from one of the two countries are able to cash benefits in the other, even if they have lived only a comparatively short time in their new country of residence. Similar arrangements are being prepared with Norway.

A scarcity of manpower in the Scandinavian countries after the war led to the drafting of a convention concerning exchange of labor. The most important of its stipulations did away, on a reciprocity basis, with the previously general rule that foreigners could accept employment only with the consent of the authorities of the state. The convention also regulates co-operation between the contracting countries' employment services, exchanges of information about the employment situation, and so forth. It was at once ratified by Denmark and Sweden. Certain Norwegian legal provisions concerning foreign residents have prevented ratification so far, but eventual adherence by that country is expected.

In measures pertaining to workmen's safety, also, a certain amount of Scandinavian co-operation has been achieved. Inter-Scandinavian conferences were held in 1928, 1937, and 1948, in Helsinki, Copenhagen, and Oslo, respectively. At these conferences workshop inspection agencies exchange information, and a commission is now at work outlining joint regulations for safety devices for machinery and tools.

But all this is only a beginning. The final step will be an over-all Scandinavian people's pension. An agreement has already been drafted which will ensure for every Scandinavian citizen full equality of social security with the native population in whichever country he may take up residence.

However, easier crossing of borderlines must not be abused by antisocial elements to secure a haven from the law. Major criminals are of course subject to extradition. In recent years it has been felt appropriate to make some provision for lesser offenders also. Accordingly a bill is in preparation that will make it possible to recover fines and execute short-term prison sentences imposed by a court of one country in all the other countries. After the war, special arrangements were made to prevent Danish and Norwegian quislings from finding refuge in another Scandinavian country.

In civil law suits the court decisions of one country can be executed in another. A Danish-Swedish convention to that effect, concluded as far back as 1861, was later adhered to by Norway.

Scandinavian co-operation is outstanding also in the organizational field. Innumerable societies and associations in practically every branch of industrial, commercial, professional, educational, and political life are organized on a broad inter-Scandinavian basis with the purpose of developing the common ties of the Scandinavian nations. Foremost among these is the Norden society, which is mainly active in sponsoring cultural activities and exchange of students and in organizing inter-Scandinavian meetings and festivals, but which also promotes economic co-operation in many ways. The Scandinavian Co-operative Association is a joint purchasing society of all Scandinavian co-operatives with a turnover of 75,000,000 kroner in 1939.

Still another field of inter-Scandinavian co-operation is foreign relations. Here co-operation assumes the form of meetings of ministers of commerce, prime ministers, foreign and defense ministers, and prominent members of parliamentary committees of foreign affairs. In Geneva, at Lake Success, or wherever international conferences are being held, Scandinavian delegates usually meet to go over problems and agenda together before the official meetings begin. This kind of co-operation is loosely organized and more a matter of habit than legal obligations. Its aim is the straightening out of possible misunderstandings or differences of viewpoint rather than an attempt to force the individual states to follow a common line. The pervading spirit was once expressed by the Danish foreign minister, Gustav Rasmussen, in the following words:

In my opinion, these meetings tell a good deal about what we mean by Scandinavian co-operation. We don't have a solemn treaty in the Latin manner with a lot of articles about how to do what. The main presupposition for the form and the course of these meetings is the fact that we think along similar lines about a lot of problems. Time and again we have found that one of us may express exactly the thoughts the others have been thinking, even if the subject has never been touched before. The similarity of language and common legislation are also pertinent facts.[2]

TOWARD A SCANDINAVIAN UNION?

So far co-operation between the Scandinavian states has been generally limited to practical matters on a day-to-day basis. In recent years, however, many schemes have been publicly discussed that aim at stronger ties of a more permanent character. Such plans range from a mere customs union to full-fledged federation.

The idea of a Scandinavian confederation is nothing new. As far back as 1846 an ardent pan-Scandinavianist, K. J. L. Almquist, outlined a scheme for a common parliament, common monetary system, common mail system, and so forth. Similar plans have been published and discussed from time to time ever since. Nothing ever came of these ideas. An immensely practical people, the Scandinavians felt no urgent need for a common government. They were not apprehensive of a common enemy, and since they were competitors on the world market with many of their foremost export products, they felt no substantial advantage in a customs union.

During World War II, however, the outlook changed. Criticism was voiced in Denmark against the prewar foreign policy of the Danish government, which had clung to the line of unconditional neutrality and had ridiculed a suggestion that the country's defense be co-ordinated with that of the other Scandinavian nations. For scores of years the Danes had paid little attention to their defense establishment. They felt that modern motorized equipment had made the defense of a small nation against a great power an utterly hopeless affair if that country was not large enough for defense in depth and got no help from a first-rate military power.

---

[2] Quoted from the Copenhagen daily, *Politiken*, Sept. 10, 1947.

In their despair over the Nazi occupation, the Danes began to wonder whether the catastrophe might have been avoided if Scandinavia had been a well-armed unit in 1940. After all, better-equipped Sweden had been spared, although it constituted a tempting bridge for German panzer divisions to Norway and Finland. Since it was obvious that even a well-armed Denmark could never by itself stop a German army, the Danes wondered whether a co-ordinated inter-Scandinavian defense might make aggression too costly to be worth while in the future. "It must never happen again" was the general feeling.

The ball was soon taken up in Sweden, where Finland's adventures had caused much anxiety and despair. In neutral Sweden it was easier to consider the matter in detail than under the nose of the Nazis. A number of schemes were worked out and discussed at great length. Just as in Denmark, prominent people—generals, high officials, and even cabinet ministers—offered their views in magazines, newspapers, booklets, speeches, radio discussions, and interviews. Professional soldiers investigated whether a common defense of so widely spread and so thinly populated areas as the Scandinavian countries was feasible and whether it would add substantially to the security of the region.

The atmosphere was generally optimistic. It was agreed that a pan-Scandinavian federation would be a great step forward. The outer states, Finland, Denmark, and Norway, would be substantially less exposed to attack. If obliged to stand by her sister nations, Sweden would be more likely to be drawn into a conflict, of course; but she would be compensated for this by the extension of her aerial-strategic frontier. Military experts stressed that in the age of the air arm it would be of paramount advantage to Sweden if her fighters and bombers could go into action 180 to 500 miles outside her coast or frontier instead of having to operate, as now, from the outskirts of the much-exposed Swedish capital.

The debate in Sweden was immediately echoed in Finland, who, as a partner in Nazi Germany's aggression, had trouble in achieving the strategic frontiers that she had hoped for. Now the Finns wondered whether it would have been wiser to have heeded Sweden's advice for caution and to have stayed out of mischief in the spring of 1941. Had a Scandinavian alliance been a fact in 1939, and not just a utopian idea, Russia might have refrained from attacking Finland.

Quite differently thought the Norwegians. A complete and drastic rebuff of these ideas came from authoritative Norwegian quarters on July 15, 1942, in the form of an inspired editorial in the mouthpiece of the Norwegian government in exile, the *Norsk Tidend* in London.

This article stated that by becoming a belligerent Norway had abandoned her previous neutrality policy for good, and that in defense matters and foreign relations Norway was primarily an Atlantic and secondarily a Scandinavian country. It said: "For us, an Atlantic power fighting the same struggle as the Atlantic powers, Great Britain and the United States, it is natural and logical to seek our security beyond a national defense, in regional agreements with our allies of today."

This rejection of the Swedish scheme did not end the discussion, though it did dismay the Swedish federalists. The debate reached its peak in 1943, with many prominent Swedish politicians, such as the former Social Democratic foreign minister, Richard Sandler, taking a leading part. Their endeavors were markedly restrained by the obvious lack of enthusiasm among the Norwegians, who were, after all, the leading protagonists in the fight for Scandinavia's freedom. The general public in Sweden took a more practical and realistic attitude and documented its Scandinavian sympathies by helping the scores of thousands of refugees who had found haven in Sweden from Nazi persecution. Others worked on concrete plans for assisting in postwar rehabilitation of the devastated areas. During the last two years of the war the discussion petered out. People began to realize that there was not much point in discussing the future setup of Scandinavia as long as nobody knew what the future would look like.

Then came the German breakup. Norway and Denmark were

liberated, refugees returned to their homelands, and within an astonishingly short time Scandinavia, which after all had suffered much less from the war than most other parts of Europe, was getting back to normal once more.

Getting back to normal meant for Scandinavian co-operation the same kind of activity as before the war: inter-Scandinavian conferences, the revival of common legislation, and the co-ordination of foreign policy through joint consultations between ministers and delegates. But it did not mean that the wartime schemes of federalization or defense alliances were revived. In the relieved atmosphere of the newly won peace such plans seemed less urgent than they had a few years earlier. Once more people concentrated on their immediate surroundings. They felt again like Danes, Norwegians, and Swedes rather than Scandinavians. The threat had gone, and all were no longer in the same boat.

CLOSER ECONOMIC CO-OPERATION

The development of the European Recovery Program early in 1947 led to wide discussion of the feasibility of a European customs union. The Scandinavian public participated in this debate. It was felt, however, that so large a union was for the time being pretty much a house in the clouds. More down to earth seemed smaller regional units, and the apparent success of the Benelux experiment led to the revival of discussion about a possible Scandinavian customs union, which was suggested by pan-Scandinavian enthusiasts long ago.

However, the adherents of this scheme did not win sufficient support. Everybody applauded the idea, and its feasibility was investigated in various committees, but nothing came of it. The great difficulty was—and still is—that the economies of the Scandinavian countries do not supplement each other. On the contrary, in many branches of basic importance they are in conflict as competitors on the world markets. Both Norway and Sweden are large-scale exporters of lumber, pulp, newsprint, and other forestry products and compete with each other; in addition, they have to keep up with Finland, whose forestry industries employ one third of the nation's labor force. In a similar way Finland and Norway are competitors in the export of iron ore and metal products, but their efforts are dwarfed by Sweden, which is one of the world's major exporters of iron ore. All three countries produce and export copper; Norway and Sweden, silver and molybdenum, and so forth.

More realistic, it was felt, was co-operation on a more limited basis. Finnish, Norwegian, and Swedish lumber exporters have achieved understanding among themselves to limit competition, and similar arrangements have been made within the aluminum industry. A current scheme foresees the construction of power stations by Danish engineers next to Norwegian cataracts, for the exportation of power through Sweden to Denmark, in order to lessen the latter's dependence on Polish and British coal.

A DEFENSE PACT?

The feeling of relative security, general in Scandinavia at the close of the war, evaporated when Czechoslovakia went Communist. Czechoslovakia was not an Eastern European country with strong social antagonisms and traditions of dictatorship, but a republic with deep democratic roots, in many ways similar to the Northern countries. The Scandinavian people were convinced that the Communist coup was due to pressure from Russia, whose armies in occupied Germany, Austria, and Hungary surrounded the country like pincers. In the general alarm it was felt that what had happened to Czechoslovakia yesterday might happen to, say, Denmark tomorrow.

Once more the necessity for unity among the Scandinavian nations became urgent. But this time the discussion was less academic and more down to earth than it was during the war. Utopian-sounding schemes like federation were discarded. Also the participation of Finland—now in the Soviet orbit—was discounted beforehand. The questions raised were pragmatic, such as these: Should the three sister countries form a Scandinavian defense alliance? If so, should the scope of such a bloc be common defense of their traditional neutrality? Or is neutrality a thing of the past which is not likely to be respected by belligerents in a future war? Should a Scandinavian bloc be tied up with a North Atlantic defense alliance as an implementation of a regional arrangement foreseen in Article 52 of the United Nations Charter?

This discussion went on, in the government as well as in public, for almost a year. An inter-Scandinavian military commission was established to study the feasibility of common defense arrangements. Negotiations broke down in January, 1949, when the foreign ministers of Denmark, Norway, and Sweden, after a meeting in Oslo, issued a communiqué to the effect that "it is not for the time being possible to agree on either the form or the effect" of an alliance.

The Swedish and Norwegian viewpoints had again proved irreconcilable. The Swedes wanted to retain their traditional strict neutrality, and the Norwegians were adamant on linking a Scandinavian alliance to the Western powers with whom the three countries have strong ideological, political, and economic ties. The Danes acted as go-betweens, trying to work out a compromise according to which an "independent" Scandinavian alliance would calibrate its arms to American standards and buy the necessary equipment in the United States. This idea, however, was dropped when it was frowned upon in Washington.

CO-OPERATION IS STILL STRONG

Full-fledged co-ordination of foreign policy in Denmark, Iceland, Norway, and Sweden became impossible when first Norway and then Denmark and Iceland in the spring of 1949 decided to sign the North Atlantic security pact, while Sweden preferred to remain aloof. This did not, however, mean a complete breakdown of inter-Scandinavian co-operation in international affairs.

During the subsequent session of the General Assembly of the United Nations at Lake Success the delegates of the Scandinavian countries met as usual and talked things over before the meetings. Their votes did not necessarily reflect the different countries' attitudes toward the North Atlantic Treaty. It sometimes happened that Denmark and Sweden voted one way and Norway and Iceland another, or that Denmark, Iceland, and Sweden agreed about a question and Norway voted differently.

It cannot be assumed that the line-up of the different Scandinavian countries on the question of joint defense will necessarily be permanent. When the plans for a Scandinavian defense pact were finally dropped during the ministers' meetings at Oslo in January, it was declared in the common communiqué that "at the present time, there is not a sufficient basis for entering into such a mutually binding alliance." Afterwards it was pointed out that evidently the qualification "at the present time" had not been sufficiently stressed in the commentaries of many foreign observers.

In the meantime co-operation is continued and even intensified in every other field as an indication that the unity of Scandinavian civilization is not only a spiritual but also a highly practical reality.

XI

We Americans and Scandinavia

By BRYN J. HOVDE
President, New School for Social Research

THERE have been relationships between the Scandinavian countries and the North American continent since America first became known to Europeans. The earliest contacts are shrouded in the mists of history, but it is well accepted by historians that the viking explorations reached the Western hemisphere though exact locations are not clearly established. The discovery of the North American continent in the year 1000 by the Norwegian viking explorer, Leif Erikson, was only the first of several visits of early Norwegian explorers. Contacts between Norway, Iceland, and Greenland were steadily maintained over a period of 350 years. In Greenland and in Iceland the knowledge of land farther west was maintained in folklore and in the tradition of seamanship down through the ages.

IMMIGRATION

No one knows precisely when the first Scandinavian immigrant set foot on the shores of North America after Columbus' discovery, but in 1638, Oxenstjerna, the chief minister of Sweden's little queen, Christina, sent a colony of Swedes to the Delaware River. They settled on both sides of this majestic stream in what later became Pennsylvania and New Jersey, and took possession of that area in the name of the king of Sweden. Sweden was not, however, in a position to hold this colony, situated as it was between the domains of the Dutch in New York and the English in Pennsylvania. Therefore, in 1655 the new colony ceased to be Swedish except in population and was incorporated in the neighboring Dutch colonies. Some of the proudest names in the colonial and subsequent history of Pennsylvania, New Jersey, and Delaware have been Swedish, and the first president, under the Articles of Confederation (1781), of the Continental Congress was John Hanson, a descendant of one of these Swedes. Meanwhile Norwegian sailors reached the Atlantic seaboard, including New York, in various private ways. Quite in accordance with custom, Scandinavian seamen jumped ship or left the crew of a vessel with the consent of the captain and settled down here and there, wherever opportunity seemed to be favorable.

It was not, however, until the end of the first quarter of the nineteenth century that immigration from Scandinavian countries to the United States assumed the proportions of a steady stream. In 1825 a small Norwegian vessel named *Restaurationen* left the Norwegian port of Stavanger crowded with fifty-three emigrants deliberately intending to find land and settle down near Rochester, New York. They were following the advice and guidance of the scout they had sent on before them in 1821, one Cleng Peerson, who had traveled widely in the United States and returned with glowing pictures of opportunities to participate in the rapid development of America. These particular emigrants were mostly Quakers, who resented the opprobrium and persecutions to which they were subjected by the Lutheran State Church. Among Norwegians in America the descendants of the *Restaurationen* emigrants have tried to assume the position of Mayflower descendants. The settlement at Rochester, New York, maintained itself throughout the following decades but never attracted any great additional numbers from Norway, and inevitably some of the original settlers there moved on with the stream of migration to the west and southwest. Except for sporadic individual emigrations, the next full shipload to leave Norway departed ten years later in 1835. From that date forward, even to the present time, Norwegians have come to the United States every year; the curve of their numbers rose steadily until about 1914 and then declined.

The beginning of Swedish emigration was later. The first large group to leave Sweden was the Eric Jansonist religious sect in 1846–1848. This group settled in Illinois but quickly dispersed for various reasons, though the original settlement continued for some time as a kind of center. This first Swedish colony had many of the aspects of other dissenting religious colonies established in America in the 1830's and 1840's, even with tendencies to communistic organization. It was not long before the Swedish stream of emigration to the United States also reached large proportions, following approximately the same curve as that of Norway, although the absolute number of Swedes to emigrate to America was greater.

Danish emigration immediately followed, though its beginnings are not so precise as Swedish and Norwegian beginnings and Danish emigration never attained the relative volume of Norwegian and Swedish emigration. Scandinavian settlement in the United States followed the general trend of popular movements in this country. Hence we find Americans of Scandinavian descent all over the country, but located en masse particularly in Wisconsin, Illinois, Michigan, Minnesota, Iowa, North and South Dakota, Montana, Washington, Oregon, and California. Goodly numbers have always remained in New York, particularly in Brooklyn.

Up and down the Atlantic and Pacific coasts and along the Great Lakes, Scandinavian and especially Norwegian fishermen and sailors have settled and contributed not a little to the advancement of American maritime occupations. But for the most part Scandinavians in America have been farmers. They generally came from agricultural communities in Scandinavia, where, until the First World War, agricultural pursuits far outranked all other occupations in the production of wealth. Only lately has Scandinavian emigration been from the urban centers, and no small part has consisted of trained engineers and craftsmen.

The causes of Scandinavian emigration have been many and highly diverse. Undoubtedly the very first emigration, at least from Sweden and Norway, was occasioned by a wish on the part of religious dissenters to escape from the bondage of countries with established religions; though persecutions in the Scandinavian countries were not severe or vicious, they did constitute a violation of freedom of worship, which was what the first immigrants to America sought to find. Another reason for leaving the Scandinavian countries was the desire to escape bureaucracy and social discrimination by Scandinavian upper classes. From the 1840's on, all three Scandinavian countries experienced a progressive revolt of the common people against aristocracy and bureaucracy. It was this revolt that established the democracy that now obtains in the Scandinavian countries, but during the great emigration years there were many Scandinavians who expressed this revolt, not by staying home and improving conditions but by emigrating. Needless to say, however, the greatest of all reasons why Scandinavians came to America was to escape restricted economic conditions, a relatively overpopulated countryside, and an economic system that afforded little opportunity for ambitious individuals with high initiative; for until the late 1850's and early 1860's there were many restrictions upon freedom of internal trade in Scandinavia and many legally established occupational monopolies. For many decades, even in 1835, America had been known to people in the Scandinavian countries as the land of economic freedom and opportunity. After the arrival of the first Scandinavian immigrants to America, letters and pamphlets began to pour from them to friends and newspapers at home describing the land to which they had come, usually in glowing terms, all carefully calculated to prove to Norwegians, Swedes, and Danes back home that the writers had been justified by success in emigrating and that America had room for their friends and relatives too. These documents spread the "America fever" like wildfire, and shipping companies as well as agents from America to recruit labor promptly created opportunities for mass movement across the Atlantic. Thus America became a beacon light to the Scandinavian peoples; as time passed there was hardly a family remaining in Norway, Sweden, and Denmark that did not have relatives in the United States. Except for Ireland, it is doubtful that any European country including England sent so many of its people, mostly its best and youngest, to America as did Norway and Sweden.

The consequences of Scandinavian emigration to the United States have been momentous to both the Scandinavian countries and the United States. The United States acquired a substantial stock of North European peoples not only capable of sustained and skillful labor, of bringing into development some of the best land in the world, and of enthusiastic response to the opportunities of individual enterprise and initiative in the heyday of that system, but with a basic education in the old countries and with a religious and democratic background that enabled them quickly to become full partners in the development of citizenship in America. How fully and quickly they felt themselves to be Americans and participants in its specific life is but inadequately illustrated by the immediate formation on the beginning of the Civil War of a Norwegian-American regiment in Wisconsin, which, under the leadership of Colonel Heg, fought with heroism and distinction to save the Union and establish freedom of labor in the United States. Not only did they develop the land and found businesses and banks, not only did many Scandinavians participate as inventors and promoters in the technological revolution after the Civil War in this country, but they early established religious congregations and synods; schools, sectarian as well as public; newspapers; and other manifestations of transitional culture. They felt themselves competent as soon as they arrived on these shores to take part in our politics, first at the local township and county levels and later at the state and national levels. The sons and daughters and later descendants of Scandinavian immigrants quickly and almost imperceptibly merged with the general public in their communities by intermarriage outside their own national group, though there are still Scandinavian communities in America that, because of their large size, remain relatively isolated and self-contained. Space does not here permit a proper survey of the contributions of Scandinavian immigrants to American life, but all American historians recognize that they have been creditable and, in proportion to numbers, significant.

By reason of emigration in such numbers, the Scandinavian countries themselves have also been markedly affected in their development. It is sufficient here to say that large-scale emigration in all three countries proved to be a safety valve for the draining off of population pressures, which, under the more primitive technological and economic conditions of the second half of the nineteenth century, created social problems of great magnitude. The overwhelming wish to emigrate on the part of many people, furthermore, brought home to successive governments in each country the need to solve these social problems and their underlying economic basis. Thus it may be said that emigration from the Scandinavian countries, large enough and long enough to be thoroughly alarming to responsible Scandinavians at home, contributed a great deal to the development of that good society so much admired today wherever democracy remains the popular ideal. There were even direct economic results of a favorable nature, such as the stream of dollar remittances from emigrating people to relatives at home and the return of some Scandinavian *émigrés* with dollar savings in their pockets. Another economic consequence that deserves to be mentioned is the boost given to Scandinavian shipping by the emigrant passengers' demand for space and even by the greatly improved architectural design of ships in the clipper period, directly imported into Norway by two young Norwegians who emigrated to the United States to master it. Actually the study of the effect of emigration upon the Scandinavian countries is an enormous subject, by no means completed by scholars of any of these countries or of America, in spite of the fact that in the first decade of the twentieth century a Swedish governmental commission devoted to this matter no less than eleven stout volumes of data.

GOVERNMENT AND POLITICS

The Scandinavian countries, with their relatively high educational standards and their close connection with general European thought, followed the same lines of political thinking as did France, England, Germany, and Western Europe generally, a line of thinking that culminated eventually in the development of contemporary democracy. In all of this thinking the American example was significant.

Under the influence of the political and social philosophy of the time, particularly as represented by Montesquieu and Rousseau, the American colonists were pictured in Scandinavian literature, as well as in Scandinavian translations from the French and English, as "simple," "natural," "virtuous," and therefore ideal. Their simple democratic life was praised and things thought to be American became highly popular in the circles of the intelligentsia. At the same time the mounting nationalism of these countries as expressed in pre-Romanticist and Romanticist writing readily identified the culture of Scandinavia, particularly that of the mountain peasants, with this idealization of the primitive, making it easy for Scandinavians to think of themselves as being nearer to the Americans than to the ultrasophisticated and therefore presumably false culture of the upper classes. When the American Revolution began it quickly engrossed the attention and excited the enthusiasm of Scandinavian literary and political circles, though in Scandinavia too opinion was much divided on the propriety of the American cause. But this very division of opinion, this taking of sides, served to increase the interest in matters American and to excite high devotions or antipathies. The writings of American leaders became known to not a few Scandinavians even before the outbreak of the Revolution in 1775. From that year forward, however, the study of the American cause became ever more widespread in Scandinavia. The writings of Benjamin Franklin, particularly *Poor Richard's Almanac,* appeared in each of the

Scandinavian countries in translation and became almost household reading. Benjamin Franklin was pictured, in Scandinavia as elsewhere, as a typical representative of the Americans, who disdained the frilly dress and the artificial manners then the mode in European upper circles, and also the affected philosophy of the time. He was thought to be a man of simple dignity, a man of the people, and a great natural scientist and philosopher. Some of the writings of Benjamin Rush became almost as popular as those of Franklin. Here, to many Scandinavians, was another product of the simple life of America, a great medical scientist who was at the same time a great political philosopher and true representative of his society. George Washington became virtually a national hero to many Scandinavians and was compared to the simple, strong generals of the Roman Republic then greatly idealized in Western society.

The Declaration of Independence of the American colonies was circulated in all three countries in good translations and was cherished by the intellectuals and many commoners alike as the greatest contemporary statement of the rights of man. In Scandinavian thinking it came to occupy a position almost above the French Declaration of the Rights of Man formulated during the French Revolution. Gradually the name of Thomas Jefferson became known to Scandinavians, principally as the author of the Declaration of Independence. His more theoretical, political, social, and scientific writings did not penetrate as deeply as those of Rush and Franklin. It should be added here that the disposition of many Norwegians, Swedes, and Danes to favor the Americans rather than the British in the struggle for independence was conditioned very largely by the mercantile and shipping interests they had with the respective contestants. The war of the American Revolution was one in which the Scandinavian merchants and shipowners made tremendous fortunes by reason of the neutrality of the three countries, the freedom with which they ranged the seas, and the enormous demand not only for Scandinavian supplies but for the goods of other countries that they could carry in their ships. The members of the nobility, particularly in Sweden, were divided. Count von Fersen became a virtual Lafayette in the American Revolution. He knew Lafayette; he fought in Washington's armies and acquired a great admiration for American revolutionary leadership. This made him highly suspect to the absolute Swedish king, Gustav III, and particularly to Gustav IV, though it may be added that in later life, when it became clear to him where the American and French revolutions were leading European development, Fersen himself became an ultraconservative.

This interest in the Americans as representatives of a simple but good democratic society, and especially the eagerness with which the commercial and shipping interests hailed the independence of the American colonies and the resultant freedom of trade, went a long way in preparing Scandinavia philosophically for the great political reforms of the late eighteenth and early nineteenth centuries. It stimulated eager discussion of subjects and institutions formerly taboo and served to strengthen the trend, already developing naturally out of Scandinavian life, toward the end of absolutism and the establishment of more democratic forms. The American constitution of 1789 was quickly translated into the Scandinavian languages and provoked continuous discussion of the defects of the existing Scandinavian regimes. It was at hand in Sweden when the constitution of 1809 was devised, but that constitution had to be formulated too quickly in view of the international emergency to be greatly influenced by the American. But the Norwegian constitution adopted in 1814 shows many effects of careful study and attempts at adapting the American constitution to Norwegian conditions. By 1814, however, the reaction had begun to set in, and for almost twenty years the American form of government was looked upon as being radical and subversive. As a matter of fact, the whole period from approximately 1775 to 1835 was one in which proponents of the existing Scandinavian orders viewed partisans of the American way as subversive. Yet a considerable amount of progress in the direction of democracy was made.

When in the late 1830's and 1840's the strength of the Holy Alliance waned and the social crisis became acute in the Scandinavian countries as elsewhere in Europe, the demand for further political reform in the direction of democracy reasserted itself. Then, too, interest in American democracy revived sharply. De Tocqueville's famous book on American democracy was widely read, both in the original and in translations, and cited over and over again in all three countries to justify changes in the Scandinavian political systems. To be sure, Norway had already (in 1814) adopted a constitution that, with interpretation and with the growing strength of the peasant political movement, enabled reforms in that country to move forward with less reference to American democracy than in Denmark and Sweden. It was especially in Sweden, where the constitution of 1809 had done little more than concede superficially to the demands of the urban middle classes, the bureaucracy, and the peasantry for limitations upon the absolute power of the king, that America became a model. By 1848 the question of Scandinavian political reforms, particularly the abolition of the Swedish four-chamber system in favor of a two-chamber system, was acute, and in that dispute both the American constitution, particularly as explained by De Tocqueville, and the Norwegian constitution, which already embodied American influence, were uppermost in the minds of those pressing for reform. The beginnings of emigration from the Scandinavian countries to America served considerably to strengthen both the demand for reform and acquaintance with America. Not even the reformers were united in their idealization of America, however. Neither the Swedes nor the Danes were uncritical worshipers of the American system. But even the most conservative reformers did from time to time justify their position in part by reference to American institutions. There is no doubt that what eventually materialized, both in the Danish constitution of 1849 and the great Swedish reform of 1865, reflected much thought on American conditions. The great Swedish parliamentary reform of 1865 and the Danish constitutional revision after the disastrous Schleswig-Holstein War of 1864 set the political pattern of those two countries for the remainder of the nineteenth century. The pattern had already been set in Norway in 1814. But even after 1865 the question of the parliamentary form of government versus the American congressional system was actively debated year by year. In the end, due mainly to natural Scandinavian conditions, the parliamentary form of government was adopted in all three countries. This was not, of course, due to any antipathy against things American, for America was never so popular in Scandinavia as between 1865 and 1900, and in the American Civil War the Scandinavian peoples almost unanimously supported the cause of the North and freedom against the cause of the South and its system of human slavery. Abraham Lincoln became, to even a greater degree than George Washington in his time, almost a national hero in each of the Scandinavian countries, and American travelers often found his picture pasted on the walls of humble peasant homes.

After 1900, however, America ceased to loom up as before in the minds of Scandinavian peoples as a great political ideal. By that time they had themselves achieved political maturity in forms practically as democratic as those on this side of the Atlantic. With the exception of Norway, suffrage was not as universal as in America, and only on that point did Swedish and Danish reformers point to America as an example. After 1914 it was rather American liberals who looked to Scandinavia for inspiration than Scandinavians who looked to America. And while it cannot be said that political reforms in America have followed the Scandinavian pattern, it requires only a superficial knowledge of American commentary since 1914 to know that American liberals have viewed the Scandinavian countries with growing interest and admiration as types of almost ideal democracy. Unfortunately Americans have not had the same detailed knowledge of Scandinavian democracy as Scandinavians have had of American democracy; hence their admiration of the Scandinavian countries has been relatively uncritical and romantic. But it would be highly mistaken to discount altogether the influence of this American adulation of things Scandinavian as a factor in the evolution of American social and political thought. Scandinavians today are highly critical of some aspects of American politics and political practice. The influence of what is generically called Wall Street has been deeply deplored in the Scandinavian countries, where many warnings have been issued against allowing similar power to develop in their own country. Furthermore, Scandinavians have viewed and still view with great disapproval our political and social discrimination against Negroes and other minority groups. Finally, the Scandinavians are unable to comprehend the irrational mentality of Americans when it comes to dealing with socialism and communism. Though almost direct neighbors of the Soviet Union, the Scandinavian countries face the problem of communism with the same dislike of that system as Americans exhibit, but with far less fear. To some extent, perhaps, this is mere fatalism before possibilities that they are too small to prevent. But it is mainly a sense of security deeply rooted in the confidence they have in their own democracy.

SOCIAL QUESTIONS

Closely related to the interest of Scandinavians in American democracy and vice versa has been their exchange of interest on social questions. Here the influence of the United States on Scandinavia was, until approximately 1900, greater than that of Scandinavia upon the United States. To Scandinavians, from American colonial times down to the beginning of the twentieth century America seemed almost the ideal social republic. An important exception must, of course, be made for the institution of Negro slavery, which the Scandinavians early began to condemn. But the high degree of economic and therefore also social equality characteristic of America from the earliest period down to the twentieth century was a constant source of stimulation and an object of imitation by many Scandinavian social philosophers and reformers. The Swedish botanist, Peter Kalm, who traveled in the American colonies in 1750, commented with great enthusiasm upon the almost total absence of poverty in those parts of America that he visited. Nothing like that existed in the Scandinavian countries then or for many decades thereafter, for not only was the land poor and technology primitive, but, in common with Western European civilization generally, the Scandinavians had from the beginning of their history developed systems of landholding and property ownership requiring for the minimal exploitation of natural resources an uneven division of wealth, so that some might produce leadership. This problem was greater in some parts of Scandinavia than in others; where land was relatively accessible and where it could be assembled in considerable estates, social inequalities were far greater than in the poorer mountainous districts of Norway and Sweden. In the mountains land was more evenly divided and social equality was greater, though poverty obtained to a greater degree. As population increased, particularly in the late eighteenth and early nineteenth centuries, its pressure upon meager natural resources under the primitive technology of the time became so great as to create an acute crisis in all three countries, though worse in Sweden and Norway than in Denmark. In the long and often bitter discussions conducted on the problem of its alleviation, America appeared often in word and symbol as the ideal for which the Scandinavian countries ought to strive. But America was more a practical factor than an example, for its very existence and its need for expansion opened the way for large-scale emigration and thus relief from the pressure of population.

The great humanitarian reforms that characterized the Scandinavian countries, particularly in the nineteenth century, brought many allusions to and even direct connections with America. The emancipation of women in the Scandinavian countries was accompanied by descriptions of the freedom women enjoyed in America, particularly in such a widely read book as Fredrika Bremer's account of her travels in America. She and others wrote novels and polemic literature favoring the equality of women with men in both economic and political spheres as well as in social and family relationships. The Scandinavian feminists were well acquainted with the American leaders from Susan B. Anthony to Carrie Chapman Catt.

The movement for prison reform in Scandinavia took its inspiration and a great deal of its technical knowledge not only from the contemporary movement in England, led by Elizabeth Fry, but from such American models as the Auburn system.

More distinctly America-connected than almost any other American social reform movement was the temperance movement. In the eighteenth century the Scandinavian countries reached an absolute high in their consumption of alcoholic beverages. Without going into a detailed explanation of the reasons for this phenomenon, it is safely recorded that conditions in many parts of Scandinavia were as bad as in Ireland. The temperance movement had its origin in America and quickly started offshoots in England and Ireland. It did the same in Scandinavia, where, in the second quarter of the nineteenth century, temperance societies were formed in great numbers. Their tracts and their leaders often alluded, as did many of the "America" letters from Scandinavian emigrants, to the high state of sobriety and consequent prosperity to be found in the United States. American temperance leaders actually traveled in the Scandinavian countries and preached the gospel there.

In the field of education too, America, particularly in the nineteenth century, provided Scandinavian leaders and reformers with much inspiration and guidance. Scandinavian education was relatively advanced from the late eighteenth century onwards, and it must not be supposed that American influence was as great as that of Prussia, or that the Scandinavian countries blindly followed the lead of either America or Prussia. In the area of education the Scandinavian countries were more independent and original than in many others and became themselves examples for all the world. This is nowhere so well illustrated as among the Scandinavian emigrants to the United States and Canada, where, after having broken the wilderness and founded settlements, they first established religious congregations and then immediately schools, both public and denominational.

Having themselves achieved cultural and political maturity by about 1900, the Scandinavian countries became examples to the United States in their dealing with some social problems. Thus Danish, Swedish, and Norwegians consumers' and producers' co-operatives became the ideal of such American reformers as Frederick C. Howe, who viewed Denmark as a "co-operative state," the very aegis of the co-operative movement. Later, in the early 1930's, Marquis Childs pointed to Sweden as the land of "the middle way," where the consumers' co-operative movement functioned as the great regulator of both the economy and society. If Childs's picture of Sweden was somewhat saccharine, it was, nevertheless, exceedingly popular in the United States and contributed not a little to the enthusiasm and almost religious devotion with which many Americans sought to build the co-operative movement here.

The area of labor relations is another in which Americans have looked to the Scandinavian countries for information and guidance. The Scandinavian labor movements were almost as slow to develop strength and maturity as the American. They are almost wholly a twentieth-century phenomenon, but to Americans interested in labor problems the Scandinavian labor movements exhibit many advances over our own. The Scandinavian labor movements are more completely developed, both as to organization and as to leadership and responsibility. Where in America we were slow to resort to legislation, either to protect or regulate labor or employers, the Scandinavians were relatively quick. The responsibility with which Scandinavian labor has viewed its function in society has often been cited as an example to American labor. Both official commissions and private students of labor questions have assembled information on Scandinavian labor and its methods, from which they have hoped that American labor itself as well as government might learn.

The movement to expand social security to an ever-widening number also achieved prominence in the Scandinavian countries earlier than in the United States and has consequently been followed over here with interest and approbation. Opponents of social security, on the other hand, have condemned the Scandinavian systems as conflicting with "the American way." The Scandinavian countries, by reason of dire necessity, developed their fundamental patterns of public health and public medicine as early as the seventeenth century, moving progressively to extend and perfect them, until today there is not a hamlet in either of these three countries where a doctor's care or a midwife's services and the use of a hospital are not provided by the public to those who need or choose to use them. American proponents of public health services have studied the Scandinavian systems with great interest and point to them as proof of the proper exercise of responsibility by society for the welfare of its members. American opponents of the public interest in the problems of health, however, have been even more vehement in denunciation of the Scandinavian systems, saying, in contravention of plain fact, that they exemplify the deterioration of medical science when it gets into public hands. This has not prevented great American foundations such as the Rockefeller Foundation from investing American money to promote medical science in Sweden or dentistry in Norway.

To American liberals today the Scandinavian countries are often the prime examples of the way in which society ought to care for itself through measures of social security, and Scandinavian concern for the welfare of its own citizens is to them a model for America to follow.

ECONOMIC RELATIONSHIPS

Passing reference has already been made to certain aspects of the relation between the Scandinavian and American economies. Commercial access to America was won by Scandinavian merchants and shipowners during the American War for Independence when the British monopoly was broken. As soon as the war had ended, in 1783, the United States negotiated its first commercial treaty with the king of Denmark, then also the ruler of Norway. That treaty embodied the most important principles of historical American policy in international trade, principles that were to be followed in subsequent treaties with many countries. The Scandinavian countries and the United States had important similar and complementary interests, such as the freedom of the seas, the most-favored-nations rule, and free trade. On the other hand, their own products were not for many decades readily interchangeable since they produced roughly the same commodities. Some American cotton and tobacco went to the Scandinavian countries, and some Swedish iron to America, where it was first known as "Norway iron" because it usually arrived in Norwegian ships. For a long time the principal Scandinavian exports to America were human beings.

The great technological revolution came to the Scandinavian countries mainly from England and Germany, but even very early America made some contributions, particularly in the important field of agricultural machinery. The first American plow was brought to Denmark in 1835 and promptly proved itself much superior to any other. Mowers and threshing machinery came later, though it was not until after 1865 that farm machinery was widely adopted even in Denmark. The steamboat, mainly an American invention, was introduced into Scandinavia via England and quickly found a place in the growing communications system in the 1820's; and thirty years later each of the Scandinavian countries installed its first electric telegraph lines, also an American discovery. The first Swedish private bank, Enskilda, was organized in Stockholm in 1856 by A. O. Wallenberg after the pattern of banks he had observed on a visit to the United States. Without such banks, which were quickly founded also in Norway and Denmark, the modernization of the Scandinavian economies would have been greatly delayed. At the World's Fair in New

York in 1853, a milepost in international technological exchange, Sweden and Norway had a small joint exhibit.

After the middle of the nineteenth century the business and technological interchanges between the United States and Scandinavia grew so numerous and regular that developments can only be sketched roughly. As Danish, and also to some extent Swedish, agriculture went over to dairying, the import of American fodders (e.g., cottonseed cakes) and grains assumed large proportions. Both in agriculture and in industry Scandinavian journals and government reports described American implements and methods in considerable detail and suggested how they might be adapted to local needs and conditions. Here as elsewhere America became the legendary land of miracle-producing machinery. The Scandinavian countries developed rapidly in modern technology. The sciences were studied and technological institutes were supported. Together with a strong tradition of superior craftsmanship, these institutes produced many highly skilled inventors and engineers, not a small number of whom emigrated to escape the limitations of the relatively small-scaled Scandinavian economies. This was particularly true in the twentieth century, though as early as the American Civil War the Swedish-American Ericsson perhaps saved the Northern navy from the Southern ironclads by inventing the *Monitor*. Kenneth Bjork has most adequately described the contributions of Norwegian technicians to the development of America in his book, *Saga in Steel and Concrete* (1947). Two such technicians, Dahm and Singstad, were mainly responsible for the solution of the engineering problems and the basic designs that created respectively the subway systems and the underwater tunnels of New York City. What the Danish-born William Knudsen has contributed to the automobile industry and American war production is well known. Similarly, of course, the spectacular expansion in Scandinavian industrial development since 1900 was due in part to the influence of American technology. It may be doubted whether history affords any better example of mutual advantage in the exchange of experts and technicians, now so important to the world, than that of America and the Scandinavian countries.

Naturally as the technological revolution made progress on both sides of the Atlantic, the volume of direct trade between America and Scandinavia increased. But prior to 1945 neither was absolutely essential to the other, for America needed little that the Scandinavian countries could produce, and trade with other parts of the world, especially Western Europe, loomed much larger in the Scandinavian total than trade with America. Nevertheless, direct trade between Scandinavia and America grew in volume and at a more rapid rate between the two world wars than earlier. Even before 1914 each of the Scandinavian countries had established direct shipping lines to America carrying both passengers and freight. And immediately upon the conclusion of the Second World War interests in the three Scandinavian countries joined hands to found the Scandinavian Airlines System on a far-flung network including America as a main point. Thus communications and travel were facilitated, resulting in closer acquaintance on both sides of the Atlantic and in valuable dollar income to the Scandinavians from the tourist trade. The American dollar has always been welcome in the Scandinavian countries. But it became essential as the most acceptable international medium of exchange or hard currency for a brief period after the First World War and again after the Second World War. Consequently in these periods, particularly in the latter, when many factors caused Scandinavian as well as other eyes the world over to be turned toward America, this country attained an unwonted prominence in Scandinavian thinking.

CULTURAL RELATIONS

The development of Western European civilization is one of the world's most significant historical phenomena. It is noteworthy that the Scandinavian countries and America have had somewhat similar offside roles in it and that these roles have coincided uniquely in point of time. The Scandinavians, of course, have always been in and of Western Europe; they have been at some distance, however, and rather gently washed by the ebb and flow of the more violent cultural tides emanating from and gushing over England and the Continent. The same has been true of America lying over the seas. Both have kept pace with the evolution of that culture and both have made their greatest contributions in the last two hundred and fifty years. With Great Britain, the Scandinavian countries and America are today the strong, outlying bastions of Western European civilization. Between them there are well-worn paths of cultural exchange and interaction. We must now take note of those that connect the Scandinavian countries and America.

One of the distinguishing features of Western European civilization is its intellectual freedom. Under that freedom the sciences have developed into another such distinguishing feature. It is not strange therefore that history reveals continuous contact between scientists in America and Scandinavia. The Swedish botanist, Linné (1707–1778), who developed the system of classifying plants, regarded America as a rich field for botanical exploration. Though the connection was not direct, American chemistry in common with that science everywhere owes much to the Swedish chemist Berzelius (1779–1848) for basic work on atomic weights and chemical nomenclature. Scandinavian and American scientists have followed one another's work ever since Benjamin Franklin and Benjamin Rush excited the interest of Scandinavian students in the eighteenth century; the awareness has been particularly marked in the twentieth. Especially in the last twenty-five years have the contacts been frequent and direct. The American-Scandinavian Foundation has fostered them with scholarships enabling students from either area to study in the other. Thus the great nuclear physicist in Copenhagen, Niels Bohr, contributed to the development of atomic energy not only by his direct participation in the Manhattan Project but also by his instruction of such American students as Harold Urey.

Neither Americans nor Scandinavians have been much given to philosophy. At this high plane of intellectual endeavor, therefore, they have had little to do with one another. But there have been many religious interactions. In the late eighteenth century and early nineteenth century each of the Scandinavian countries experienced a religious awakening of the lower classes in both town and countryside, expressing itself in revivalistic meetings, pietistic orthodoxy, and lay leadership. This was not due to any marked foreign influence, for the revival remained on the whole within the framework of the established Lutheran Church, though often deplored by the regular clergy. There were, however, some secessions from the state churches, and it was mainly with these that American ties were established, though it must be borne in mind that the Lutheran churches founded in America by Scandinavian immigrants maintained many contacts with the state churches in the homelands.

Mention has already been made that a group of Norwegian Quakers emigrated in 1825. Norwegian Quakerism came first from England, but as early as 1818 it was strengthened by a visit from the French-American leader, Stephen Grellet. The Danish Baptist Church owed its beginnings in 1839 to a sailor who had learned that doctrine in America. A Swedish sailor, Olaus Nilsson, greatly influenced by the Baptist seamen's mission in New York, became the leader of the Baptists in Sweden, where the first congregation appeared in 1848. Though he and some of his flock soon emigrated to America, where Nilsson became a circuit rider, his work was continued successfully in Sweden by Anders Wiberg, who had also been in America. Methodism too established itself in Scandinavia and maintained close relations with the American as well as the British brethren. In the twentieth century religious bonds between Scandinavia and America have been established and strengthened by the ecumenical movement in which the Swedish archbishops, Söderblom and Eidem, and the Norwegian bishop, Berggrav, have been active. American Protestant religious leadership has recently been considerably influenced by the Danish Søren Kierkegaard, rather belatedly discovered since he died in 1855. There is evident in Scandinavian-American religious relations, as in others in the last few decades, an interest of the whole peoples in one another, not limited as formerly to the interest of the emigrants in their original homes. This, of course, is evidence of their growing consciousness that they belong to the same basic Western European civilization.

The interest of the Scandinavian and American peoples in one another's literature and art is further proof of their recognition of a common culture. Ole Bull practically conquered America with his violin and Jenny Lind with her voice, and the music of Edvard Grieg caused the name of Norway to be more often spoken in America than all her ships and sailors. Ibsen was perhaps the first Scandinavian (Norwegian) to be widely read in America, followed hard by the Swedish Strindberg. From their time forward the giants of Scandinavian letters and, as time passed into the nineteen-twenties and thirties, even a number of writers of smaller stature became popular, particularly the Norwegian Knut Hamsun, the Swedish Selma Lagerlöf, and the Danish Johannes V. Jensen. Some American publishers, like Alfred Knopf, have drawn heavily upon Scandinavian literature for American readers. Similarly, the recent high degree attained by Scandinavian architecture, furniture, and craftsmanship has been admired and imitated here.

America, however, has only recently come to be viewed in Scandinavia as ranking high in literature and art. For many decades after the American Revolution little or nothing was known in Scandinavia about American developments in the fine arts. There was some acquaintance with Longfellow and Emerson and Mark Twain; but it was the American novel, represented by Dreiser, Anderson, Hemingway, and Steinbeck, and the American drama of O'Neill and Lillian Hellman that finally caused Scandinavian bookshops to stock up on American literature. And, of course, American motion pictures. American music, especially jazz, and its counterpart, the dance, have become very popular since 1914.

AMERICA AND SCANDINAVIA, PARTNERS IN DEMOCRACY

Since 1940 the American and Scandinavian peoples have been drawn very close by their need of one another in the struggles against authoritarian political systems. The proud Swedes to be sure stand somewhat aloof, partly because they were luckily neutral in the war and partly because they lie so near to Finland and Finland is so very much exposed to the Soviet Union. But their hearts are also with the Western nations. The Scandinavian peoples know that but for the United States their liberties would have been lost in the war with Nazi Germany, even those of neutral Sweden. They know also that it is to the Americans that they must look for the preservation of those liberties against Soviet imperialism. But the Scandinavians view America with some misgivings also, first because they are not quite sure what use she may make of her new-found power, and second because they fear she may not be present when they need her.

No European countries have made greater and more successful efforts at self-help than the Scandinavian in postwar reconstruction. Sweden, physically undamaged by war, has contributed as much per capita as the Americans to aid her neighbors and many other war-devastated countries. By wise investment policies Norway and Denmark have largely replenished their capital plants on land and sea, and they are producing now at considerably more than prewar rates. Their Labor and Socialist governments have accomplished these results by systems of planning and controls and by austerity that many Americans decry but nevertheless urge upon all European beneficiaries of Marshall Plan aid. Of that aid the Scandinavian countries have requested comparatively little. What they have needed has been due primarily to circumstances beyond their own control, for they cannot alone mend the broken strands of world trade nor bridge the dollar gap. For these recoveries they must wait upon world-wide improvement. Meanwhile the Scandinavian peoples are building the defenses of democracy at home by extending the stake of every citizen in the common welfare and by developing his understanding through education and cultural growth.

For the Scandinavians, as for the Americans, the era of national isolation is over. Not only is this true on the cultural side when students, professors, and experts are exchanged as never before. It is true also in the political sense. Sweden is in this respect a somewhat special case. She is, like Norway and Denmark, a loyal member of the United Nations, which they would all wish to see become the guardian of their peace. And no more than her sister countries can Sweden place her whole reliance on the Security Council, which they all recognize to be locked in dire dissension. Yet after Norway and Denmark refused Sweden's offer of a binding Scandinavian alliance to preserve their neutrality in any future war, Sweden was still unwilling to join the North Atlantic defense alliance. In a sense, therefore, Sweden faces the East alone, relying upon her own not inconsiderable but incomplete industrial war potential and upon an army that has not seen action since 1814. Norway and Denmark, on the other hand, are under the protection of the North Atlantic defense alliance, of which the United States is the strongest member. But perhaps this isolation is more apparent than real, for it is highly doubtful that a Soviet attack upon Sweden would go unchallenged by the North Atlantic states.

CONCLUSION

The peoples of Scandinavia and the United States pass the middle of the twentieth century bound together by almost every tie that is possible between sovereign states. They are very near in their cultures and eagerly exchange their material goods and have the same interest in those of the whole wide world. They represent to a paramount degree the same rights of person and of civic action, even though upon the American escutcheon there is still the blot of racial prejudice. They have the same desire for peace, though not at any price.

Appendix:

Statistical Tables of Scandinavia

According to the current rate of exchange 100 Danish kroner correspond to 103.20 Norwegian kroner and 74.78 Swedish kronor. This difference in the rate of exchange does not correspond exactly to the difference in the cost of living, the Swedish currency being somewhat overestimated, in particular since the raising of the Swedish krona in 1946.

Table 1. Area and population.

Region	Year	Area	Population	Population per sq. mi.
		sq. mi.	*thousands*	
Denmark *	1947	16,576	4,146	250
Norway †	1947	125,194	3,145	25
Sweden	1947	173,396	6,842	39
Greenland	1945	840,006	21	0.03
Faeroe Islands	1945	540	29	54
Spitzbergen	1947	24,553	0.6	0.02

* Excluding Greenland and the Faeroe Islands.
† Excluding Spitzbergen.

Table 2. Birth rate, death rate, infant mortality, and population growth. Figures given are per thousand inhabitants; for infant mortality, per thousand live births.

Year	Denmark				Norway				Sweden			
	Birth rate	Death rate	Infant mortality	Population growth	Birth rate	Death rate	Infant mortality	Population growth	Birth rate	Death rate	Infant mortality	Population growth
1939	17.8	10.1	58	7.4	15.9	10.2	37.2	5.5	15.4	11.5	39.5	4.9
1940	18.3	10.4	50	7.1	16.3	10.9	38.7	5.3	15.0	11.4	39.2	4.7
1941	18.5	10.3	55	8.1	15.9	10.4	43.0	4.7	15.6	11.3	37.0	5.4
1942	20.4	9.6	47	10.4	17.9	10.8	35.9	7.1	17.7	9.9	29.3	8.0
1943	21.4	9.6	45	11.8	19.1	10.5	35.4	8.6	19.3	10.2	28.9	10.0
1944	22.6	10.2	48	12.4	20.5	10.8	36.7	9.8	20.3	10.9	31.1	11.4
1945	23.5	10.5	48	11.8	18.8	9.5	—	9.4	20.4	10.8	29.6	11.5
1946	23.4	10.2	46	13.8	22.5	9.2	—	13.3	19.6	10.5	26.3	13.4
1947	22.1	9.7	41	11.0	21.6	9.3	—	—	18.9	10.8	—	11.5

Table 3. Net reproduction rate.

Year	Denmark	Norway	Sweden
1939	940	849	830
1940	987	858	812
1941	985	813	843
1942	1,095	936	960
1943	1,165	995	1,063
1944	1,242	1,073	1,140
1945	1,297	—	1,147
1946	1,319	—	—
1947	1,269	—	—

Table 4. Life expectancy.

	Denmark (1941–1945)	Norway (1921–1930)	Sweden (1936–1940)
	years	years	years
Men	65.62	60.98	64.30
Women	67.70	63.84	66.92

Table 5. Rural and urban population.

	Urban areas	Rural areas	Total	Urban population in per cent of total population
Denmark	2,634,231	1,411,001	4,045,232	65.1
Norway	1,330,217	1,483,977	2,814,194	47.3
Sweden	4,070,177	2,603,572	6,673,749	61.0

Table 6. The active population classified according to occupation.

Occupation	Denmark (1940)	Norway (1930)	Sweden (1940)
	%	%	%
Agriculture, fishing, and forestry	28.5	35.3	28.8
Mining	—	0.6	1.0
Manufacturing and technical industries	32.2	25.9	34.7
Trade	14.3	12.5	13.6
Navigation	1.3	3.9	1.2
Transportation and communication other than navigation	4.5	5.3	5.6
Army and navy	0.2	0.3	1.2
Public service	1.4	1.1	1.2
Clerical occupations	5.9	4.3	6.4
Domestic service	11.0	10.4	5.2
Miscellaneous	0.7	0.4	1.1
Total	100.0	100.0	100.0

Table 7. Foreign trade in 1946 according to kinds of merchandise; expressed in millions of kroner of the country concerned.

Kind of merchandise	Imports						Exports					
	Denmark		Norway		Sweden		Denmark		Norway		Sweden	
	millions	%	*millions*	%	*millions*	%	*millions*	%	*millions*	%	*millions*	%
Foodstuffs	63.7	2.2	353.4	16.2	506.2	15.0	1,113.4	69.0	333.6	27.8	76.7	3.0
Stimulants	123.2	4.3	87.9	4.0	112.7	3.3	15.6	1.0	1.0	0.1	12.4	0.5
Feeds	104.9	3.7	7.2	0.3	36.1	1.1	1.2	0.1	5.2	0.4	3.6	0.1
Oil (fuel, vegetable, etc.)	422.6	14.8	281.3	12.8	451.2	13.3	14.8	0.9	112.7	9.4	14.2	0.6
Chemicals, perfumes, soap, etc.	143.2	5.0	77.7	3.5	241.1	7.1	36.9	2.3	19.3	1.6	98.3	3.9
Fertilizers	79.6	2.8	34.7	1.6	48.0	1.4	0.1	—	100.1	8.3	—	—
Rubber, etc.	40.4	1.4	19.2	0.9	75.8	2.2	1.0	0.1	2.5	0.2	2.4	0.1
Wood, wood products, paper	257.9	9.1	63.0	2.9	64.6	1.9	19.0	1.2	342.2	28.5	1,230.0	48.4
Hides, leather products	33.0	1.2	43.3	2.0	145.0	4.3	19.1	1.2	36.1	3.0	29.2	1.1
Textiles	703.5	24.8	342.6	15.5	618.5	18.3	14.2	0.9	6.9	0.6	75.9	3.0
Minerals, metals, etc.	467.0	16.4	328.3	14.9	580.2	17.2	51.6	3.2	171.9	14.3	513.2	20.2
Machines and electrical articles	111.9	3.9	141.4	6.4	218.1	6.5	125.3	7.7	7.8	0.6	316.4	12.4
Transportation equipment	169.8	6.0	332.2	15.1	121.7	3.6	55.9	3.5	38.6	3.2	114.1	4.5
Other raw materials	46.3	1.6	26.5	1.2	} 161.3	4.8	125.3	7.7	7.3	0.6	} 56.2	2.2
Miscellaneous products	79.2	2.8	58.0	2.6			15.4	1.0	16.3	1.4		
Total	2,846.2	100.0	2,196.7	100.0	3,380.5	100.0	1,608.8	100.0	1,201.5	100.0	2,542.6	100.0

Table 8. Foreign trade in 1947 according to areas of production and consumption; expressed in millions of kroner of the Scandinavian country concerned.

Area	Imports						Exports					
	Denmark		Norway		Sweden		Denmark		Norway		Sweden	
	millions	%	millions	%	millions	%	millions	%	millions	%	millions	%
Northern countries	509.2	16.7	538.8	14.2	411.5	7.9	458.6	20.0	397.0	21.9	456.9	14.1
Denmark	—	—	183.0	4.8	169.8	3.3	—	—	141.4	7.8	137.2	4.2
Norway	157.6	5.2	—	—	166.1	3.2	124.5	5.4	—	—	245.8	7.6
Sweden	213.2	7.0	322.4	8.5	—	—	208.8	9.1	193.5	10.7	—	—
Western Europe	1,397.9	45.6	1,496.3	39.4	1,884.7	36.1	1,286.8	56.1	764.7	42.3	1,427.7	44.1
The United Kingdom	670.4	21.8	737.3	19.4	701.1	13.4	624.5	27.2	263.5	14.6	527.0	16.3
France	100.9	3.3	151.6	4.0	200.1	3.8	59.9	2.6	115.4	6.4	183.4	5.7
Benelux countries	301.4	9.9	360.4	9.5	495.2	9.5	263.3	11.5	190.4	10.5	415.8	12.8
Iberian countries	35.3	1.2	39.3	1.0	76.1	1.5	23.7	1.0	58.5	3.2	72.8	2.2
Italy	99.4	3.3	112.6	3.0	190.3	3.6	79.0	3.4	60.0	3.3	92.0	2.8
Switzerland	83.2	2.7	25.0	0.7	220.5	4.2	174.0	7.6	17.8	1.0	107.3	3.3
Germany	107.3	3.5	69.9	1.8	0.9	—	53.2	2.3	49.2	2.7	—	—
Eastern Europe	262.4	8.6	204.9	5.4	526.4	10.1	351.0	15.3	207.9	11.5	310.2	9.6
USSR	93.0	3.0	52.4	1.4	121.0	2.3	79.2	3.5	61.1	3.4	41.3	1.3
Poland	91.5	3.0	59.1	1.6	173.6	3.3	173.6	7.6	43.7	2.4	98.8	3.0
Czechoslovakia	63.9	2.1	69.4	1.8	156.2	3.0	66.6	2.9	64.1	3.5	92.5	2.9
Europe (total)	2,169.4	70.9	2,240.0	59.0	2,822.6	54.1	2,096.4	91.4	1,369.6	75.7	2,194.8	67.8
North and South America	800.1	26.2	1,370.4	36.1	2,274.8	43.6	128.5	5.6	246.8	13.7	817.0	25.2
United States	605.0	19.8	949.9	25.0	1,813.9	34.7	86.6	3.8	88.8	4.9	365.0	11.3
Canada	20.3	0.7	100.7	2.7	34.4	0.7	8.2	0.4	23.0	1.3	11.5	0.4
Argentina	87.8	2.9	159.8	4.2	211.4	4.0	8.0	0.3	46.0	2.5	191.0	5.9
Africa	12.4	0.4	51.2	1.3	20.9	0.4	25.0	1.1	54.8	3.0	98.3	3.0
Asia	58.2	1.9	117.0	3.1	78.9	1.5	42.6	1.8	98.1	5.4	81.0	2.5
Near East	1.8	0.1	50.7	1.3	21.9	0.4	16.9	0.7	19.6	1.1	20.2	0.6
Far East	56.4	1.8	66.3	1.8	57.0	1.1	25.7	1.1	78.5	4.3	60.8	1.9
Australia	18.0	0.6	20.2	0.5	22.0	0.4	1.8	0.1	37.7	2.1	48.5	1.5
Miscellaneous	—	—	—	—	0.9	—	—	—	2.0	0.1	0.2	—
Total	3,058.1	100.0	3,798.8	100.0	5,220.1	100.0	2,294.3	100.0	1,809.0	100.0	3,239.8	100.0

Table 9. Distribution of farms according to size.

Size	Denmark (1945)		Norway (1939)		Sweden (1944)	
ha *	*no.*	*%*	*no.*	*%*	*no.*	*%*
1–2	7,000	3.4	44,025	22.9	58,825	16.5
2–5	38,618	19.0	78,237	40.8	107,776	30.4
5–10	51,293	25.2	45,013	23.5	94,844	26.7
10–20	49,524	24.3	18,782	9.8	58,477	16.5
20–50	47,599	23.4	5,432	2.8	27,740	7.8
Over 50	9,579	4.7	392	0.2	7,390	2.1
Total	203,613	100.0	191,881	100.0	355,052	100.0

* One *ha* equals 2.5 acres.

Table 10. Industrial employment.

Year	Denmark	Norway	Sweden
1938	100	100	100
1939	109	103	104
1940	101	98	102
1941	104	103	101
1942	111	105	107
1943	116	106	110
1944	117	104	112
1945	109	96	118
1946	121	114	122
1947	128	128	122

Source: International Labour Office, *Yearbook of Labour Statistics,* 1947–1948 (Montreal, 1949).

Table 11. Industrial wages per hour.

Year	Average Denmark		Nor-way	Sweden		Index Denmark		Nor-way	Sweden	
	Men	Women	Men	Men	Women	Men	Women	Men	Men	Women
	ører	*ører*	*ører*	*ører*	*ører*					
1938	151	94	157	137	80	100	100	100	100	100
1939	156	96	159	142	84	103	102	101	104	105
1940	173	108	172	153	93	115	115	110	112	116
1941	188	119	176	164	101	125	127	112	120	126
1942	196	123	181	179	109	130	131	115	131	136
1943	211	130	188	186	114	140	138	120	136	142
1944	222	140	192	189	119	147	149	122	138	149
1945	237	155	217	198	127	157	165	138	145	159
1946	262	174	252	215	138	174	185	161	157	172
1947	277	186	278	244	162	184	198	177	178	202

Source: International Labour Office, *Yearbook of Labour Statistics,* 1947–1948 (Montreal, 1949).

Table 12. Cost-of-living index.

Year	Denmark	Norway	Sweden
1938	100	100	100
1939	103	101	103
1940	127	118	116
1941	148	139	131
1942	153	147	142
1943	155	150	144
1944	158	152	145
1945	159	155	145
1946	158	159	146
1947	163	160	155
1948	177	159	158

Table 13. Distribution of taxpayers according to size of income, 1946.

Denmark *		
Income, kroner	Number of taxpayers	Per cent of total
0–799	108,595	5.39
800–999	49,495	2.46
1,000–1,999	347,382	17.24
2,000–2,499	163,885	8.14
2,500–2,999	153,756	7.63
3,000–3,999	309,615	15.36
4,000–4,999	266,248	13.23
5,000–5,999	205,974	10.22
6,000–6,999	134,296	6.67
7,000–7,999	82,104	4.08
8,000–9,999	91,636	4.55
10,000–14,999	63,257	3.14
15,000–19,999	17,492	0.81
20,000–29,999	11,844	0.59
30,000–49,000	5,581	0.28
50,000 and over	3,095	0.15
Total	2,014,435	100.00
Sweden †		
0–599	188,770 ‡	5.69
600–999	196,206	5.91
1,000–1,999	560,600	17.17
2,000–2,499	259,381	7.81
2,500–2,999	244,479	7.36
3,000–3,999	486,563	14.66
4,000–4,999	441,253	13.29
5,000–5,999	311,924	9.41
6,000–6,999	187,917	5.66
7,000–7,999	118,627	3.57
8,000–9,999	131,542	3.96
10,000–14,999	108,456	3.27
15,000–19,999	33,953	1.02
20,000–29,999	23,348	0.70
30,000–49,999	11,624	0.35
50,000 and over	6,289	0.19
Total	3,319,938	100.00

* Net income (income after deduction for state and local taxes paid in 1946).
† Gross income (income after deduction for local taxes paid in 1946).
‡ Figures in this column estimated.

Table 14. Total income tax * in the Scandinavian capitals, for the fiscal year 1949–1950, expressed in kroner of the country concerned.

Taxable income	Copenhagen †		Oslo		Stockholm	
			Single persons			
kr.‡	kr.	%	kr.	%	kr.	%
1,000	0	0.0	—	—	0	0.0
2,000	124	6.2	—	—	0	0.0
3,000	252	8.4	—	—	177	5.9
4,000	405	10.1	646	16.2	408	10.2
5,000	570	11.4	837	16.7	656	13.1
6,000	803	13.4	1,089	18.2	929	15.5
7,000	1,028	14.7	1,363	19.5	1,218	17.4
8,000	1,250	15.6	1,644	20.6	1,520	19.0
9,000	1,496	16.6	1,924	21.4	1,832	20.4
10,000	1,732	17.3	2,263	22.6	2,163	21.6
11,000	1,978	18.0	2,608	23.7	2,501	22.7
12,000	2,234	18.6	3,004	25.0	2,805	23.4
13,000	2,493	19.2	3,405	26.2	3,110	23.9
14,000	2,754	19.7	3,806	27.2	3,447	24.6
15,000	3,014	20.1	4,222	28.1	3,788	25.3
20,000	4,518	22.6	6,619	33.1	5,758	28.8
30,000	7,866	26.2	11,738	39.1	10,200	34.0
			Man and wife and two children			
kr.‡	kr.	%	kr.	%	kr.	%
1,000	0	0.0	0	0.0	0	0.0
2,000	5	0.3	0	0.0	0	0.0
3,000	82	2.7	0	0.0	0	0.0
4,000	211	5.3	48	1.2	177	4.4
5,000	342	6.8	281	5.6	361	7.2
6,000	507	8.5	497	8.3	554	9.2
7,000	709	10.1	713	10.2	762	10.9
8,000	935	11.7	930	11.6	987	12.3
9,000	1,171	13.0	1,146	12.7	1,218	13.5
10,000	1,411	14.1	1,399	14.0	1,458	14.6
11,000	1,654	15.0	1,661	15.1	1,708	15.5
12,000	1,902	15.9	1,923	16.0	1,962	16.4
13,000	2,164	16.6	2,227	17.1	2,230	17.2
14,000	2,436	17.4	2,512	17.9	2,501	17.9
15,000	2,700	18.0	2,915	19.4	2,805	18.7
20,000	4,145	20.7	5,025	25.1	4,533	22.7
30,000	7,450	24.8	9,585	32.0	8,847	29.5

* Church tax included with state and local income taxes.
   † Net income after certain deductions for insurance not exceeding 400 kr.
   ‡ In Danish, Norwegian, and Swedish currencies, respectively.
Sources: Taxation tables of the city of Copenhagen and information from the Norwegian and Swedish embassies in Copenhagen.

Table 15. Government expenditures and receipts for the fiscal year 1946–1947, expressed in thousands of kroner of the country concerned.

	Expenditures					
	Denmark		Norway (budget)		Sweden	
	thousand kr.	%	*thousand kr.*	%	*thousand kr.*	%
Political bodies of the state	8,507	0.5	12,185	0.6	11,083	0.4
Foreign service	18,001	0.9	16,249	0.8	17,965	0.7
Defense	210,491	11.2	361,819	17.6	729,128	26.3
Administration of justice	150,192	8.0	74,831	3.6	42,768	1.5
Higher courts, sanitation, civil defense	80,148	4.3	49,132	2.4	155,284	5.6
Education, libraries, etc.	169,578	9.0	118,251	5.8	378,652	13.7
Church administration	10,721	0.6	6,590	0.3	5,778	0.2
Agriculture, fishing, forestry	136,487	7.2	47,066	2.3	329,785	11.9
(including subsidies)	(90,667)	(4.8)	—		—	
Trade, industry, shipping-supply	72,888	3.9	557,587	27.0	89,844	3.2
(including subsidies and supply bodies)	(33,033)	(1.8)	(492,826)	(24.0)	(51,057)	(1.8)
Social services	449,730	23.9	164,965	8.0	557,975	20.1
Public works, transport, communications	24,643	1.3	382,479	18.6	185,477	6.7
(including special reconstruction aid)	—		(240,334)	(11.7)	—	
Collection of taxes, customs, duties, etc.	485,885	25.7	192,100	9.3	152,259	5.5
(including special entries due to the war)	(295,000)	(15.7)	(150,415)	(7.3)	—	
Pensions	65,363	3.5	44,703	2.3	111,747	4.1
Other items	—	—	27,826	1.4	1,769	0.1
Total expenditures	1,882,634	100.0	2,055,783	100.0	2,769,514	100.0

Table 15 (continued)

	Receipts					
	Denmark		Norway (budget)		Sweden	
	thousand kr.	%	*thousand kr.*	%	*thousand kr.*	%
Net income from domains and public works	12,947	0.7	—114,900	—5.6	236,414	8.5
Net income from interest and from various funds (less depreciation)	—11,277	—0.6	—88,890	—4.3	—253,110	—9.1
Taxes on income and property	764,898	40.6	359,952	17.5	1,178,090	42.5
Customs duties and excise taxes	1,076,315	57.1	1,274,550	62.0	1,845,186	66.7
Stamp taxes, fees, etc.	36,879	2.0	41,352	2.0	76,958	2.8
Current income (less current expenses)	—17,868	—0.9	284,138	13.8	—450,859	—16.3
Other items	20,740	1.1	299,671	14.6	136,830	4.9
Total receipts	1,882,634	100.0	2,055,783	100.0	2,769,514	100.0

Table 16. Distribution of current public expenditures between state and local governments in the fiscal year 1943–1944, expressed in millions of kroner of the country concerned.

		1. Administration	2. Defense (including civil)	3. Social and health services	4. Transport and communication*	5. Church administration and education	6. Promotion of business	7. Other items	Total
		Denmark							
State	millions	141.2	70.4	383.7	34.8	107.1	—†	488.8	1,226.0
	%	63	99	54	30	50		76	62
Local	millions	81.9	0.9	330.0	82.6	107.1	—†	156.1	786.6
	%	37	1	46	70	50		24	38
Total	millions	223.1	71.3	713.7	117.4	214.2	—†	644.9	1,984.6
	%	100	100	100	100	100		100	100
		Norway							
State	millions	97.5	18.5	94.0	117.0	66.1	86.7	630.9	1,110.7
	%	68	100	42	65	44	85	74	66
Local	millions	46.8	—	131.7	63.7	85.3	15.2	224.0	566.7
	%	32		58	35	56	15	26	34
Total	millions	144.3	18.5	225.7	180.7	151.4	101.9	854.9	1,677.4
	%	100	100	100	100	100	100	100	100
		Sweden							
State	millions	257	2,019	472	768	125	607	350	4,598
	%	55	99	52	86	23	71	84	75
Local ‡	millions	211	21	444	124	408	244	67	1,519
	%	45	1	48	14	77	29	16	25
Total	millions	468	2,040	916	892	533	851	417	6,117
	%	100	100	100	100	100	100	100	100

* Not all expenditures in connection with transport and communication are included for Denmark and Norway.

† Cannot be specified.

‡ Calendar year 1943.

Table 17. Prime ministers and political parties of the governments of the Scandinavian countries since 1930.

Date	Prime minister	Political party
Denmark		
April 23, 1929, to July 8, 1940	Thorvald Stauning	Labor party and Liberals
July 8, 1940, to May 5, 1942	Thorvald Stauning	All parties excluding Communists
May 5, 1942, to November 5, 1942	Vilhelm Buhl	All parties excluding Communists
November 5, 1942, to May 4, 1945	Erik Scavenius	All parties excluding Communists (August 29, 1943, to May 4, 1945, the permanent secretaries of the departments administered on behalf of the government)
May 4, 1945, to November 7, 1945	Vilhelm Buhl	All parties and representatives of the resistance movement
November 7, 1945, to November 9, 1947	Knud Kristensen	Farmers' party
November 9, 1947, to the present	Hans Hedtoft	Labor party
Norway		
February 14, 1928, to May 8, 1931	Johan Mowinckel	Liberals
May 8, 1931, to March 3, 1932	P. Kolstad	Farmers' party
March 3, 1932, to March 3, 1933	J. Hundseid	Farmers' party
March 3, 1933, to March 19, 1935	Johan Mowinckel	Liberals
March 19, 1935, to June 21, 1945	Johan Nygardsvold	Labor party (June 11, 1940, to June 7, 1945, in England)
June 21, 1945, to October 30, 1945	Einar Gerhardsen	All parties excluding Christian party
October 30, 1945, to the present	Einar Gerhardsen	Labor party
Sweden		
June 7, 1930, to September 24, 1932	Carl Ekman	Conservatives
September 24, 1932, to June 19, 1936	Per Albin Hansson	Labor party
June 19, 1936, to September 28, 1936	Axel Pehrsson-Bramstorp	Farmers' party
September 28, 1936, to December 13, 1945	Per Albin Hansson	Labor party and Farmers' party
December 13, 1945, to July 31, 1945	Per Albin Hansson	All parties excluding Communists
July 31, 1945, to October 5, 1947	Per Albin Hansson	Labor party
October 5, 1947, to October 11, 1947	Osten Undén	Labor party
October 11, 1947, to the present	Tage Erlander	Labor party

Table 18. Distribution of seats in the Scandinavian parliaments.

Denmark: the lower house (Folketinget)

Election year	1929	1932	1935	1939	1943	1945	1947
Labor party (socialdemokratiet)	61	62	68	64	66	48	57
Farmers' party (venstre)	43	38	28	30	28	38	49
Conservatives (konservative)	24	27	26	26	31	26	17
Liberals (radikale venstre)	16	14	14	14	13	11	10
Communists (kommunister)	—	2	2	3	—	18	9
Others (andre partier)	4	5	10	11	10	7	6

Denmark: the upper house (Landstinget)

Election year	1928	1932	1936	1939	1943	1947
Labor party (socialdemokratiet)	27	27	31	35	34	33
Farmers' party (venstre)	28	28	22	18	18	21
Conservatives (konservative)	12	13	15	13	14	13
Liberals (radikale venstre)	8	7	7	8	8	7
Communists (kommunister)	—	—	—	—	—	1

Norway: (Stortinget)

Election year	1930	1933	1936	1945	1949
Labor party (arbejderpartiet)	47	69	70	76	85
Conservatives (højre og frisinnede venstre)	44	31	36	25	23
Liberals (venstre og rad. folkeparti)	34	25	23	20	21
Communists (kommunister)	—	—	—	11	0
Farmers' party (bondepartiet)	25	23	18	10	12
Christian party (kristeligt folkeparti)	—	—	2	8	9
Others (andre partier)	—	2	1	—	—

Sweden: the lower house (Andra kammaret)

Election year	1928	1932	1936	1940	1944	1948
Labor party (socialdemokratiet)	90	104	112	134	115	112
Liberals (folkepartiet)	32	24	27	23	26	57
Farmers' party (bondeförbundet)	27	36	36	28	35	30
Conservatives (högern)	73	58	44	42	39	22
Communists (kommunister)	8	8	11	3	15	9

Sweden: the upper house (Första kammaret)

Election year	1929	1933	1937	1941	1945
Labor party (socialdemokratiet)	52	58	66	75	83
Liberals (folkepartiet)	31	23	16	15	14
Farmers' party (bondeförbundet)	17	18	22	24	21
Conservatives (högern)	49	50	45	35	30
Communists (kommunister)	1	1	1	1	2

Source: Hal Koch and Alf Ross (eds.), *Nordisk demokrati* (Copenhagen, 1949).

Selected Bibliography

SELECTED BIBLIOGRAPHY OF BOOKS IN ENGLISH

ON SCANDINAVIA

GENERAL

Andersson, Ingvar. *Introduction to Sweden.* Stockholm: Forum, 1949.

Childs, Marquis W. *Sweden, the Middle Way.* New York: Pelican Books, 1948.

Danstrup, John. *A History of Denmark.* Copenhagen: Wivel, 1948.

Gedde, Knud, and Anderson, K. B., (eds.). *This Is Denmark.* Copenhagen: Jul. Gjellerups Forlag, 1948.
Distributed in the United States by Scandinavian Book Service, Box 169, Audubon Station, New York 32, N.Y.

Hovde, Bryn J. *The Scandinavian Countries, 1720–1865.* 2 vols. Boston: Chapman and Grimes, 1943. Ithaca, N.Y.: Cornell University Press, 1948.

Koht, Halvdan, and Skard, Sigmund. *The Voice of Norway.* New York: Columbia University Press, 1944.

Larsen, Karen. *A History of Norway.* New York: American-Scandinavian Foundation, 1948.

National Travel Association of Norway. *Norway.* London: J. M. Dent, 1944.

Outze, Børge, (ed.). *Denmark during the German Occupation.* Copenhagen, London, and Chicago: Scandinavian Publishing Co., 1946.

Royal Danish Ministry for Foreign Affairs. *Denmark.* Copenhagen: Royal Danish Ministry for Foreign Affairs, 1947.

Royal Ministry for Foreign Affairs. *Sweden, a Wartime Survey.* Stockholm: Royal Ministry for Foreign Affairs, 1942.

Social Denmark: A Survey of Danish Social Legislation. Edited by Socialt Tidsskrift. Copenhagen: Socialt Tidsskrift, 1946.
Distributed in the United States by Crown Publishers, New York.

Swedish Tourist Traffic Association. *Sweden, Past and Present.* Stockholm: Swedish Tourist Traffic Association, 1947.

SCANDINAVIAN DEMOCRACY

Arneson, Ben A. *The Democratic Monarchies of Scandinavia.* New York: Van Nostrand, 1939.

Bellquist, Eric C. "Political and Economic Conditions in the Scandinavian Countries," *Foreign Policy Reports* (New York), vol. XXIV (May 15, 1948), no. 5.

Cole, Margaret, (ed.). *Democratic Sweden.* London: Geo. Routledge and Sons, 1938.

Herlitz, Niels. *Sweden, a Modern Democracy on Ancient Foundations.* Minneapolis: University of Minnesota Press, 1939.

Landsorganisationen. *The Postwar Programs of Swedish Labor.* Stockholm: Landsorganisationen, Barnhusgatan 18, 1946.

SCANDINAVIA IN A CHANGING WORLD ECONOMY

Delegations for the Promotion of Economic Co-operation between the Northern Countries. *The Northern Countries in World Economy.* Copenhagen: Einar Munksgaard, 1937.

Institute for Industrial Research. *Sweden's Trade Policy after the War.* Stockholm: Institute for Industrial Research, 1946.

Kragh, B. *Sweden's Monetary and Fiscal Policy before and after the Second World War.* Supplement to Index. Stockholm: Svenska Handelsbanken Index, 1946.

GOVERNMENT ECONOMIC PLANNING IN SCANDINAVIA

Prewar

Braatoy, Bjarne. *The New Sweden.* London and New York: Thos. Nelson and Sons, 1939.

Clark, Harrison. *Swedish Unemployment Policy, 1919–1940.* Washington: Public Affairs Press, 1941.

Möller, Gustav. *Swedish Unemployment Policy.* New York: Royal Swedish Commission for the New York World's Fair, 1939.

Montgomery, Arthur. *How Sweden Overcame the Depression.* London: P. S. King, 1939.

Social Denmark, pp. 301–323.

Postwar

Norway

Galenson, Walter. "Nationalization of Industry in Great Britain and Norway," *American-Scandinavian Review,* XXXVI (Sept., 1948), 234–238.

Klein, Lawrence R. "Planned Economy in Norway," *American Economic Review,* XXXVIII (Dec., 1948), 795–814.

Det norske Nationalbudget, 1947, 1948, 1949. Oslo, 1947, 1948, 1949.

Memorandum on a Norwegian Long-Term Program. Oslo, 1948. (Mimeographed.)

Denmark

Economic Survey of Denmark, National Budget for 1949. Copenhagen, 1949.

The Long-Term Program of Denmark. Copenhagen: Danish Information Office, 1948.

Sweden

Lindbom, Tage. *Sweden's Labor Program.* New York: League for Industrial Democracy, 1948.

Översikt över Det ekonomiska läget. (Meddelanden från Konjunkturinstitutet, serie B. 8; 1948). With a summary in English.

Översikt över Det ekonomiska läget. Meddelanden från Konjunkturinstitutet, serie B. 9; 1946–1949). With a summary in English.

Ekonomiska utredningar varen 1949. Meddelanden från Konjunkturinstitutet, serie B. 10). With a summary in English.

LABOR RELATIONS

Childs, Marquis W. *This Is Democracy.* New Haven: Yale University Press, 1938.

Galenson, Walter. *Labor in Norway.* Cambridge, Mass.: Harvard University Press, 1949.

Lindbom, Tage. *Sweden's Labor Program.*

Norgren, Paul H. *The Swedish Collective Bargaining System.* Cambridge, Mass.: Harvard University Press, 1941.

Robbins, J. J. *The Government of Labor Relations in Sweden.* Chapel Hill, N.C.: University of North Carolina Press, 1942.

Social Denmark, pp. 258–277.

SOCIAL WELFARE

Anderson, Mary. "Social Legislation, Progress in the United States and Sweden," *American-Scandinavian Review*, XXX (March, 1945), 32–40.

Armstrong, B. N. *The Health Insurance Doctor*. Princeton, N.J.: Princeton University Press, 1939.

Child Welfare Committee, League of Nations. *Child Welfare Councils, Denmark, Norway, Sweden*. (Official no.:C.8.M.7. 1937, IV.1.)

Dam, Poul, and Larsen, Jørgen, (eds.). *Danish Youth, Work and Leisure*. Copenhagen: Joint Council of Danish Youth Organizations, 1948.

Erlander, Tage. "Swedish Social Policy in Wartime," *International Labour Review*, XLVII (March, 1943), 297–311.

Family and Child Welfare in Norway. Oslo: Joint Committee on International Social Policy, 1949.

Gille, Halvor. "Recent Developments in Swedish Population Policy," *Population Studies* (London, 1948), vol. II, nos. 1–2.

Gloerfelt-Tarp, Kirsten, (ed.). *Women in the Community*. London and New York: Oxford University Press, 1939.

Hohmann, Helen Fisher. *Old Age in Sweden*. Washington: Federal Security Agency, 1940.

Höjer, Karl J. *Social Welfare in Sweden*. Stockholm: Forum, 1949.

Jensen, Orla. *Social Services in Denmark*. Copenhagen: Det danske Selskab, 1948.

Myrdal, Alva. *Nation and Family*. New York: Harper and Bros., 1941. London: Kegan Paul, 1945.

Myrgaard, Arvid. "Sweden's Public Health System," *American-Scandinavian Review*, XXXV (Dec., 1947), 304–320.

New National Pension Scheme in Sweden. Stockholm: Svenska Handelsbanken Index, 1947.

New Universal Social Security Plan for Norway. Oslo: Joint Committee on International Social Policy, 1949.

Ratzlaff, Carl J. *The Scandinavian Unemployment Relief Program*. Philadelphia: University of Pennsylvania Press, 1939.

Social Denmark, chs. 1–3.

Social Insurance in Norway. Oslo: Norwegian Joint Committee on International Social Policy, 1949.

Social Services for Children and Young People in Sweden. Stockholm: Swedish Institute, 1947.

The Swedish Institute. *Public Health and Medicine in Sweden.* Stockholm: Forum, 1949.

The Youth of Norway Today. Oslo: Norwegian Joint Council, 1947.

HOUSING

Cooperative Housing Abroad. Final Report of Subcommittee no. 1 of the Committee on Banking and Currency, House of Representatives, Pursuant to H. Res. 331 (approved October 13, 1949), February 10, 1950 (Washington: Government Printing Office, 1950).

Cooperative Housing in Europe. A Report of the Banking and Currency Subcommittee Investigating and Studying European Housing Programs, January 31, 1950 (Washington: Government Printing Office, 1950).

Graham, John. *Housing in Sweden.* Chapel Hill, N.C.: University of North Carolina Press, 1940.

Silk, Leonard. *Sweden Plans for Better Housing.* Durham, N.C.: Duke University Press, 1948.

Social Denmark, ch. 7.

Swedish Housing. Stockholm: Swedish Institute, 1949.

PRODUCER AND CONSUMER CO-OPERATIVES

Drejer, A. Axelsen. *Co-operation in Denmark.* Copenhagen: Central Co-operative Committee (Andelsudvalget), 1947.

Grimley, O. B. *The New Norway.* Oslo: Griff-forlaget, 1937.

Gullander, Åke. *Farmers Co-operation in Sweden.* London: Crosby Lockwood & Son, 1948.

Hedberg, Anders. *Consumer Co-operatives in Sweden.* Stockholm: Ko-operativa Förbundets Bokförlag, 1948.

Lamming, N. *Sweden's Co-operative Enterprise.* Manchester, Eng.: Holyoake House, 1940.

Ravnholt, Henning. *The Danish Co-operative Movement.* Copenhagen: Danish Information Handbooks, Det danske Selskab, 1947.

Social Denmark, pp. 360–371.

ADULT EDUCATION

Coit, Eleanor. *Government Support of Workers' Education.* New York: American Labor Education Service, 1940.

Cole, Margaret. *Democratic Sweden.*
Forster, F. Margaret. *School for Life: A Study of the People's Colleges in Sweden.* London: Faber, 1944.
Lund, Ragnar, (ed.-in-chief), *Scandinavian Adult Education,* Copenhagen: Det danske Forlag, 1949.
MacKaye, David. "Grundtvig and Kold," *American-Scandinavian Review,* XXX (Sept., 1942), 229–239.
Möller, J. C., and Watson, Katherine. *Education in Democracy: The Folk High Schools of Denmark.* London: Faber, 1944.
Skrubbeltrang, F. *The Danish Folk High Schools.* Copenhagen: Det danske Selskab, 1947.
Stensland, Per G. "Adult Education," *American-Scandinavian Review,* XXXIII (June, 1945), 118–128.
Stolpe, Herman. *Cog or Collaborator: Democracy in Co-operative Education.* Stockholm: Kooperativa Förbundet, 1946.

SCANDINAVIAN FOREIGN POLICY

Heckscher, E. F., Bergendahl, K., Keilhau, W., and others. *Sweden, Norway, Denmark, and Iceland in the World War.* New Haven, Conn.: Yale University Press, 1930.
Hedin, Naboth. "Sweden: The Dilemma of a Neutral," *Foreign Policy Reports* (New York), XIX (May 15, 1943), 50–63.
Hopper, Bruce. "Sweden: A Case Study in Neutrality," *Foreign Affairs* (New York), XXIII (April, 1945), 435–449.
Jones, S. Shepard. *The Scandinavian States and the League of Nations.* Princeton, N.J.: Princeton University Press, 1939.
Koht, Halvdan. *Norway, Neutral and Invaded.* New York: Macmillan Co., 1941.
Royal Danish Ministry for Foreign Affairs. *Memorandum Containing Royal Danish Government Views regarding the Future Settlement of Germany.* Copenhagen, 1947.
Seidenfaden, Erik. "Scandinavia Charts a Course," *Foreign Affairs,* XXVI (July, 1948), 653–654.
Tingsten, Herbert. *The Debate on the Foreign Policy of Sweden: 1918–39.* Oxford: Oxford University Press, 1949.

CO-OPERATION BETWEEN THE SCANDINAVIAN COUNTRIES

Bukdahl, Jørgen. *The North and Europe.* Copenhagen: Aschehoug, 1947.

Leistikow, Gunnar. "How Scandinavia Co-operates," *Forum*, CIX
(June, 1948), 332–336.
The Northern Countries in World Economy, ch. 14.
Toyne, S. M. *The Scandinavians in History*. New York: Long-
mans, 1949.

BIBLIOGRAPHIES

American-Scandinavian Foundation. *A List of Books by Scandi-
navians and about Scandinavia.* New York, 1946.
Hedin, Naboth. *Guide to Information about Sweden.* New York:
American-Swedish News Exchange, 1947.

Index